PEAVEY
GUITARS

The Authorized American History

By

Willie G. Moseley

For information contact Nautilus Publishing, 426 South Lamar Blvd., Suite 16, Oxford, MS 38655.

ISBN: 978-1-936946-51-8

The Nautilus Publishing Company
426 South Lamar Blvd., Suite 16
Oxford, Mississippi 38655
Tel: 662-513-0159
www.nautiluspublishing.com

Front cover design by Connor Covert
Cover Photo Credits
Front:
Chip Todd: Hollis Calvert
T-60 guitar: Peavey Electronics Corporation
1958 guitar drawing: Peavey Electronics Corporation
Mystic guitar: Willie G. Moseley
Hartley Peavey: Peavey Electronics Corporation
HP Signature guitar: Peavey Electronics Corporation

Back:
Foundation bass: Bill Ingalls Jr.
Rudy Sarzo: Peavey Electronics Corporation
Hard Rock Casino sign: Willie G. Moseley
T-60 headstock, serial #00000000: Willie G. Moseley
Mark Farner: Peavey Electronics Corporation
T. Model Ford: Wikimedia Commons
President George Bush: Peavey Electronics Corporation
Author: Bill Ingalls Jr.

(all photos in text courtesy of Peavey Electronics Corporation unless otherwise credited)

Library of Congress Cataloging-in-Publication Data has been applied for.
Printed in United States of America

10 9 8 7 6 5 4 3 2 1

It almost goes without saying that
this story is dedicated to Hartley and Chip

TABLE OF CONTENTS

LEXICON

ACTIVE CIRCUITRY: Solid-state circuitry built into certain guitars and basses, which provides additional sonic options beyond standard/passive volume and tone controls. Such selections can include volume boost, tone enhancement, compression, etc. Active circuitry is usually powered by one or two 9-volt batteries installed in the instrument body.

ARCH-TOP: Somewhat self-explanatory; some hollow or semi-hollow instruments have a curved top that is sometimes carved. The term is usually associated with guitars rather than basses, and isn't necessarily used when discussing solidbody instruments, although "carved top" *is* used regarding solidbody instruments (see separate definition).

BINDING: Material that is usually made from flexible plastic; "binds" edges of wood together, but sometimes its use is strictly cosmetic.

BRIDGE: Metal, wood, or plastic part on the top of an instrument where strings "transmit" vibrations to the body of the instrument for sonic reproduction. A bridge usually has small grooves in it to accommodate each string. Most bridges on electric guitars and basses allow adjustment of string height, and many also have adjustable "saddles" for individual strings, to allow intonation/fine tuning.

BOLT-ON: Refers to a type of attachment of a neck to a body (as found on most Peavey instruments).

BOUT: Upper and lower portions of a traditional guitar or bass body, separated by an indention/"waist." The two sections have a connotation that implies viewing an instrument that is on display vertically— "upper bout" refers to the part of the body nearer to the neck joint, while "lower bout" refers to the portion nearer the end of the body, where the bridge, controls on electric instruments, etc. are usually found.

CARVED TOP: This term usually describes a contoured top found on many guitars and basses, including solidbodies. The carve may be part of the same wood as the body, or may be a different wood that is attached.

CENTER DETENT: A mechanical middle/halfway "stopping point" for reference on a rotary control.

COIL TAP SWITCH: Cuts out one of two coils in a humbucking-type pickup (see "PICKUP"). As will become apparent in the Peavey guitar story, the company developed unique coil circuitry for its earliest instruments.

CONTOUR: Beveling on solidbody instruments. Such contouring usually consists of a "belly cut" on the back, and a "forearm bevel" on the top, to enhance comfort—and both of those terms are self-explanatory. As noted earlier, contouring can also refer to a carved top on an instrument body.

CONTRABASS: A six-string bass, with a lower-tuned and higher-tuned string in addition to the standard four strings on a standard bass. Regular tuning for a contrabass is B-E-A-D-G-C.

CUTAWAY: Portion of instrument near neck/body joint that appears to have been "cut out" to allow access to higher area of the neck. Such shaping creates a "horn" on the body silhouette. Instruments may be single-cutaway (Peavey Odysseys and Generations), symmetrical double-cutaway, or offset double-cutaway (most solidbody Peaveys).

dB: Abbreviation for "decibel." Usually found in citations of volume and/or frequency response/tone in electronics (including some stringed instruments with active circuitry).

FLAT-TOP: Another self-explanatory term; this is the classic configuration of an acoustic guitar.

FRET: A metal strip on a fingerboard/fretboard. Each space between frets serves the same sonic function as a piano key by changing the pitch of a string by one note. The metal strips that delineate each space are usually made of "fret wire," an alloy.

FRET MARKERS: Also known as "position markers." Decorative dots, blocks, or other inlay on the fretboard playing surface and/or side of the neck for visual reference.

FRETBOARD: Also known as a fingerboard. Top surface of a guitar or bass neck where notes are selected and played. Rosewood, maple, and ebony are among the most popular fretboard woods laminated to the top of a neck. A maple fretboard is often part of a maple neck itself instead of being a laminated part.

HEADSTOCK: Top end of instrument where the tuning keys and brand name are (usually) found. Also known as a "peghead."

Hz: Abbreviation for "hertz." Usually found in citations of frequency response/tone in electronics (including some stringed instruments with active circuitry).

JACK: Receptacle for guitar cord.

kHz: Abbreviation for "kilohertz." Usually found in citations of frequency response/tone in electronics (including some stringed instruments with active circuitry).

LUTHIER: A individual builder who hand-makes stringed musical instruments, usually in a small shop.

NAMM: Acronym for "National Association of Music Merchandisers," an organization of retail music businesses. New instruments and other musical wares usually debut at "NAMM shows," which are held twice a year.

NECK-THROUGH: Construction style that utilizes a long piece of wood (sometimes made of several laminated layers) that runs the entire length of the instrument. Usually, the sides of the body are glued onto the neck/center portion. Peavey's original neck-through concept was known as "Unity."

NUT: Small grooved part for string spacing and height, located between headstock and fingerboard. Usually made of bone, plastic, metal, or, in more recent times, space-age composite material.

P/J: A pickup configuration that references, at least *visually*, a Fender Precision model pickup (split/offset; two pickup sections for two strings each) and a Fender Jazz model pickup (straight bar). Many manufacturers have utilized this pickup layout (and designation), so the term's usage has become generic.

PAN KNOB: A more recent variant of pickup selection on guitars and basses. Rotary control that allows a player to gradually blend one pickup with another, instead of abrupt on-off changes (see TOGGLE SWITCH). Many times, a pan knob will have a center detent; in the case of a two-pickup instrument, the center stopping point indicates that both pickups are blended together in equal amounts of output.

PASSIVE CIRCUITRY: Standard/"non-active" electronics in an instrument; no battery required.

PHASE SWITCH: Reverses polarity of a humbucking pickup to evoke unique sounds.

PICKGUARD: Somewhat self-defined item, usually made of plastic or metal, that shields a guitar or bass body from pick damage (if the player happens to use a pick); also known as a "scratchplate."

PICKUP: Microphone-like device consisting of magnet(s) and wiring that "picks up" string vibrations. "Single-coil" pickups have a self-explanatory designation, while "humbucking" pickups have two coils, wired in opposition to each other to cancel out annoying electrical noise. If an instrument has a coil-tap switch, one coil of a "humbucker" can be turned off to evoke a single-coil sound.

While most pickups are mounted under the strings on the top of a guitar or body, some instruments have transducer-type pickups built into a bridge (and usually aren't visible; re: Peavey's Ecoustic model).

POTENTIOMETERS: "Pots" aren't visible, but are critical to the function of an electric guitar or bass—they're the electronic controls underneath a volume or tone knob.

RADIUS: Curvature of fretboard. The lower the number, the more pronounced the curvature of the fretboard will be. Peavey's groundbreaking T-60 guitar and T-40 bass each had a 12" radius.

SCALE: Distance from nut to bridge. Scales found on Peavey's domestic electric guitars are either 24 3/4" or 25 1/2", both of which are considered industry standards. Two early models, the T-15 and T-30, had shorter scale of 23 1/2". Bass scales for Peavey include 34" (the industry standard) or 35".

SET-NECK: Refers to the glued-in neck style found on some guitars or basses, such as Peavey's Odyssey.

STRING TREE: Hardware attached to headstock to stabilize strings between nut and tuning keys.

TAILPIECE: Anchor point for "ball end" of string. Most Peavey electric instruments feature a bridge and tailpiece that are combined into one unit.

THINLINE: A hollow or semi-hollow guitar or bass configuration with a body that has a shorter depth (usually around two inches) than most acoustic stringed instrument bodies. Peavey has never produced thinline instruments domestically.

TOGGLE SWITCH: Turns individual pickups off and on. The most common configuration is found on a two-pickup instrument, with a three-position toggle switch that works either pickup individually or both at the same time. Toggle switches are also used to control other functions of a guitar or bass, particularly on active instruments.

TRANSDUCER: All pickups are transducers; i.e., devices that transduce mechanical energy (string movement, for electric guitars and basses) to electrical energy (electrical impulses through circuit wires). However, in present-day guitar jargon, "transducer" usually refers to a type of pickup that fits under, or is built into, the bridge of an acoustic instrument.

TRUSS ROD (and TRUSS ROD COVER): Most modern guitars and basses have a metal truss rod inside the neck to alleviate string tension (which, if not controlled, could cause the neck to warp). The truss rod is usually adjustable, and on most Peavey guitars and basses, a small plate located on the headstock (just behind the nut/headstock juncture) covers the access point. On some latter-day domestic Peavey models, the truss rod adjustment was done at the neck joint.

VIBRATO: A device with an "arm" that is manipulated by a player's hand to change the pitch of a note or a chord on stringed instruments. Nicknamed "whammy bars," they are usually associated with electric guitars rather than basses, but bass vibratos do exist. Peavey instruments have had vibratos developed by the company, as well as aftermarket vibrato systems.

ZERO FRET: An extra piece of fret wire positioned where the neck joins the headstock; utilized to facilitate better-sounding chords. Peavey models don't have this feature.

CHAPTER 1

Pre-company

"I had no intention of doing getting into the guitar-making business. If my competitors had left their dealers alone, and had been the professionals that they claimed to be, I never would have done it."

—*Hartley Peavey, August 2014*

The founder of Peavey Electronics Corporation has been forever feisty about his hometown, Meridian, Mississippi, and its place in not only the history of American-made musical equipment, but in American music itself.

Meridian, a.k.a. the "Queen City," has been proclaimed as the birthplace of Jimmie Rodgers (1897-1933), one of the founders of the country music genre, but Hartley Peavey promotes what he considers to be Meridian's perhaps-overlooked importance by evoking geographical references.

"It's educational and enlightening to consider where most kinds of American music evolved," Hartley says assertively. "You can draw a square that's about 250 miles long on each side, where the 'bottom' borders the Gulf of Mexico, the 'west side' is just on the other side of the Mississippi River, the 'north side' is the northern border of Tennessee, and the 'east side' goes down from the eastern border of Tennessee. Inside you've got Louisiana, Mississippi, Tennessee, Alabama, and maybe a little bit of Missouri.

"Think of the musical styles that came from that area—jazz from New Orleans, country and gospel from Nashville, Delta blues, and 'blends' of all of those types of music, including rockabilly, and, eventually, rock and roll.

"And where is Meridian in that 'square'? Dead center. We're in the middle of the heartland of American music."

For an aspiring musician, having been born into a family where at least one of the parents is a player and/or singer himself/herself can be beneficial, but Hartley's abilities to make musical gear would ultimately take him much further than any bona fide talent he had as a guitarist.

Hartley's father, Joseph B. "Mutt" Peavey, had graduated from Meridian High School in 1932, during the throes of America's Great Depression. He'd played saxophone in the high school band, and the only job Mutt could find in those trying times was as a member of a swing band. That musical aggregation toured the Southeast, playing as far south as Miami.

However, Mutt grew tired of the nomadic lifestyle of a road musician. He returned to Meridian in 1938, and dabbled with employment at J.J. Newberry, a "five-and-dime" store.

His father, J.L. Peavey, had sold pianos at a local store, Gressett Music House, and Mutt was inspired to open his own retail shop. His new retail venture, Melody Music Company, initially began as a partnership with a local band director named Lane. Mutt's original investment was $50 and a used piano donated by his father. After the partnership ended, the store name acquired "Peavey's" at the head of its moniker.

1938 would prove to be an eventful year in another way, as Mutt met a young secretary from nearby Clarke County named Sarah Davis. After a brief courtship, they married late that year.

Their first son, Hartley, was born on December 30, 1941, and a second son, Robert, would follow eight years later. Mutt was almost 30 years old when Hartley was born, and did not have to serve in the military in World War II.

"They had some sort of a 'rating system' involving age and how many dependents a person had," Hartley explained. "Because of Mutt's age and because of me, he didn't get drafted."

Diversion of raw materials to the war effort meant that new musical instruments were hard to acquire, so Mutt survived by selling used instruments. He would journey into rural areas, buying used player pianos and other instruments to refurbish. His experience with the Great Depression had made him quite conservative in his business dealings.

"He ran his store very pragmatically," said Hartley. "He could squeeze a nickel 'till the buffalo screamed."

After the war, Mutt's business diversified into a full-line store, stocking not only pianos, but brass and reed band instruments, electric organs, phonographs, televisions, "…and a few guitars," Hartley said.

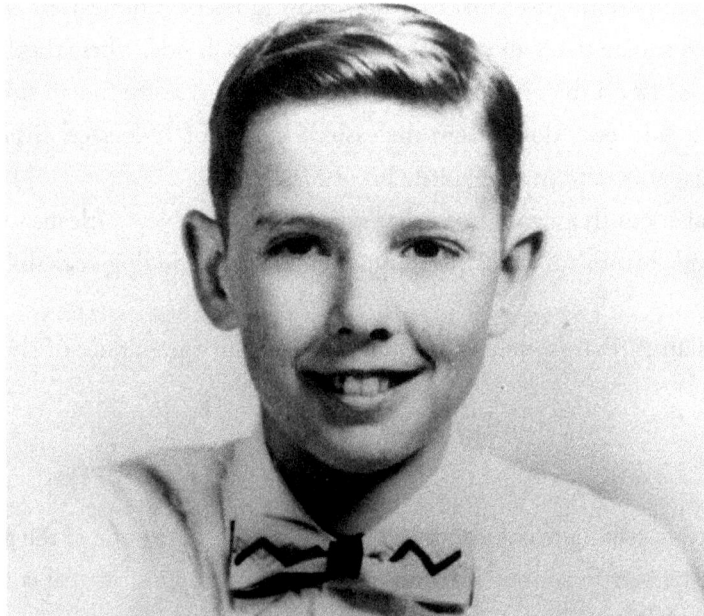

As a youngster, Hartley gravitated towards his paternal grandfather, who was known as "Pop." J.L. Peavey was a tinkerer and inventor, and his workshop projects fascinated his grandson, who would head to Pop's shop almost every day after school.

Accordingly, it's fair to say that "Pop" Peavey probably had more influence than anyone else on Hartley's early motivation for what became his ultimate career—more so than Hartley's own musical father.

When Pop died in 1955, Hartley, for all intents and purposes, inherited his grandfather's hand tools.

"My dad was a very musical kind of guy, but he wasn't mechanically-inclined," Hartley said.

Hartley used the inherited tools to build model airplanes and science projects in the basement of his family's house. He was talented enough to get enrolled at Ross Collins Vocational School (now Ross Collins Career and Technical Center) just before entering the seventh grade. Hartley was the youngest student who ever enrolled at the school.

The opportunity at Ross Collins Vocational School had come about at the behest of his great-uncle, Dick Wiggins, who taught at the school.

"He was a master machinist and a mechanical genius," Hartley remembered. "He invented the hydraulic lift for automobiles, but never patented it. Somebody from Memphis saw it and got the patent, and made megabucks."

Wiggins wrangled an age waiver for Hartley, who joyfully engrossed himself with learning the wonders of mechanical drawing, sheet metal, radio repair, and the operation of milling machines and lathes. Some of the courses he took at Ross Collins were taught by his uncle, Dick Wiggins, Jr.

Hartley was also soon voraciously reading magazines like *Popular Science, Mechanics Illustrated,* and *Popular Mechanics* (including issues that dated back to the late Thirties), and his award-winning school science projects validated his knowledge and talent.

"I was pretty handy," he remembered. "I'd win some science fairs, not because I was smart, but because my projects looked really good. There were a lot of things I wanted, but couldn't afford, so I built them myself, using sheet metal and other materials."

By the time he graduated from high school, he would also have six years of education at the trade school under his belt.

"I took virtually every course they had," he said. "Every shop course except for auto shop and welding shop, and I would have taken those too, if I'd had the time."

Hartley is still a proponent of acquiring useful skills at vocational schools.

"The irony is that the guidance counselors advised me not to go to trade school," he said, "but if I hadn't attended Ross Collins for all those years, I wouldn't be where I am today."

Hartley also had dreams of being a musician, however, and like millions of other American youngsters who came of age in the Fifties, he was interested in the new and rapidly-evolving genre of rock and roll.

He began working at his father's music store in the mid-Fifties. One of his early mentors was Ed Shealey, the owner of a small repair business located above the store. Shealey serviced home entertainment items sold by Mutt Peavey's store.

"My father's store was also a Magnavox dealership," Hartley said, "and when I was in junior high school, I'd go upstairs to Ed Shealey's electronics shop after school. I did odd jobs that nobody else wanted to do, and Ed would let me watch was he was doing, which was fascinating."

In 1958, Hartley began converting Magnavox monaural/hi-fi audio systems to stereo at his father's store, around the time the two-channel/separate-sounds-in-separate-speakers sonic innovation was just being introduced into the American marketplace.

"My father got me to do that because he didn't want to pay Ed Shealey to do it," he remembered. "Then, he told me he wanted me to learn how to repair automatic record changers, and those were a monumental pain in the ass."

In addition to the employment opportunity at the family business, jobs at local radio stations had the bonus effect of developing Hartley's love of rock and roll, as well as rhythm & blues music.

"We used to sell records in our store, and I remember getting goosebumps the first time I heard Ray Charles' 'What'd I Say'," he said. "We actually had a full-time record salesperson; her name was Rose Jackson, and I told her what to order. In those days, record salesmen would come by, and they'd have records in the trunks of their cars. We *did* order some that were shipped in, but some distribution companies actually worked directly with stores back then."

As for radio work, Hartley recounted, "I did some deejay work as a teenager as well, and one of the stations where I worked switched to a country format two or three weeks after I started there. I was all ready to quit, but then I realized they were getting all kinds of records coming into the station, and they were literally throwing away of these great rock and blues records.

"Greed got the better of me; remember those old Allstate Insurance ads showing a pair of hands, and the slogan 'You're in good hands with Allstate'? Well, I was like that with my own hands, holding them out to gather in records. I'd walk home every day with a *ton* of great records—classic labels like Blue Note and Excello."

Hartley was also able to further his appreciation for blues music thanks to a local jukebox operator, who had machines that played different formats of records.

"He would put all of his jukeboxes that played 45s in the nicer places, and he'd put his older jukeboxes that played shellac 78s in the juke joints," Hartley recalled. "Almost all of the major jukebox manufacturers' machines had maybe a 20-watt amplifier with a couple of 6L6 tubes. I did some repair work for him, and when he rotated his 78s out of the juke joints, he'd give them to me."

(Decades later, when the B.B. King Museum was built in Indianola, Mississippi, Hartley would donate 13 records by "Blues Boy" King—all of which were 78 r.p.m. on the RPM label—to the facility. They were placed on display along with other early B.B. King recordings.)

Perhaps not unexpectedly, stereotypical generational differences regarding loud, raucous music developed between father and son, and were only intensified by the fact that Mutt was a talented musician himself.

"My father had no faith in rock and roll, and thought it would never last," Hartley remembered. "He was a traditionalist; he wanted me to play in the school band, and he promised to buy me a car—which was also important to a teenager—if I played in the band. I started out on clarinet, which a lot of sax players do. I didn't like it; I thought it was a sissy instrument, and it seemed like I was always biting holes in the reeds. Ultimately, I played trumpet in the marching band, but I still hated it. I didn't want to march at football games or dress up in a monkey suit with a tassel on my head, but I was willing to do anything for that car!"

Mutt Peavey would ultimately buy Hartley a new 1957 Chevrolet. The model was built in an era when American automobiles were known for visually-striking/"large" aesthetics, and Hartley's '57 Chevrolet was a definitive example—it had a two-tone finish, and huge tailfins that epitomized the design propensities of those times.

"It was a Chevy Bel-Air four door hardtop," Hartley remembered fondly. "The body was red and the roof was white. I put lowering blocks on it, and it had fender skirts and a 'bar-style' grille for a while. It had Moon hubcaps, and dual 'glass pack' mufflers. Unfortunately, it came with that awful two-speed 'Powerglide' transmission. I loved that car, though!"

One intriguing bonus was the fact that the bright red color of Hartley's car matched the paint on the front of Peavey's Melody Music.

Mutt grudgingly recognized that the advent of rock and roll only was increasing the interest in guitars. However, the veteran store owner wasn't enthusiastic about developing an electric guitar-playing clientele.

Hartley: "My dad didn't like Fender; he liked Gibson, and he didn't like electric guitars. Typically, he had only one electric guitar in our store, and it was known as *the* electric guitar. He had a whole row of Gibson acoustics; he didn't like Martin, either. He was just a Gibson guy; I don't know whether he liked the (sales) rep or whatever. At any one time, he probably had fifteen to twenty Gibson acoustics on display."

"The electric guitar was on a shelf behind a glass counter, along with trumpet mouthpieces, clarinet reeds and other accessories. He actually kept one Les Paul for about five years. It was a Custom with three humbucking pickups on it—the one they called the 'Fretless Wonder', and I couldn't figure out why they used that nickname, because it had frets on it. My dad wouldn't even let anybody touch it. Sometimes he'd open the case so somebody could see it better, but if a customer reached out for it, he'd slam the lid back down."

"To my dad, an 'amplifier' was a small box with an eight-inch speaker, but he'd have to stock one of those to go with the one electric guitar. Occasionally, he'd bring in a lap steel guitar."

While Hartley credits several different individuals for his initial motivation regarding electronics, he can zero in on a singular incident that made him want to be a guitar player.

"I was in a high school fraternity called Theta Kappa Omega—TKO," he recounted, "and we thought we were the bad boys. My father was a Mason, and he wanted me to join DeMolay, but I wasn't interested.

"As I recall, the Laurel (Mississippi) chapter of the TKOs might have been the ones who booked Bo Diddley there in late '57 or maybe early '58—I remember it was cold—and a bunch of us from the Meridian chapter went down there to see the show. We actually booked Bo later in Meridian, as well as Larry Williams, and Chuck Berry. We booked Lloyd Price one time, but he never showed up. All of the fraternities and sororities were trying to out-do each other with the bands and singers they booked."

The pounding, exciting performance in Laurel by Bo Diddley—who actually had a musical beat named after him—fascinated the Meridian teenagers (from both a sonic and visual perspective), as well as the rest of the audience.

"He played a Les Paul-shaped guitar that was covered in rabbit fur, and he had an amplifier that was about the size of a desk!" Hartley recalled. "Being inquisitive, I managed to look inside the back of the amp when he was taking a break. He had a Fender amplifier chassis that had a tremolo circuit, and a bunch of speakers sitting on top of planks instead of being mounted to baffle board. Damnedest thing I've ever seen.

"I went home and pestered my father to give me a guitar, but he said I had to learn to play before he'd give me one. He also noted that guitar players didn't play their bills.

"He finally loaned me a cheap Stella acoustic, and later, a Suzuki classical guitar. It was the first Japanese guitar I'd ever seen, and I didn't know you weren't supposed to put steel strings on it, which I proceeded to do. Of course, the bridge came right off!"

Hartley also fell in love with the look of one of Bo Diddley's custom-made Gretsch guitars.

"It looked like a rocket ship," he said, "and it had fins on it like a Cadillac. I drew out my idea for a similar-looking guitar, on butcher paper."

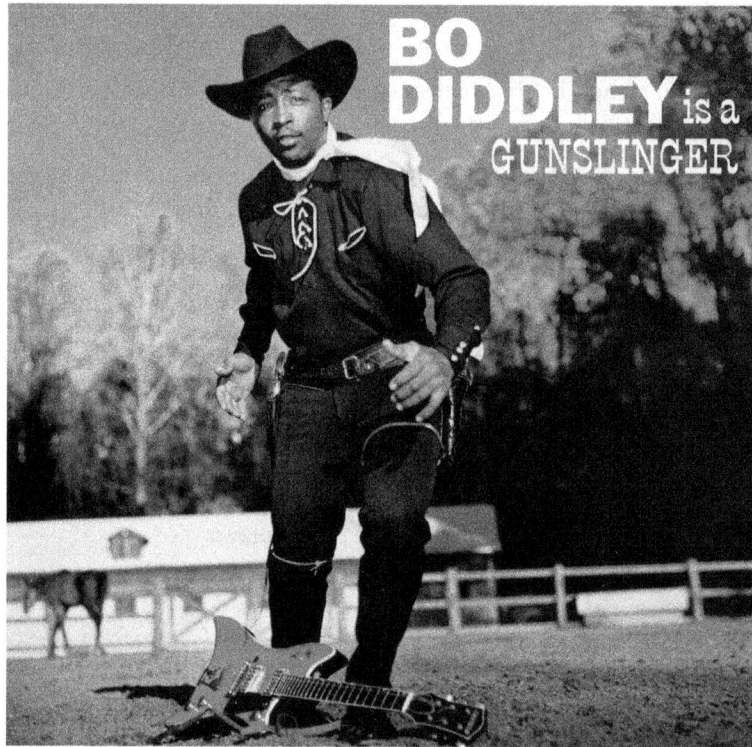

Hartley was fascinated by the Space Age design of Bo Diddley's custom-made Gretsch electric guitar, seen on this album cover *Wikipedia*

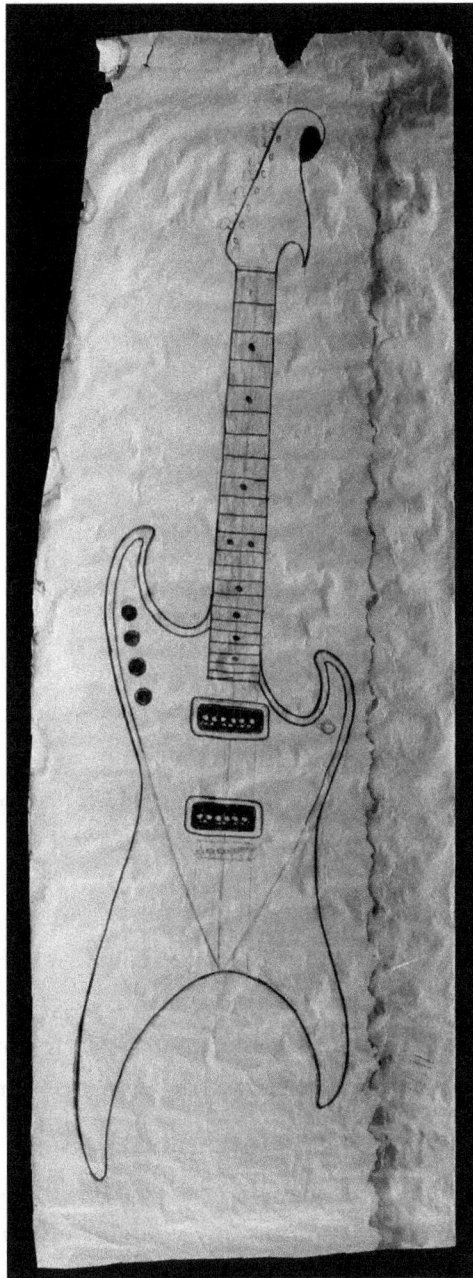

**Primeval design for a modernistic solidbody electric guitar,
drawn by Hartley on butcher paper, ca. 1958**

The drawing of the futuristic guitar was detailed enough to include two DeArmond DynaSonic pickups, as found on Diddley's Gretsch. It would be retained for decades, and its body silhouette would show up in the design of a Peavey electric guitar in the early Eighties.

When he was a senior in high school, Hartley created a zig-zag-shaped drawing of his surname that he envisioned as a corporate symbol if he ever went into the electronics manufacturing business. It would ultimately become known as the famous Peavey "lightning bolt" logo.

Hartley's original drawing of the "lightning bolt" logo is now framed, and is on display at the Peavey museum in Meridian. *Willie G. Moseley*

Like the rest of the Deep South, Meridian was still segregated, and as was often the case, underage white kids would sneak into black clubs to listen to music they weren't allowed to hear elsewhere.

"I only did that once," said Hartley. "There was a place in Meridian called 'Lake Erie Beach', down off of 10th Avenue. I don't where they came up with that name; it was far away from Lake Erie, and it wasn't close to any beach, either. It was kind of understood that there was a table there where white kids could go."

Hartley began playing in bands when he was a student majoring in Business at Mississippi State University in Starkville. He played several different guitars, and recalled that his first decent instrument was a mahogany Gibson Les Paul Special. Like many aspiring guitarists, he had various experiences with various models.

"I liked the way Gibsons sounded, but I didn't like the way they looked," he remembered. "I thought Fenders were cool, so I carved out a place in the back of the Les Paul, as well as a forearm bevel, and painted it with white Krylon paint."

Hartley asserts that in those times, guitarists in most bands were considered good if they could play the solos on hit songs note-for-note. He described himself as a "robot," because he attempted to hone his skills by slowing 45 r.p.m. records down to 33 1/3 r.p.m. in order to better learn guitar notes.

"There were a few songs I could play where some people thought I was actually pretty good, but if you wanted to jam, forget it," he said. Perhaps his focus on the rigid disciplines and guidelines involved with electronics figured into his apparent inability to be "loose" whenever he played guitar, but his interest in rock and roll was also nurturing his interest in sound amplification.

Working in the basement of his parents' home, Hartley had begun to build guitar amplifiers for himself as well as his bandmates, and such craftsmanship was appreciated by other musicians with whom he played.

Hartley's original workbench from his childhood home has been meticulously reassembled for display in the Peavey museum. *Willie G. Moseley*

"A buddy of mine named Sonny Roth told me he'd give me some lessons if I'd build him an amp, so I did," he remembered. "I built an amp from a Mullard schematic that had four twelves (12" diameter speakers) and a couple of horns. It had an RIAA (Recording Industry Association of America) E.Q. (equalization) curve that was a piece of crap—it was for an amplifier that reproduced the sounds of radio broadcasts or records—but it worked.

"As it turned out, I ended up building gear for almost every band I played with, then I'd go to practice one day, and they'd have some new guitar player who could blow me away, so I'd be out of a job.

"The first time this happened, I said something to myself like 'That's life'; the second time it happened, I said something like 'Boy, this is a string of bad luck!' But the third time it happened, I said, 'You know, I think these people are trying to tell me something.'"

Another Meridian musician who was a few years older than Hartley was guitarist George Cummings. Although they never played in a band together, the two became friends, and George, who described Hartley as "my ol' beer-drinking, water-skiing, and jazz record-collecting buddy," was one of the earliest musicians to recognize Hartley's abilities in building amplifiers.

"I was with Hartley in the basement of his father's house when he first started building projects like speaker cabinets and exploring the electronics of amps," Cummings recalled. "He was the brains behind it all; I just helped him glue and screw things together. We made some big speaker cabinets that I still have, and they still sound good. This was in the early Sixties, and I was playing in bands around Meridian while going to college on a football scholarship. Hartley was learning to play guitar and was a decent player, but building things was his passion."

Hartley also recalled the water-skiing excursions with Cummings and other friends to the Tombigbee River, about 55 miles from Meridian. The beer of choice was usually Jax, a budget brand. The Jax brewery was located in New Orleans on the bank of the Mississippi River, near the French Quarter.

The budding amplifier builder traded off various other instruments over the course of his playing days, and he ended up turning the Les Paul Special over to Cummings, in a swap for a Fender Stratocaster.

"I saw him reshape a Gibson mid-Fifties Les Paul Special and paint it white," Cummings said, confirming Hartley's recollection. "I had just gotten a Strat in trade from a friend, and Hartley and I traded even."

"I had recalled that I'd given it to him," Hartley said of the Les Paul, "but George reminded me years later that he'd *traded* it to me for an old blue piece-of-**** Stratocaster. I'd always wanted a Stratocaster, but this one was a horrible guitar. It buzzed and hummed, and had a one-piece white pickguard with a V-shaped neck. The trade actually probably happened when I was in college, although George never went to Mississippi State."

Cummings forged his guitar career in a band called the Chocolate Papers, which toured the Southeast, and later became the house band at the Gus Stevens Restaurant, an 800-seat supper club on the Mississippi Gulf Coast. Headline acts at the venue included Elvis Presley, Andy Griffith, Mel Tormé, Jayne Mansfield, Rudy Valee, Jerry Lee Lewis, and Mamie Van Doren. The club achieved some notoriety in 1967, when Mansfield was killed in an automobile wreck after performing there.

The Chocolate Papers would later provide original members of Dr. Hook and the Medicine Show, which had hits like "The Cover of the *Rolling Stone*" and "Sylvia's Mother." Cummings co-founded the band, and played lead guitar. In the studio, he also relied on an old steel guitar that Hartley had given him.

"(Hartley) had loaned me a Gibson lap steel, which I hauled around for years until I finally decided to try to play it," Cummings detailed. "I wound up using it on a lot of the Dr. Hook records we made in the Seventies."

**Publicity photo of the Chocolate Papers. George Cummings is on the right, with the
Les Paul Special formerly owned by Hartley, and a lap steel Hartley also owned is seen on the left.
Note the middle-digit comment by Cummings' right hand, on the guitar's headstock.** *George Cummings*

F

As an aspiring player, Hartley also had his eye on other guitars owned by other acquaintances, including the aforementioned Sonny Roth.

"Sonny had a 1959 (Fender) Jazzmaster with an aluminum pickguard, and I *very* much coveted that guitar," he remembered. "Eventually, I made a copy of it, making the body out of two pieces of three-quarter-inch plywood glued together; I bought a Fender replacement neck, and fabricated the metal parts at Ross Collins Vocational School. It had a black pickguard, and I painted it white with a can of Krylon spray paint. It actually looked and played well.

"I ended up trading it to a local country musician –*even*—for a 1959 Gibson ES-345 Stereo with a Bigsby (vibrato), and I still have that Gibson. The guy who owned claimed that 'It wouldn't play right.' He sent it back to Gibson several times and they couldn't find anything wrong with it –and there *is* nothing wrong with it."

Hartley eventually did acquire a Jazzmaster, but recalled, "While I was at Mississippi State I saw a guy with a brand new (Fender) Jaguar, and I went crazy, and sold my Jazzmaster to buy a white Jaguar. *Big* mistake! That Jag was nowhere near the guitar the Jazzmaster was; it buzzed almost as bad as that blue Strat, and those slide switches on the Jag for pickup selectors *sucked*, big time. I tried to buy my Jazzmaster back from the guy I sold it to, and he wouldn't sell it back to me. Decades later, I was eventually able to buy my own Jazzmaster, and I loved it."

F

In 1960, Mutt sold his store to Mississippi Music, which had other retail locations in the Magnolia State. However, he retained the ownership of the building in which the store was housed, becoming a landlord for the business that had bought him out.

Hartley stopped playing in bands when he was a junior at MSU, and took what he termed as a "personal inventory," trying to decide what he wanted to do after college. He knew that he was good at building amplifiers, and he still loved music and musicians, despite his dearth of personal musical talent.

"I'd played in bands for about three years before I quit," he recalled, "and during that time, I'd noticed that almost every musician I ever talked to told me something like 'I wish somebody would make quality equipment for working musicians at fair prices.'"

Such a collective opinion would become the impetus and inspiration for Hartley Peavey's future, and the *quality-equipment-for-working-musicians-at-fair-prices* phrase would become his mantra.

A "pre-company" amplifier built by Hartley. This one is reportedly the first to feature the Peavey "lightning-bolt" logo, and is on display at the Peavey museum, courtesy of R.T. Lowe. *Willie G. Moseley*

CHAPTER 2
A decade of amplification and expansion

Unlike many college seniors who are about to venture into the working world, Hartley Peavey knew exactly what he wanted to accomplish, even if his attitude seemed to be overly-ambitious or even brash. A member of Mississippi State University's Class of 1965, he would garner a business degree, but was still focused on building amplifiers, primarily because he enjoyed such labor, and he was good at it.

Accordingly, he persuaded his father to help him found Peavey Electronics with an $8000 loan, and the new company, with one employee, set up shop in the empty, dingy attic above Mutt's former music store. Mississippi Music would continue to operate downstairs, as the red-headed college grad erected a workbench upstairs, and began hand-crafting guitar and bass amplifiers, one at a time, in a hot and almost-claustrophobic work environment.

Hartley's "test instrument" was his white Fender Jaguar.

"It was the only guitar I had," he explained, "and I never had a bass for a test instrument."

Hartley with his earliest test instrument

The earliest amplifiers Hartley had built during his would-be musician days had utilized vacuum tubes, but he was intrigued and inspired by the relatively-new and still-evolving technology of transistors and solid state amplification. A trip with his father to an electronics company in Opelika, Alabama convinced Hartley that solid state was the way of the future.

The initial Peavey amplifiers included a guitar model and a bass model. Hartley's first amplifier sale was, perhaps not unexpectedly, to Mississippi Music.

The young entrepreneur began traveling to area music stores, personally pitching his amplifiers in Jackson, Tuscaloosa, and Montgomery, among other locales. However, increasing amp building responsibilities (including the addition of employees) kept him more confined to Meridian, and he eventually contracted with a manufacturer's representative (a fancy name for "traveling salesman") who also sold watches, but the association didn't last long.

And the story of how Hartley acquired his first long-term salesman is a classic tale that he loves to recall:

"Around 1966 or '67, the manager of the music store below my shop called me one day and asked me to come down; there was a sales rep down there claiming he had the best-sounding amp in the world. The salesman said it would blow any other amp away; that it was better than Fender, better than Vox, better than anything. The music store didn't have a guitar player on the premises, so they called me downstairs to try it out.

"I walked downstairs, and there sat this 'tuck-and-roll' pleated Kustom monster on casters, with two Altec speakers in it. The salesman was bragging about it, and told me to turn it on. When I hit the switch, the amp went '*KA-POOK! Ssssssss...*' It was noisy as hell, and it had no definition. The salesman wanted to know my honest opinion, and I told him I didn't think it sounded worth a ****. The salesman got agitated, obviously, and when I told him I had an amp that sold for less than half of what the Kustom would retail for, he dared me to bring it out; he said something like 'Roll it on out here, sport.'

"I brought down my 65-watt solid state amp with four ten-inch Utah speakers in it—I couldn't afford Altecs—I turned it on, and blew his ass out of the room. I mean, the blood drained from his face! He didn't say a word; he just packed his bag and rolled his Kustom amp out the door. I went back upstairs, feeling sorry for the salesman, and a bit embarrassed, but he made me do it.

"A few minutes later, the salesman's brother, who was traveling with him, came up to my shop. The Kustom amp salesman's name was Bob Belfield, and his brother, Don, was also a traveling salesman, but didn't have a job at the time. Don was also in the store when my amp blew away the Kustom, and he came scurrying upstairs, begging me to let him sell my amplifiers. I didn't know how desperate he was, and he didn't know how desperate I was, because I didn't have any money. But he took my amp on the road, which left me more time to build amps, so it worked out well for both of us."

Bob Belfield would also later become a Peavey rep. Hartley remembered the siblings as having outgoing and mercurial personalities, noting that Don and Bob got into a fistfight on the display floor at a National Association of Music Merchandisers (NAMM) show, a once-a-year event (at that time) where music manufacturers displayed their wares for retailers (Hartley had attended his first NAMM show with his father in 1954).

The feisty facet of the Belfield brothers' personalities was compatible with Hartley's own personality, and their sales efforts were critical in the company's early days.

"They were 'characters'," Hartley recalled. "The first NAMM show I went to after I started the company was at the Conrad Hilton Hotel in Chicago, and I was amazed at how Don walked through the lobby, calling everybody by their first name."

The Belfields were highly successful in getting the Peavey name out beyond the Deep South. Don was so successful that he bought an airplane that he often used on his sales routes.

"It's a thousand wonders that Don didn't get killed in that thing," Hartley said. "He had a Mooney Mark 20, which is not a big plane, but it was very fast. One time, he landed without putting the landing gear down. When I asked him why he didn't completely crash, he said 'Well, hell, I saw sparks flyin' every which way, which was the prop hittin' the runway.' Instead of belly landing, which he should have done, he went around. With the tips of your propeller bent back, you can break the crankshaft or destroy the engine mounts, or whatever. He was ungodly lucky, because that's the way you get killed. And like a fool, I actually flew with him, more than once."

While the new Peavey amplifiers looked sharp and sounded good, they obviously didn't have the brand recognition of national companies. Paying close attention to dealers' comments (even if they declined to stock his amplifiers), Hartley took advantage of a developing niche in sound reinforcement—portable public address systems for combos, which consisted of a central, multiple-channel amplifier for microphones and two vertical columns with speakers, were just coming onto the amplification market.

"A dealer in Montgomery told me something like 'Son, I'm not interested in your amplifiers, but if you had a sound system, I'd be *very* interested in that,'" Hartley remembered. "On the drive back to Meridian, I got to thinking: 'I can do that', so I designed a four-channel, 100-watt sound system. This was around 1967 or '68, and about the only two sound systems you could buy back then were the Shure Vocal Master, which was 100 watts, six channels, and it had 'cheesy' columns made by Argos. It cost a thousand dollars. Kustom also had a four-channel system for about nine hundred bucks. Remember, this was back when gas was 32 cents a gallon!

"I had paid attention to my father's pricing at retail, so not knowing any better, I priced my stuff at about a 30 percent gross margin over cost, hoping to end up with ten percent net. You could get my sound system two ways, with two columns with twelve-inch speakers or two columns with ten-inch speakers. The system with 'twelves' was $599 list, and I couldn't build them fast enough."

Peavey's sales and product lineup did indeed mushroom in the late Sixties and early Seventies, and musicians at all levels responded to the upstart company's straightforward approach to sound reinforcement equipment.

The company's first factory would open in early 1968, and was followed by a second factory in 1971.

Two other brothers, Jim and Jack Wilson, would also boost the Peavey moniker as reps in the western half of the U.S. in the earlier days of the company.

Jim preceded Jack, and Hartley recalled that Jim "...had this big Winnebago (motor home) that he drove all over the place. He was the only rep of ours from the Mississippi River to the Pacific Ocean, and he made a ton of money. He literally opened up the West for Peavey, and he was one of the best salesmen I ever had. Jim put Jack to work covering some of his area, because he couldn't possibly cover it all himself."

Jack specialized in doing clinics for the company, which demonstrated Peavey products at a specific dealer's store for local musicians. Some years later, Jack would become an artist relations official, as Peavey lined up endorsers. Other veteran reps clamored to sell Peavey products to dealers.

The clinician for the eastern half of the U.S. was Marty McCann, who was from Pennsylvania, and had a background in electronics. He was a part-time musician who played a variety of music for specific ethnic groups in his area ("I played a lot of polkas"). McCann's "day job" was with U.S. Steel, and he began repairing amplifiers for an area music store, Zambo Music, as a sideline income. He would later become a full-time employee at that retail business.

"We threw the first Peavey rep out of the store," McCann recalled. "We had all of the 'entry-level' amps we needed in those days. But somebody else had been selling Peavey to a few local musicians, and every once in a while, something would come into my repair shop. This was around 1969, and if you called Peavey with a question, sometimes Hartley Peavey himself would answer the phone. He was always polite; he always tried to help me solve my problem, and then he would pump me for information about how his competitors were doing in my area—'What's Fender doing? What's Gibson doing?' He would actually give me tips on how to fix his competitors' amps!"

McCann finally met Hartley at a NAMM show, and Zambo Music placed its first order for Peavey amplifiers at the same event.

"We'd had other brands of amps and P.A.s that kept blowing up," said McCann, "and we had to cannibalize a lot of our new stock to keep what we'd already sold working, so the boss bought about $10,000 worth of Peavey gear, and it did real well for us."

McCann's employer, Duane Zambo, ultimately got out of the retail business and went on the road as a musical instrument rep. His lines later included Peavey.

Marty was doing sound system installation work and managing bands when he was seriously injured in a head-on automobile collision, and was hospitalized for five and a half months.

"At that time, Hartley was looking for someone to do education, and Duane told Hartley about me," Marty said. "Duane didn't know I was in the hospital at the time. He finally got ahold of me when I was at home, with my leg in traction; some people thought I wouldn't be able to walk again. I came down to Meridian *in a body cast* and interviewed for the job. Hartley will still tell people that I was so pathetic that he felt sorry for me, and hired me. I went to work at Peavey in June of 1975."

The Peavey lineup of amplifiers and sound reinforcement gear continued to grow. In 1972, the company took somewhat of a step backwards, as a series of tube amplifiers were introduced. The electric guitar market was already demanding a "retro" sound, and although Hartley insisted—and still insists—that Peavey isn't a "retro" company, he recognized that the tube amp niche was an area where his company could easily be competitive. Not surprisingly, Peavey tube amps were covered in tweed, to emulate the look of classic tube amplifiers from the Fifties.

Peavey had been expanding, and already had two factories when the company purchased an office building on 'A' Street in Meridian in 1973. An enormous plant was built across the street in the same annum. The new facility had almost 250,000 square feet of floor space. The company began export operations that year, and also introduced powered mixers.

By the early Seventies, Peavey had made some serious inroads into the amplifier and P.A. business. 1974 saw the introduction of Peavey microphones, but one important step introduced that year by the Meridian company, now considered a giant in its field, were product education seminars for dealers and sales reps.

However, Hartley began to hear reports about companies that made both guitars and amplifiers requiring dealers to purchase both product lines; i.e., the companies informed dealers that in order to purchase their guitars, they had to buy the same brand of amplifiers as well. Hartley had no doubt that the success (and value) of his own amplifier line had prompted other companies to institute such policies.

The Seventies weren't particularly a good decade for the Big Two of electric guitars, anyway. Gibson (owned by a company called Norlin) and Fender (owned by the CBS conglomerate) both suffered from quality control problems, and had also introduced new products that had stiffed in the marketplace. The encroachment of imported guitars and other equipment was also a factor, but the many of the guitars and amplifiers made by the two most-recognized guitar companies in the U.S. were unpopular, and the notion that dealers would be required to purchase merchandise in a regimented manner, dictated by the manufacturer, was anathema to most retailers.

"By the early Seventies, CBS had really screwed the pooch," Hartley said of Fender products of that era. "They pissed off all the dealers with their high-handed techniques. They rushed through a bunch of engineers and redesigned all of their amplifiers, supposedly to be better, but they lost the sound. They were trying to sell solid state amps, which were horrible.

"Gibson has always tried to get in the amplifier business, and they never really have, although they've come close a couple of times. Their SG brand of amps looked like flight cases, but had these awful-looking, big ol' knobs, like something you'd see on a washing machine. They were not what the market wanted. Their best effort was their 'Lab' series, which were decent amps. In fact, B.B. King used a Lab amp."

Hartley maintains that his products were appreciated by his accounts as well as working musicians in the early Seventies, and he held forth in detail about his then-competitors:

"You had people who were big music dealers, but they didn't know anything about the product," he said, "but in those days, it *wasn't necessary* to know anything about the product. When I got into the business, a lot of my dealers were already big Fender or Kustom amp dealers—or maybe both—so I had to take the 'second tier', or in some cases, the 'third tier.' Most of them eventually made Peavey their first tier line, because they could push my products profitably.

"Both Fender, under CBS, and Gibson, under Norlin, were desperate. The offerings of both of these companies was at an all-time low, and they were losing traction with the dealers…and at the same time, Peavey was gaining traction. But apparently the Fender and Gibson reps felt empowered to use the same 'strong-arm tactics' they used in the 'good ol' days' in the Sixties. Fender Strats and basses were still in relatively high demand, and they apparently felt this would provide leverage with their dealers. Same thing was true of Gibson and their guitars.

"The reps were going in and demanding that dealers stock at least one of their amps or P.A. systems for every Peavey amp or P.A. system the dealers had in stock.

"Technically, that was illegal; it's called 'tying,' and I endured it for a couple of years. I've never been a fan of lawyers or suing people, so in my naiveté, I decided that if those reps were going to use their instruments as a mace on the heads of their dealers—which were also *my* dealers—I'd just 'fight fire with fire'—I decided to build guitars."

P

Hartley had actually toured the Gibson factory in Kalamazoo, Michigan many years earlier, when he was in the area for a Chicago NAMM show.

"God, what an archaic situation that was," he recalled. "I could tell that the way they were making guitars was primitive."

He had also toured Fender's facilities in California:

"One of my reps, Paul Robinson, had been a Fender rep, and was good friends with one of the CBS/Fender top dogs, who gave us a tour of the Fender factory years earlier, when we were out on the West Coast—it might have been for one of the first NAMM shows in California. It was kind of interesting, but it was also kind of surprising, because it, too, was so primitive. I was astounded at the way they were making necks, because they had a piece of aluminum in the shape of a neck; they'd take a neck blank, saw it out with a band saw, then do the final shaping by hand on a pin router, which has been around since the 1800s. If the worker was feeling good that day, you'd get a nice thin neck, but if he didn't, you could get a Louisville Slugger (baseball bat). They didn't press frets in from the top; they tapped them in from the side, which I thought was bizarre. I saw lots of inefficiencies and poor work flow."

The Fender official who had invited Hartley and Robinson to tour the California factory had expected a reciprocal tour of the Peavey factory, and eventually showed up one day in Meridian. He was given what Hartley termed a "whirlwind" tour.

"He wasn't impressed, since at that time we were still in our old Plant #1 on 10th Avenue, and our old Plant #2, where we were making the cabinets."

Hartley had an interest in guns, and had always been impressed with the close fit in the construction of firearms. He began to speculate about applying such techniques to the construction of guitars.

"Even the *best* woodworkers who build something by hand are hard-pressed to maintain a tolerance of 1/32 of an inch," he opined, "and a lot of so-called 'hand craftsmanship' is 'adjusting for slop'. I thought that if I could eliminate the tolerance limitations on guitar bodies and necks, I could eliminate the handwork."

The earlier tours of the Gibson and Fender factories let Hartley know how he *didn't* want to make guitars, and he began to envision the use of innovative CNC (computer numerical control) machinery and other cutting-edge technology in his preliminary quest for consistent quality in unique woodworking tasks (guitar bodies and necks aren't shaped like speaker cabinets). What he was seeking to do had never been accomplished in the guitar manufacturing business, and for that matter, such construction techniques had never even been *tried,* to his knowledge.

The construction of the gigantic factory on 'A' Street had left Peavey's first and second factories empty, and plans were made to locate loudspeaker production in the first factory, and guitar production in the second vacant facility. Peavey had also been experiencing difficulties with speaker suppliers, and in a parallel response, Hartley decided that his company would make its own loudspeakers. Such a two-pronged transition proved to be difficult, and caused a lot of stress—financial and otherwise—for the company founder.

"The mistake I made was trying to do the loudspeaker program and the guitar program at the same time," Hartley said. "I bit off more than I could chew, and I almost went bankrupt.

"1976 was a time of real stress for the company and me, but I had some very talented guys working with me on both of the new programs.

"We hired a machinist named Sam Moore, and little did I realize he was a mechanical genius! Sam designed and built most of the tooling for our speaker factory, and luckily, he applied his genius to help us in guitar and bass production, too. We probably couldn't have done either program without him.

"Hollis Calvert, a good country picker, had joined the company as a draftsman; he and a guy from our advertising department, Pat House, would help with the shapes of bodies and headstocks. Other guys who helped out a lot were R.T. Lowe, Charlie Gressett, and Jerald Pugh."

Still, Hartley also knew he would have to hire a special person to create his guitar line from scratch, and such an individual would need to share his own appreciation of what modern technology could do to facilitate uniformity and quality in guitar construction. The word was put out to Peavey reps to keep their eyes open for someone who was talented in building and/or repairing guitars, and who had a knack for electronic technology and computers as well.

It seemed like a tall order, but Peavey's first successful salesman, Don Belfield, soon informed Hartley about a guitar repairman in south Texas.

CHAPTER 3
Chip Todd

"Don't be fooled by his easy-goin' Texas drawl," one Peavey veteran said of Chip Todd. "Behind that, he's a mechanical genius."

Indeed, Todd is the holder of numerous patents, some of which are shared with Hartley Peavey. However, other patents of Todd's have nothing to do with guitars, and he has maintained a personal logbook for decades, filled with many other unique ideas that he's never patented.

Charles Hugh Todd III was born in 1939 in Beaumont, Texas, the son of a physician and a schoolteacher. Beaumont is the nation's fourth largest seaport by tonnage. Much of the area's economy is, perhaps not surprisingly, Texas oil-based, and famous natives of Beaumont have included astronaut Robert Crippen, Olympic champion Babe Didrikson Zaharias, pro athletes Bubba Smith and Frank Robinson, and numerous musicians, including J.P. Richardson ("The Big Bopper"), funk bassist Larry Graham, blues/rock brothers Johnny and Edgar Winter, and country performers Mark Chesnutt and Clay Walker.

Like Hartley, Chip wasn't particularly musical, and as he entered his teens, he became fascinated with racing cars and boats.

"I was constantly hopping up cars," he remembered, "and my friends in high school had a betting pool that I wouldn't live to be 21. I even drove a hearse and an ambulance—back when the funeral homes had the ambulance services—and we raced to wrecks, for obvious reasons."

Todd even built his own engines for his drag racing cars.

Graduating from Lamar State College [now Lamar University] with a Commercial Art degree in 1964, Todd began working at a television station in nearby Port Arthur as the art director. His first experience with guitar building was, by his own admission, an experimental learning experience.

"I was looking for a way to repay an engineer who fixed our TV, and wouldn't take pay for doing it," he recalled. "I found out that he played guitar in a Mexican band, and decided to build him a guitar. I went to the Port Arthur branch of Swicegood Music and asked them if they had a guitar that needed painting. The manager, who later became a close friend, brought out an 'old' [Fender] Stratocaster. I took it home and disassembled it, noting what I could about its construction. I painted it and returned it for a charge of a whopping $25. The guitar I then made for my new friend was mahogany, and was quite a beauty, but, looking back, I realize that it was probably unplayable."

Moving to California to do graduate work in sculpture, Todd met automobile racing legend Mickey Thompson, who hired the Texas transplant to work at his speed parts manufacturing company. He worked his way up the company quickly, and ultimately designed an innovative monocoque Indianapolis 500 race car for Thompson, who was so impressed by Todd's talent that he co-sponsored Chip's return to Lamar State to get a Mechanical Engineering degree in 1968.

While he was back in Beaumont, the manager of the Beaumont Swicegood Music store (the company's flagship location) approached Todd about doing repair work on used guitars that the stores had in stock.

"Swicegood had been in business for 35 years with stores in Port Arthur, Beaumont, and Orange, and had never sold a traded-in instrument," he detailed. "The Beaumont store was close to us, and had a large metal building with hundreds of cases and boxes of instruments stacked to the roof. He told me that I could take four of them home, fix *one* for them, and the other three would be my pay. The nostalgia craze hadn't hit—yet—and there were [Fender] Broadcasters, [Gibson] Firebird Vs, first model Les Pauls; an unbelievable array of old guitars and all types of instruments.

"It didn't take long to figure out what did what, and how. They also got me the job of repairing the school system's instruments, which included bass violins, cellos, and music stands. I was making more doing the repairs than I would earn as an engineer, and I had a monopoly without a foreseeable end."

Todd's interest in modern technology and transportation led to a job with a monorail company in Dallas, which soon folded. He contacted Gibson sales representative Mudge Miller about the feasibility of a guitar repair company, and was advised to open such a business in Houston. Chip's shop quickly became an authorized warranty station for Fender, Gibson, Ovation, and other companies.

"I opened a solo shop," he recounted, "then Charles Parker Music, right downtown, offered me the entire second floor with my own entrance, free of rent. I hired Kevin Perry and Priscilla Price to make it a three-person shop, and was doing well."

A particular repair on an acoustic guitar was the impetus for Don Belfield's aggressive "bird-dog" efforts on behalf of Peavey.

"That repair was to an Ovation acoustic guitar that had been dropped," Todd detailed. "It had landed on the front binding at the butt end, splitting the binding away from the soundboard and damaging the spruce front. It had been played after the damage was done, causing dirt and sweat to further damage and discolor the area. I worked some Tite-Bond III—the completely waterproof version of Tite-Bond—into the cracks, and reinforced it from the inside with a strip of bias-cloth that was filled with the glue.

"I had to remove some of the dirty wood, so I grafted some fresh splinters in place of the removed wood. Since that could be seen, I feathered walnut-stained lacquer around the whole front edge in a sunburst fashion which faded out to about an inch from the binding. It was just a thing that I did regularly for front edge repairs."

Belfield was in Brook Mayes Music in Houston when Todd returned the Ovation to the store, and was impressed enough to follow Todd back to his shop to check out his operation. The veteran Peavey rep then flew his airplane to Meridian to inform Hartley of his discovery.

"Evidently, Hartley was interested enough to send [Belfield] right back to Houston to feel me out," said Todd. "He called, took me to an impressive restaurant for lunch, and talked me into leaving my shop with Kevin long enough to visit Hartley."

Todd may have already been a whiz regarding mechanical engineering and guitar repair, but he was woefully uneducated regarding sartorial protocol for business interviews.

"I asked [Belfield] what to wear, and he said 'a leisure suit'," Chip remembered with a chuckle. "I didn't know what a 'leisure suit' was, so I went to a man's store nearby, and asked for one. It was a black men's store, and the salesman talked me into a denim two-pieced suit. I still can't believe that Hartley didn't do a double-take when I showed up in that awful suit!"

On the flight to the interview in Meridian, Belfield cautioned his passenger not to expect an immediate offer, because Hartley was methodical, and would probably take about a week to decide on whether or not to offer employment to Todd.

"Until we were airborne, I didn't really realize the scope of Peavey's plan to build guitars," Chip noted.

And as it turned out, Belfield's admonition was completely wrong.

"When Don introduced me, Hartley didn't beat around the bush," Todd remembered, "and he immediately asked 'What do you think of a zero fret?'

"I answered, 'It's a good idea that the Japanese loused up by losing their nerve at the last minute, making it larger than the regular frets.'

Hartley was impressed by Chip's mechanical engineering credentials as well as the fact that Todd was a gunsmith.

"He was a big ol' tall, lanky guy who seemed to know what he was doing," Hartley said. "He happened to be a gun enthusiast, and that helped a lot, because I've always been a gun guy. We had a lot in common."

"We did some small talk," Chip remembered, "but I noticed that Hartley was already selling Meridian to me, and he made me an offer pretty quickly. We really didn't have any negotiations; he pretty much hired me on the spot. I asked for a couple of weeks to close up my business. Hartley took me out to eat that night, and got me a motel room."

"As Don and I were flying back to Houston the next day, Hartley added another $5000 to the salary we had agreed to, and it was almost a year later, at tax time, that I realized that he'd done that. When I thanked him, he said, 'I wondered how long it'd take you to notice.'"

Chip Todd closed out his repair shop in early June, 1975, turning over the business to his top guitar repairman, and setting him up with the companies with which the business had warranty responsibilities.

Todd reported for work in Meridian two weeks later.

CHAPTER 4
Design and start up

Todd set up his desk in a Peavey factory lobby, and recalled that he was the only employee of the guitar division for the first year, as he and Hartley brainstormed, drew up plans then scrapped them, and drew up other plans. Todd shared the room with Marty McCann, but he and Hartley spent long hours with each other, focusing on their mutual goals, and they both thrived on such interaction.

"Chip came in with an open mind," Hartley said. "He wasn't stuck in his ways, and for that matter, none of us knew of a proper way to make guitars; we had no preconceived notions of how it should be done. Had it not been that way, what we did would have never happened. Being totally ignorant was a blessing in disguise."

"Little did I know how much time Hartley was willing to invest in the guitar's design," Chip remembered wistfully. "I found this period to be exhilarating, and I believe Hartley did, also. We spent more time together than Siamese twins."

Hollis Calvert, who had started at Peavey in 1971 in the Quality Control section, was transferred into guitar production. It helped that he was a talented and experienced guitar player.

"I had met Hartley early on," Hollis remembered. "We were in the same National Guard unit. He was just starting his company, and we got to be friends. He wanted me to check out the sound of his first amps; they sounded great, and were actually better than what I was playing through."

Calvert was a draftsman by trade, and he created ink drawings of Hartley's first circuit designs before he was even hired by the Peavey company. He also recalled taking Hartley to Nashville to help him get acquainted with noted players in Music City. Hollis already knew some of the session musicians, including Leon Rhodes, Jimmy Capps, Charlie McCoy (band leader for *Hee Haw*), Jeff Newman, Curley Chalker, Lloyd Green, Hal Rugg, and others. When the company began planning its guitar manufacturing venture, the input of Hollis and several other employees, as well as local players, was sought.

Hollis Calvert at his first NAMM show in the early Seventies.
He was involved in designing and constructing the display. *Hollis Calvert*

"It wasn't difficult to convince us that this new concept of a guitar—at an affordable price, with great features—was something we needed to do," he said. "We had tons of meetings where there was a lot of input from local players on tone, playability, weight, cosmetics."

Calvert was also impressed with the focus of new employee Chip Todd.

"Chip and I hit it off right away," he recalled. "He was from the engineering community, and had always enjoyed music—the guitar in particular. Chip was attacking the design of our first instrument from an engineering perspective, especially on the structural side, but he was also concerned about comfort, and ease of playing. He knew what the instrument was supposed to do, and how to make it do it."

Among the new employees who went to work with the new guitar venture was R.T. Lowe of Laurel.

For the 14 years he worked at Peavey, Lowe would make a daily commute from Laurel to Meridian and back (over 100 miles round trip) from a rural home on land homesteaded by his great-grandfather.

As a child, R.T. listened to the Grand Ole Opry on the radio, and got a guitar when he was ten. He also paid attention to the music broadcast by WNOE, a rhythm and blues/rock n' roll station in New Orleans. Another influence was his uncle, Mundell Lowe, who was also born in Laurel, and went on to become the staff guitarist at NBC Studios in New York City.

By his sixteenth birthday, R.T. was playing bass in a band that sported a horn section. Later, while in the Air Force, he played in a band in Las Vegas, and he would also serve in Vietnam. He ultimately returned to Mississippi, and took a job working on organs with Mississippi Music, the retail chain that had bought Hartley's father's store.

"Peavey was in the early stages as a small factory," Lowe recalled. "I was sometimes a critic, but the handwriting was on the wall about what Peavey would become. I visited Hartley and Hollis often. I wanted to be a Peavey rep; Hartley told me he needed techs, but he had a line of salesmen around the block."

Lowe was hired when news of the guitar plans were made public. He worked temporarily for Frank Morris in Peavey's Service Department, before heading over to the new guitar division.

"Hartley and Chip had designed the basic look of the guitar and bass on paper," he remembered, "and many of the components were already in-house, in quantity."

Hartley and Chip first decided on the type of machinery they would need to accomplish uniform construction of bodies and necks.

Hartley had been to a woodworking show in Louisville, Kentucky, and had noticed a machine made by a Chicago-area company called Ekstrom-Carlson.

"They were making router profilers, which were (computer) numerical control machines," Hartley detailed. "They had a three-axis, or X-Y-Z, machine. We used that Z axis to carve the top of the guitar body as it was being cut out of the body blank; I didn't want it to be a flat-top guitar. With that machine, one operator can make 250-300 solid guitar bodies a day. Bass bodies had more lineal outline, so they took a little longer."

The Ekstrom-Carlson machine Peavey purchased had six work stations. Guitar bodies could be loaded as body blanks, carved, and unloaded all in an ongoing process, so the machine would never stop.

Like Hartley, Todd also appreciated the precision with which firearms were built, so it wasn't surprising that the twosome zeroed in on a machine that was known for carving gunstocks to carve their guitar necks.

"I approached it with an open mind," Hartley said. "I wanted to do it the *best* way; I didn't give a damn how they hand-built guitars back in Germany in 1850, and the best way to carve necks was certainly not the way Gibson or Fender were doing it!

"We started looking into a device called a Geiger copy lathe—which is essentially a rotary pantograph—to carve necks. On a gunstock, the piece of wood is just several thousandths of an inch from the size of the final product; all they have to do is a bit of final sanding.

"I ended up going to Germany to buy one. The Geiger copy lathe we bought had five spindles, one for the pattern and four for neck blanks. It would cut on one side of the neck blanks, then rotate them 180 degrees for sanding. You'd take four pieces of wood that looked like two-by-fours, and in about five minutes they were guitar necks that were 90-something percent complete."

Peavey's Geiger copy lathe, loaded with necks. *Chip Todd*

The neck blanks were actually two pieces of maple laminated together, and a patented manufacturing process with a pre-installed truss rod was used when the necks were created.

"We installed the truss rod into the neck blanks before they were carved," Hartley said. "Nobody had ever done that before, as far as I know. A truss rod is literally a bent piece of steel, and it pre-tensions the neck. If you install a truss rod *after* a neck is carved, you get an artificial force that is added. We carved the necks with the truss rods already installed, so that meant that when we carved the surface of the neck, it was already pre-tensioned. The bilaminated necks with the pre-tensioned truss rods were very stable. You'd have to do something really stupid to make one of them warp, and whatever you did probably wouldn't work, anyway. Those necks were *that* sturdy."

As was the case with most manufacturers, Peavey's guitar neck truss rod could be adjusted by accessing it through the headstock/neck juncture. However, the Peavey truss rod cover, which was slightly bullet-shaped, had a curved/"bent" appearance, and it is thought this look was also an industry first.

Hartley also reaffirmed the efforts of machinist Sam Moore in the early days of Peavey's guitar venture.

"Sam built a lot of the guitar-making machines we had," he said. "He was a crusty ol' bastard, but he could make anything. He would argue with you about anything. He and I would argue in order to purify our perspectives."

P

A matching guitar and bass were planned from the outset. Todd recalled that the guitar and its parts were designed first, and that coming up with matching or corresponding parts for the bass was relatively easy.

The fret spacing on the necks was, according to Todd, "…calculated, not copied, using the factor of the twelfth root of two as the basis. This gives the mathematically-correct notes, and has been the correct basis for centuries of fretted instruments. We even used internally-designed fretwire."

In spite of an immediate meeting of the minds regarding a zero fret when Chip had first met Hartley, that item was not placed on Peavey instruments.

"We didn't do it, because a zero fret—at least, at that time—had a horrible reputation, because of all the crap that was coming in from overseas," Hartley said.

The scale of the new guitar was 25 1/2" with a 12" radius on its 21-fret fingerboard, and the bass had a 34" scale, and a 12" radius on a 20-fret fingerboard.

As for the shape of the body, Hartley recalled: "Chip and I thought 'If you took a Les Paul, a Stratocaster, and maybe a Mosrite, and put 'em in a bag and shook 'em all up, what would fall out?' That was what inspired the body shape. It looks a little clunky to me today, especially with the lower cutaway."

"I had been partial to fairly symmetrical body shapes," Todd said, "and knew that any 'fanciful' offset body shape would reek of Fender in everybody's minds. The lead guitar's body shape changed daily for quite some time, as we'd change a line and move it back and forth."

Northern ash was selected for the bodies of the instruments (both body and neck blanks were supplied by Hulsart Lumber of Tuscaloosa, Alabama; George Porter of the Joyner Machine company located that supplier of behalf of Peavey). That wood was chosen for its high mass and distinctive grain pattern. High altitude and cold weather wood has a grain that is denser, with smaller growth bands due to the shorter growing seasons, as opposed to the broad summer growth bands of southern ash.

While the instruments were somewhat heavy, "…so were other guitars from other manufacturers in that generation," Hartley said. "Everybody believed that the heavier guitars were, the more they'd sustain. At that time, everybody wanted a very dense body."

There were several valid reasons the original guitar and bass debuted in a plain, natural satin finish. Hartley recounted that in that era, many new instruments were being stripped to a natural finish.

"A lot of players—especially out on the West Coast—would take a nice, new, shiny Stratocaster or Les Paul and strip all the paint off of it," he said.

Chip cited additional details:

"We knew that 'weight equals sustain' was B.S., but we were the new kids on the block and didn't want to start a fight. We wanted a natural finish to show the grain, and that finish would also show that we weren't using cheap wood and hiding it with opaque paint. We chose to use a thinned lacquer wash-coat to keep the walnut grain filler from dyeing the wood, and the dark color filler made the attractive ash grain highly visible."

Multiple piece bodies were carved, as is the case with other manufacturers, to eliminate bowing of the body blanks. The direction of the grain was staggered, where possible, to aid in stability.

Strings loaded through the rear of the bodies, going all the way through to the bridge on the other side. The six holes on the guitar body and the four holes on the bass body had metal ferrules inserted to prevent the ball end of a string from damaging the wood.

This rear view of Peavey's first guitar model shows that the body is made from several pieces of wood laminated together. The rear-load string holes with ferrules are also seen. *Heritage Auctions*

Ditto this rear view of the first bass model. *Heritage Auctions*

Perhaps surprisingly, one of the most difficult aesthetic tasks was the design of the headstock. Original guitar prototypes tried out both "3 + 3" headstocks (equal number of tuners on each side) and six-on-a-side tuners.

"We both felt that the six-in-line tuning machines layout made an easier-to-tune arrangement," said Todd, "but it didn't take but a few hours of laying down pencil lines and erasing them to discover that any appreciable deviation from the familiar 'Strat' peghead shape was not pleasing to the eye. We spent way more time on the peghead design than any other feature. We felt that we succeeded in honoring CBS's design patent rights, yet had come up with a pleasing shape. In more than one way, my education and experience as a commercial artist paid off with the design."

"It took us longer to do the headstock than anything else on that guitar," Hartley agreed, "but to me, that 'harpoon' peghead is still one of the best-looking ones out there."

While the prototypes of the guitar and bass would be hand-fretted by Todd, another custom-built, first-of-its-kind machine that Peavey would order was used in standard production to install frets on necks without human hands touching the fret wire. The complex mechanism keyed off the top surface of the fretboard, slotted all fret slots as well as the topnut slot, advanced fretwire from 28 rolls in the attic, pressed all frets in at one time (with 45 tons of hydraulic pressure), sawed along both sides, and sanded the beveled fret ends.

P

Hardware for the new instruments was planned in a meticulous-yet-pragmatic manner.

"Early in our design sessions—and Hartley was *very* active in the designs—we talked ahead," Chip remembered. "We were erasing and moving lines around about future components, and which paths to take. Even though neither of us liked individual height adjusting saddles, Hartley felt that we needed to have some things, like body weight and adjustable saddles, to establish our credibility; again, we were 'the new kids on the block'. I knew what I wanted in knobs, and Hartley liked what I came up with. The 'lightning bolt P' on them was a given. Both of us also wanted a beefy bridge plate to take advantage of the die-casting."

P

One of the most innovative facets of Peavey's earliest guitars was the revolutionary roll-off coil-tap circuitry for their humbucking pickups. The (passive) circuit was built into tone controls, and was the idea of legendary pedal steel guitarist Red Rhodes (1930-1995), who sketched out the idea for Hartley.

"Red ran a repair facility in Hollywood called 'Red's Royal Amp Repair," Hartley recounted, "and he told me he had a circuit for what he called '…the best tone control ever, and it can make a pickup humbucking, single-coil, or anywhere in between, with no additional components—no pre-amp, no batteries,' or so he said. We were in a restaurant, and he drew it on the back of a napkin. I told him I didn't believe it would work, and he said, 'Well, before you start tellin' me it won't work, go try it.' So I did…and it did!"

The basic premise of Rhodes' unique design is that a humbucking pickup with two coils can gradually have one of its coils faded out by rotating the tone control, allowing for the pickup to be a humbucking pickup, a single coil pickup, or an "anywhere-in-between" pickup, with one coil blended in to whatever extent the user wishes. It would ultimately be trademarked, and was marketed as "The Circuit." Hartley and Red would share the patent.

The controls on the new guitar and bass were installed as a separate volume and tone control for each pickup. However, unlike a similar setup on a Gibson guitar (and some similar brands), volume controls on Peaveys were independent; i.e., on most two-volume, two-tone-control guitars, rotating one volume knob back would reduce the volume on *both* pickups, but Peavey volume controls worked each pickup individually.

"That's the way it always should have been," Todd insisted. "I've never understood the reasoning for the other way."

Another innovation was the pickup "fly winding" process, which included yet another innovative mechanism.

For decades, the standard way of creating a pickup involved manually winding the wire around a rotating oblong bobbin, and both wiring and bobbin were in motion—the bobbin would rotate as tensioned wire was being wrapped around it. Certain "handmade" or "hand-wound" pickups are desirable to some musicians because of their so-called legendary sounds.

However, human hands, or even machines that are being manually controlled by humans, could make mistakes, as tension gaps in the wiring could occur during the winding process. The sounds of different examples of the same model of hand-wound pickups can vary greatly if there were aberrations in the way they were wound.

"In the old days, wire would indeed be tensioned by hand," Hartley explained. "When it's being wound, the angle of the wire when a spinning bobbin is in a vertical position is very different from when it's in the horizontal position, and you could get kinks, backlashes, and all kinds of other problems in them. If you put a strobe [light] on the wire while it's being wound, you can see that it's actually being *whipped* on there, like what happens when you take a garden hose and snap it; the 'wave' travels down the hose, and the wire is doing the same thing. And that's a bull**** way of doing it. A perfect coil should be wound so tight it should feel as hard as a rock, but conventional 'spinning bobbin' coils feel spongy, and that's why they have to be soaked in lacquer or wax. That's like putting a Band-Aid on them; it's not a cure."

The wiring on Peavey pickups was installed from a company-designed machine that actually rotated around the bobbin, which was stationery. Wiring was installed in a much smoother, more uniform, and dependable manner, as tension gaps were eliminated.

"We did it a better way," Hartley said. "When we wound our pickups, the tension on the wire was constant. We ended up sealing the coils anyway, but we didn't have to. Nothing would move or shift in our pickups, so they didn't get microphonic and squeal."

Instead of individual polepieces for each string, the coils on the pickup had a (concealed) blade across their entire length to assure that no signal was lost if a string was bent (which could happen if a pickup had individual polepieces for each string).

Hartley does have 20/20 hindsight about one facet of the new pickup design, and wishes he had a time machine to correct it:

"Since we were designing a guitar that was totally different, we saw no reason to make the mounting the same size as a 'normal' humbucker. This was in a time before the so-called 'aftermarket' pickup companies; DiMarzio was probably the first, and they started around the same time we started making guitars, so there was a timing factor, as well. In retrospect, we should have made them the standard sizes."

That being said, he is also assertive about the pickups' placement on the guitar body:

"You can look at most humbuckers, and they're mounted in a little frame with two screws. You can take your fingers and rock the damn things back and forth, and that's crazy. In the T-60, you'll notice that we mounted the pickups with four screws. If you try to rock those, you can't do it; they're rigidly mounted."

R.T. Lowe recalled that the pickup coil roll-off circuit might have initially been perceived as "…somewhat of a gimmick, but to do what we hoped to do, a gimmick gave us an edge. The circuit complicated the pickup design because at every setting, we had to outperform everyone. Only cosmetic excellence and amazing performance at a fair price point would work."

Lowe was ultimately drafted to solve a problem that developed with the pickup early in the research and development stage. Initial experiments with the pickup revealed anemic performance.

"The bobbins, base plates, covers, and plastic inserts that fit in the 'window' of the cover were in stock," he said. "I began by trying to redesign the magnetic circuit only, but the problem was bigger. I bought lots of tools and equipment, and continued to work on it for months. At the same time, we began design of fixtures and assembly lines, and ordered tools for rapid assembly; the plan was to build 300 a day."

Curiously, the prototype pickup that Lowe was fine-tuning had been given a "Super Ferrite" moniker, and some early pickups had that name embossed on one of the two exposed ovals of the black plastic insert (with the Peavey "lightning bolt" logo on the other). However, Lowe recalled that the part "…forced the magnetic circuit too far for the strings to achieve superior output. Only a few of these (pickups) survived intact."

**Early variant of Peavey's first guitar pickup, with
"Super Ferrite" embossed on the insert.** *Chip Todd*

When Lowe announced that the plastic insert could not be used, such a pronouncement was not popular ("We had zillions already purchased," he said).

As a solution, the company designed a vacuum-formed "cup" that "potted" (sealed) the pickup, allowing it to protrude through the oval-shaped windows of the chrome frame. Earlier production pickups would have concealed blades; later examples had exposed blades, but the difference in the two styles was strictly cosmetic.

Other controls on the guitar and bass included a mini-toggle three-way pickup switch, and a mini-toggle phase switch, to switch the polarity on a humbucking pickup in order to offer unique alternative sounds.

The pickguard on the original instruments was three-layer, black/white/black. One simple and practical innovation on the scratchplate was a small, dot-shaped route through the top black layer into the middle white portion by each control knob, offering a point of reference.

"I think I probably brought that up, as it's what I did at my repair center in Houston," Todd recalled. "Since you bevel the edges to show the white outline, it wasn't a big deal to put it into the design."

⟜

"We were constantly changing and fine-tuning," Hartley said of the creation of the first Peavey guitars and basses, "which means there were a lot of fights, but it also means we thought we got it right. And I always listened to what someone had to say, and I still do. Do I have an ego? Yes, but my ego does not mean I need to suppress somebody else's. There've been plenty of times when I consider myself to have been a 'catalyst'— something that speeds up or enhances something else without being changed itself, and that was certainly evident when we got into the guitar business."

Todd: "We were working on intuition and logic, about how each operation could be done economically, yet accurately. There was never any machining or other step made before we were 100% convinced that it was correct, and that it involved very few 'unknowns'. Because of my degree and experience, I was able to concoct a mental image of the projected steps, and I'd refine those as we progressed."

⟜

One incident around the advent of Peavey's venture into guitar-making and building their own speakers beget an ID badge policy that is still in effect to this day.

"One of our 'friendly competitors' sent a guy here to check out Peavey," Hartley remembered. "He snuck in the back loading ramp and was caught walking through the 'Yellow Building', which is what we call Plant #3. They threw him out, and damned if he didn't go to the front side of the building and attempted to walk in through the incoming loading dock, and he got as far as the metal shop. He was spotted again, and was asked to leave.

"He then went to the main gate in the middle of the building and tried to talk his way in past the main gate. He was thrown out again. He then had the audacity to come over to the main office across the street, and try to get a factory tour from there. I had already been advised of the B.S. he tried across the street at our main factory, and I told him '*Hell, no!*"

As it turned out, the intruder was from a small Midwest amplifier company that would go out of business later in the decade, as Hartley recalls. Considering his company's ventures into new territory with speakers and guitars, he decided to introduce employee ID badges.

"*Everybody* would wear ID tags, and *nobody*—including me—was to be permitted to enter our facilities without their name badge," he recounted. "Since we are a 'first name only' company all the badges have the employee's first name on the badge, and their last name in small letters."

Mid-Seventies: Hollis Calvert displays his new company ID badge. *Hollis Calvert*

As for whether or not the earliest guitar and bass prototypes met expectations, Todd recounted, "I believe that both of us could see exactly how the prototypes would be; otherwise Hartley wouldn't have announced that the instruments would be at a NAMM show."

Three prototypes—a guitar with six-on-a-side tuners, a guitar with "3 + 3" tuners, and a bass—were assembled in Todd's garage, with Lowe assisting, just before the NAMM show. An additional option, a rosewood fingerboard, was installed on the bass. Todd recalled that the preparation went right down to the wire:

"With the time to pack up the prototypes and fly to Chicago only one day away, I had to call Hartley, who was already there, and ask him what to put on the peghead. That was scary, because I knew I would have to do it with some rub-on lettering left over from my commercial artist days. He told me to put whatever I wanted on the pegheads, which was a great surprise. I just took the easy way and put my initials on them, figuring we could come up with some explanation, if needed. I chose 'CT-1' for the six-on-a-side guitar, 'CT-2' for the three-keys-per-side instrument, and 'CT-B' for the bass. Some people might have thought that was egotistical, but Hartley had given me a loose rein."

CHAPTER 5
Introduction and initial production

The hand-fretted Peavey guitar and bass prototypes did indeed sport "CT" as well as the "lightning bolt P" from the company logo on their headstocks. The instruments debuted at a 1977 NAMM in Chicago, although Hartley showed them off in a hotel suite instead of on the main exhibition floor.

And Peavey retailers were very, very interested.

"The dealers went into full arousal," said R.T. Lowe. "The market was ripe, and at the same time, [it was] in serious turmoil—rising prices and strong arm tactics."

"These were the dealers who had bitterly complained about the heavy-handed tactics of 'The Big Two'," Hartley averred. "On the other hand, the reaction and the attitude of my competitors to our guitars was the same it's always been—'Aw, that's just a crazy redneck.' But what difference does that make, and what am I gonna do? Do I have a Southern accent? Yes. Am I located in Mississippi? Yes. If you think I'm a redneck, I'll just have to prove things differently."

"I believe they were surprised that we would introduce the line with a matte-finished model," Todd said of dealers who perused the guitars at the NAMM show, "but they liked how it showed the grain off. That was rather rare in deluxe instruments, which we considered our guitars to be."

Dealers also offered suggestions to Peavey employees about the new instruments.

"One dealer took me aside and tactfully whispered in my ear, 'You have a way to go with the fretting'," Todd recounted. "I agreed with him, and explained that I had built the three instruments in my carport in two days, and that I had only had ten minutes per instrument to fret them. I also mentioned the fretting machine we were having made, that would blow away any fretting on the market. Some months later, that dealer called me after production started to agree with what I had told him in Chicago about fretwork."

Todd also remembered that a few dealers asked about binding, and were told that it was possible on future instruments.

The CT-1 guitar and CT-B bass that went to Chicago are now on display at the Peavey museum in Meridian.

**Prototype Peavey guitar and bass; the earliest known examples.
Note the rosewood fingerboard on the bass.** *Willie G. Moseley*

Hartley recalls that at that first NAMM show, the orders for instruments "…far exceeded our ability to make them."

Refinements were, of course, interpolated soon after the original prototypes returned from the Windy City exhibition. Several other prototypes would be created before production actually commenced.

Another prototype, with "T-60" on the headstock, had striking concentric graining on its body. It was nicknamed "the bull's-eye guitar" because of its similarity to a target. It would be used in early promotions, and was later seen in a collage of Seventies images in a 1995 issue of *Monitor*, Peavey's quarterly magazine; the article was part of the salute to the company's 30th anniversary.

The T-60 "Bull's-eye" prototype

"Of course, we progressed from rushed hand fretting to the unbelievably accurate machine fretting," Todd recounted. "The graphics on the peghead had to be finished, and the machine-fit at the neck/body joint was improved."

Among the many locations where Hollis Calvert would work with the company during his career was in Artist Relations ("I'd been into that just about from the day I arrived," he said), and in an ongoing assignment, he was called upon to solicit input for refinements from musicians. Hollis contributed ideas himself, recalling that he suggested the 1/16" pinstripe around the perimeter of the headstock.

"I was one of the few who were actually working regularly with bands in the local area," he recalled, "and I could get prototypes into actual stage situations. We would get suggestions concerning neck width at the nut, sustain, shape and curvature of the neck, the tone circuit, and the gain of the pickups. My best input actually came from my relationship with players in the Nashville area—all of the *Hee Haw* players, many of the session players, and some recording artists that were willing to give us a listen."

Peavey did an appropriate public advertising buildup for the introduction of the instruments, which were ultimately christened the T-60 guitar and T-40 bass. "Coming soon"-type preview ads hyped the three years spent on development, resulting in professional grade instruments, available at reasonable prices; i.e., the vibe of the ad was right in line with Hartley's adopted mantra.

T-40 preview ad

Another early ad showed Hartley with his new product. Its headline proclaimed that Hartley had worked for over two decades (from 1957, when he started playing guitar) to create a viable and affordable electric instrument, and Hartley detailed his philosophy within the ad in an extended and eloquent first-person pitch.

**Hartley's straightforward pitch in this ad offered numerous "how" and "why"
details about his company's new instruments**

Production bass body, showing the multiple laminate body with routing for pickups, controls, and neck installation. Holes are drilled for pickguard installation, and the control pocket is shielded. The ground wire is also visible. *flatericbassandguitarblogspot.com*

Chip also got Peavey's sales reps for ready to market the new guitar and bass by conducting detailed seminars on how the T-60 and T-40 were made, and how the instruments operated.

Chip explains the features and benefits of Peavey's revolutionary instruments to the company's sales force. *Hollis Calvert*

Production versions of the T-60 and T-40. *Heritage Auctions*

Peavey's initial entries into the electric guitar market quickly caught on among players at all levels. The tone circuitry was indeed different, and it was versatile.

The coil-blend tone control circuitry was hyped in the owner's manual as follows:

"How The Circuit Works: Our unique tone circuitry enables dual or single coil operation of each pickup independently through the rotation of the pickup tone controls. Rotating the tone controls fully clockwise (position #10) achieves the single coil mode and produces a greater degree of 'highs' from the instrument. Rotating the tone controls counterclockwise to approximately the #7 position brings the second coil into operation for full-range, humbucking tonalities. Further counterclockwise rotation of the tone controls (from position #7 to 0) yield conventional tone contouring action."

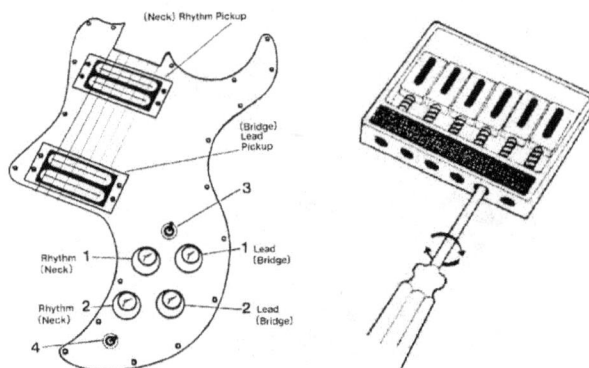

Line drawings of the control layout and bridge intonation adjustment from the T-60's owner's manual

Soon after production began, Peavey opted to install an innovative item on the pickguards of T-60s and T-40s. Like other manufacturers, the company sought to protect the scratchplates of new instruments by covering them with a clear sheet of vinyl plastic film. What was different about Peavey's protector was the way it was installed, and that it was labeled with the function of each control.

"We had heard many complaints from dealers about scratches on pickguards of new guitars when customers played them in the store," Hartley detailed. "We listened, and decided to do something unique—our removable non-adhesive pickguard protector. It is the only one I know of that style that has ever been used on new guitars. This was *way* different from the protective layer of plastic or paper that comes laminated to the raw 'sheet stock' of most pickguard plastic materials to protect the surface during the manufacturing process. Many of the imports just leave this protective coating on the pickguard, *then* attach the pots, pickup rings, switches, etc. This approach is a mess, because when you try to pull this protective layer off, it's held to the guitar because of the various components mounted to the pickguard.

"Our approach was to have a vinyl plastic that was pre-screened with descriptive labels and die cutouts *around* the various components mounted to the pickguard. Our protective layer had no adhesive, stuck to the pickguard by static pressure, and could easily be peeled off. Our approach was far better, because we die cut around the controls, switches, and pickups."

Some notable players actually opted to leave the protector on the pickguard instead of removing it.

As it turned out, however, the peel-off protector could cause problems if an instrument was displayed in a store window—direct sunlight meant that the black pickguard absorbed heat, and sometimes the warmth would cause the vinyl plastic to stick to the pickguard, making the protector difficult to remove and/or leaving unsightly patterns on the pickguard if and when the protector sheet was removed. Peavey ultimately opted to discontinue the unique protector.

Peavey's unique non-adhesive pickguard protector, seen on a T-60.
flatericbassandguitarblogspot.com

Obviously, clinicians such as Marty McCann were expected to the get the word out about the new guitar and bass.

"I wasn't so much a 'guitar clinician' as I was a 'clinician who introduced Peavey's guitars'," McCann recalled. "All of the reps had guitar samples as well, but some of the reps never played guitar at all. I'd take the instruments to stores to demonstrate them—along with a lot of sound gear—and would quickly get them into the hands of guitar players who had come in. I could play a little rhythm guitar and a few chords, but I wasn't a professional. I'd encourage the good players to pan the tone control to note how the coil sound changed."

McCann eschewed a tactic that other reps (of Peavey and other brands) employed, which was to take a new instrument to area clubs at night.

"I thought that put musicians in an uncomfortable situation," he said. "They might play it for two or three songs, but they shouldn't have been expected to play it the rest of the night. What I did instead was to give one to a guy who had come by a dealer's store, and if the dealer told me that this particular individual was a good player, or renowned in the area, I'd tell the guitarist, 'Take this home and play with it a couple of days before you take it out on a gig'. Shortly after the guitars caught on, (Peavey) hired clinicians to work exclusively with guitars. After the guitar clinicians were hired, I went back to doing just sound reinforcement clinics, which is what I'd been hired to do in the first place."

McCann still owns the T-60 he used in his clinics. Its serial/shipping number is 00000000.

Unstrung icon: Marty McCann's early T-60, serial #00000000. *Willie G. Moseley*

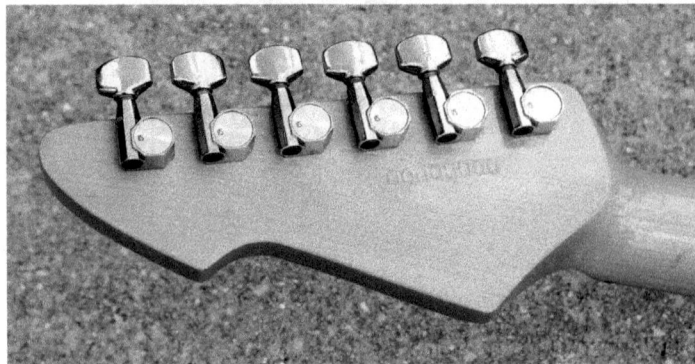

The back of the headstock of McCann's guitar shows its primeval serial number. *Willie G. Moseley*

McCann also recalled that Hollis Calvert could ably demonstrate Peavey's new electric stringed instruments if called upon.

"He could emulate *so* many guitar players," Marty enthused. "When he'd demo the guitars, he'd say something like 'Now, if Chet (Atkins) was playing this T-60…' Hollis would dial in something that sounded like Chet; that's how good he was. I enjoyed *watching* him play guitars as much as I enjoyed *listening* to him. His left hand looked like a spider doing a ballet."

Once production instruments were available, Calvert made sure noted players, including session musicians in Nashville, received samples of the new instruments.

"Overall, I would present a guitar directly to the players," he recalled. "Some of the contacts early on were with session players, such as Leon Rhodes, Jimmy Capps, Phil Baugh, Steve Wariner, etc. They didn't use the T-60 on every session, of course…different songs and different artists required different sounds. But those guys represented our 'foot in the door'."

Through session contacts, other players (including members of the Grand Ole Opry house band) became interested. Calvert recalled making many trips to Music City, where the instruments would get a private showing in a hotel room.

"Usually, the guitars were demoed with the (Peavey) Session 400 amplifier, which we were also promoting," he detailed. "That amp became the Opry standard for many, many years."

Nashville guitar ace Fred Newell was the house guitarist on the long-running "Nashville Now" television, and was already a user of Peavey amplifiers. Although he didn't bond with the T-60, he was impressed by its construction and innovations, and recalled other legendary country players playing the new Peavey model.

"Phil Baugh used one, and that was the first one I'd seen," Newell recalled. "The fact that it was so precisely-made was impressive, and I thought it sounded pretty good. The idea of a coil roll-off circuit built into the tone control was brilliant, because it gave guitars more versatility. Their earlier basses did well, too. In fact, they probably 'caught on' around Nashville better than the guitars."

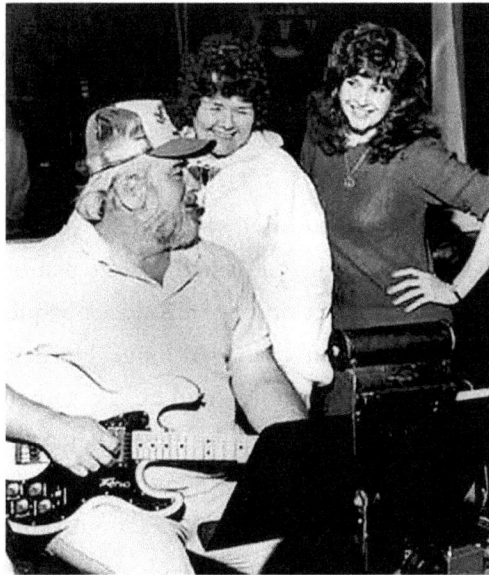

Nashville studio player Phil Baugh is shown with an early T-60 as Bonnie Guitar, center, and Cheryl Arnold, right, look on. Baugh was playing in a session for Arnold's album. *bluemariahband.com*

"They flew me down to Meridian one time to show me how they were making guitars," Newell added, "and I was amazed at how those computerized machines could carve guitar bodies. Every single one that came out of there was perfect!"

Newell would later utilize several other Peavey guitar models in his multi-faceted career.

One pleasant surprise that came about was Peavey's discovery that legendary rockabilly singer/guitarist Carl Perkins of "Blue Suede Shows" fame was using a T-60 out of personal preference.

Calvert: "We found out he had been seen playing a T-60; we made contact, and presented a special T-60 to him in Meridian at the Jimmy Rodgers Festival, in the Temple Theater."

Hollis also recalled one noted player who had been using the T-60 but "… he called after a couple of years of using our guitars, saying that he was going to endorse another company, because they committed to running ads featuring him with an instrument. At that time, our budget would not support such endorsements."

The reception among non-famous/hobbyist/semi-pro musicians was encouraging as well. Peavey's new instruments epitomized the company's goals of value at a fair price.

"Dealers were letting us know what their customers were saying," Calvert remembered.

Refinements were made to the original models after they hit the marketplace, in response to the logical input from dealers and musicians.

McCann recalled that one of the initial comments from dealers in the field was that the treble cutaway was not deep enough on the T-60, so the body carving CNC program was slightly modified. Soon, the treble cutaway horn joined the neck at approximately the 19th fret instead of the 17th fret.

By 1979, rosewood fingerboards would become an option for an extra $25. The bass would eventually get a lined fretless neck option (rosewood fretboard only).

Todd: "We had postponed the introduction of rosewood fretboards, because it would involve masking tasks that were considerably more stringent."

Additional colors (in a gloss finish instead of a natural satin/matte finish) were soon added, and lighter woods such as poplar was introduced for solid-color guitars and basses. By mid-1979, colors included white, black, and sunburst. Within a few years, other finish options were Blood Red, Royal Burgundy, Frost Blue (metallic), and Sunfire Red (metallic).

"We had agreed that a matte finish, from the outset, would help get the 'cabinet sprayers' up to the more-challenging job of guitar spraying," Todd detailed. "Gloss bodies were planned to follow matte bodies, and the change from ash to the lighter poplar was a perfect time to introduce opaque and glossy paint jobs."

"The whole idea of a 'heavy body and sustain' didn't last long," Hartley said of the use of body woods. "I remember trying to get Merle Haggard to use our guitars, and he said something like 'Well, you need to make me something that's *this* light, and he handed me his (Fender) Telecaster, and I swear, it felt like it was made out of balsa! It was the lightest Tele I've ever felt, so we tried to go in that direction."

Follow-up orders were encouraging as well, and Peavey was soon making approximately 200 guitars a day. The company eventually added a robot, nicknamed Onan, which was programmed to buff guitar necks and perform other tasks.

Some sources have claimed that soon after Peavey got into the guitar business, the company was manufacturing more guitars domestically than any other company. Hartley wasn't certain about such a citation, but noted, "That's not important. What was important is that we were making a damn good guitar at a fair price—not a *cheap* price—and it was different; it was not like everybody else's. Our bilaminated neck was different, and we had a different tone circuit."

Production runs of T-60s or T-40s were somewhat akin to furniture "cutting" schedules.

"(Woodshop manager) Jerold Pugh would get the proper vacuum nests set up on the Ekstrom-Carlson router for the run," Todd recounted. "R.T. Lowe would be notified at the same time, and would order the parts, designating when they were needed. Jerold would keep purchasing updated regarding how many neck and body blanks he had in the dry room."

In the first years of Peavey guitar production, the bobbin winding machine was run by Joan Moulds, who, according to Todd, was proprietary about her job duties.

"Joan was quite uncomfortable with anyone else messing with her machine," Chip recalled.

Hartley had decided to include a case with each guitar, which was practical for more than one reason—"case included" is a positive marketing term, and the company could also save on shipping insurance costs. However, soon after the T-60 and T-40 were introduced, their cases would have a disproportionate share of problems, which the company corrected.

The original Peavey guitar cases were vacuum-formed, rectangular-shaped items, for which Chip designed the exterior embellishments. However, quality problems developed, and employee Louis Bailey was tasked with finding a plastics company that did blow-molding, in an effort to create an alternate (and unique) case.

This early ad shows Peavey's original, rectangular-shaped case.

"Blow-molding is the most efficient way to make a hollow structure," said Hartley.

Bailey and Todd visited a factory that was a potential outsourced case manufacturer, and were impressed. Todd set about designing a case that was unique in several ways, in addition to its oval silhouette.

"I started a design on a blow-molded case that had a split handle," Chip said, "so that picking the case up—without remembering to close the latches—wouldn't be a catastrophe. I fashioned the integral 'seal' to close it with a wedging effect, to help prevent rain or other moisture from entering the case. I had built rifle cases for my father like that, so it was quite easy to incorporate those features. We also nixed ribbon lid restraints and opted for steel rod stays."

The interior of the blow-molded cases feature a compartment for storage of strings, picks, and other items. The underside of the instrument's body rested on a pad of urethane foam, and a long strip of the same material ran along the underside of the lid, to cushion and stabilize the neck and strings.

**Peavey's second effort in designing and marketing guitar cases
was the iconic, oval-shaped, blow-molded case.**

**Parallax view of an early T-40 in an early oval blow-molded case.
Note one half of the split handle at the far left, the storage compartment under the neck,
and the urethane foam strip on the interior of the lid.** *flatericbassandguitarblogspot.com*

However, one common (and messy) problem for the earliest instruments that came with blow-molded cases had nothing to do with guitar or bass parts or construction. The urethane foam inside the case tended to deteriorate, turning into a sticky, black mung that got all over the instrument. To some observers, such gunk-afflicted guitars or basses might have looked like they had been in a fire.

"What we didn't know was that the formulation of foam that people were using at the time meant that it would be eventually destroyed by ozone," Hartley said. "We had similar problems when we used the same stuff in speaker surrounds."

The stereotypical solution for many owners of cases in which the foam had deteriorated was to remove the decomposed material from instruments and the inside of the case with cleaning substances such as Goo Gone, a lemon oil-based product. The silhouette of the body would then be traced on a piece of terry cloth (an old towel being the definitive example), cut out, and placed in the bottom of the case. A corresponding strip of the same material (from the same towel?) was installed on the upper lid, along the length of the strings.

The manufacturing solution for *new* blow-molded Peavey cases was to upholster the entire interior with a plush-type fabric, which Hartley dubbed "...'teddy bear plush', because it was the same material teddy bears are made from."

An even-more-parallax view of a later T-40 in a plush-lined blow-molded case.
The refined T-40 had pickups with exposed blades, and larger toggle switches, as seen here.
flatericbassandguitarblogspot.com

One of the more noticeable, unique, and potentially-controversial ads that involved the T-60 showed the Peavey guitar, listing at $375 with a case (having undergone a minor $26 price increase over its original price), between a Gibson Les Paul Standard, listing at $898 without a case, and a Fender Stratocaster, listing for $685 without a case. The ad asked a one-word question: "Why?"

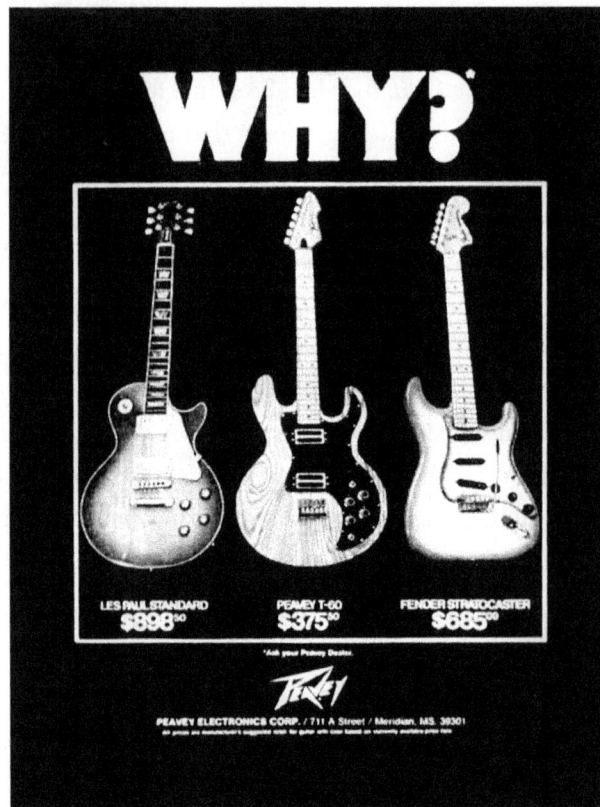

"I think the best advertising I ever did was that 'Why?' ad in *Guitar Player*," Hartley would recall with a grin. "That was how I got back at my competitors."

However, the Peavey founder recalled that there was no threatened litigation about the ad.

"All it was, was the truth," Hartley insisted. "All I did was present the facts. The competition went nuts, which was exactly what I hoped to accomplish. It is, without a doubt, our most effective ad ever!"

A later version of the same ad reflected price increases in the Les Paul and the Stratocaster, with the same image showing the earlier prices of the competing models "X-ed out"/"hand-corrected" to new prices of $918.50 (Les Paul) and $790 (Stratocaster).

While the new guitar and bass had a no-frills look, many practical musicians—famous and wanna-be famous—ultimately picked up on their versatility. Musicians from more than one genre began to be seen playing Peavey guitars and basses.

Jerry Reed and a member of his band both played natural-finished T-60s with rosewood fretboards on a 1982 episode of the PBS concert program "Austin City Limits."

Steve Wariner (a Chet Atkins protégé) sported a red T-60 on the cover of his first album.

Wikipedia

Texas bluesman Johnny Copeland (1937-1997) gigged with a white T-60. A multiple winner of W.C. Handy blues awards (including one for his 1981 debut album *Copeland Special*), he also utilized his Peavey guitar on the legendary *Showdown!* album with Albert Collins and Robert Cray in 1985, for which the three guitarists won a Grammy for Best Traditional Blues Recording.

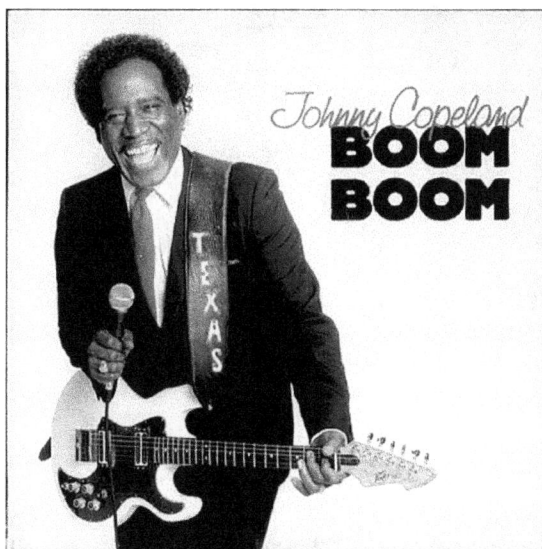

Perhaps the earliest noteworthy use of a T-40 bass happened on September 9, 1979, at a "Woodstock Reunion 1979" concert in Brookhaven, New York, on Long Island. Among the bands was Canned Heat, a veteran blues and boogie aggregation that had performed at the original Woodstock concert a decade earlier. Bassist Larry "The Mole" Taylor used a T-40 (which still had the pickguard protector on it) at the '79 concert, having acquired it a few months before the event.

"I didn't have a lot of money at the time," Taylor recalled with a chuckle, "but I was looking for a certain sound; something clear but 'mid-rangey', and that bass had it. It sort of had its own character, sound-wise. I just saw it in a store, and thought it was pretty interesting. I actually bought it and had to make payments on it."

Taylor recalled using his T-40 "…for about a year and a half, and I don't know why I changed. It didn't look too fancy, but it had some good sounds, some of which I didn't know about until I bought it and really got into playing it. It was pretty versatile, and I wish I still had it."

Canned Heat's set at the Woodstock reunion was later released as a live album.

Canned Heat bassist Larry Taylor, center, plays a T-40 bass between singer Bob Hite (1943-1981), left, and guitarist Michael "Hollywood Fats" Mann (1954-1986), right, at the "Woodstock Reunion 1979" concert *Wikimedia Commons*

One of the first endorsers of the T-40 was Ross Vallory, bassist for Journey, who appeared in more than one Peavey ad.

And while a Peavey ad featuring Molly Hatchet bassist Banner Thomas promoted a bass amplification system ("Take It From The Bottom"), it wasn't surprising that he was also shown playing a T-40.

Another Southern rock band that was just beginning to break through in the mid-Seventies was .38 Special, which was a Jacksonville-based aggregation that was considered by some to be a "little brother" band of Lynyrd

Skynyrd, as guitarist/singer Donnie Van Zant of .38 was a younger sibling of Skynyrd lead singer Ronnie Van Zant (1948-1977).

However, .38 Special was more of a "radio-ready" band, and their lead guitarist was Jeff Carlisi, son of a career Navy aviator who had fought in World War II. While Jeff would acquire an architecture degree from Georgia Tech, he opted for a career in rock and roll.

Jeff had become aware of Peavey amplifiers in the late Sixties, and while he wasn't initially impressed, he later became a "convert" when Peavey made and marketed its Mace amplifier head.

"In 1974, I was out of school, and had gone back to Jacksonville; [it was] the beginnings of .38 Special," he remembered. "Skynyrd had bought a place downtown and turned it into a small studio, and it was near our own rehearsal space. One day, they were rehearsing, and we stopped by to say hi, and all of a sudden we noticed all of their Marshall amplifiers were gone. They had Peavey amps. They told me 'Peavey's really got its act together; these are reliable and they sound great.' So if Skynyrd had Peavey, we had to have it. They had Maces, so we had to get Maces, too. We actually bought our very first Maces ourselves but word got back to Peavey about the Skynyrd 'baby brother' band, or whatever you wanted to call us back then."

The company offered .38 Special some gear as an artist endorsement around the time the band was beginning its recording career.

"The first guy I met in Meridian was Hollis Calvert," Carlisi remembered, "and he said that Peavey was impressed that we were using their amps without being solicited. He just basically said 'What do you need?' There was no contract, no piece of paper to sign, no attorneys."

Carlisi agreed to a photo ad for Peavey that ran in 1977. He was shown in front of a wall of Mace amplifiers of more than one configuration, playing his hand-built Rhyne electric guitar (the body silhouette of which had been traced from an original Gibson Explorer owned by Lynyrd Skynyrd's Allen Collins).

Carlisi's 1977 Peavey ad showed off a wall of the company's Mace amplifier series. *Jeff Carlisi*

Peavey stayed in touch with .38 Special (and other endorsement bands), keeping such clients up to date about new gear. One contact informed the group that the company was going into the guitar-making business.

"I don't think I'd even thought about it," Carlisi said. "I thought they were only interested in making amps. But they sent stuff our way, and I got a T-60 in a natural finish."

Carlisi's first impression was that the company had forgotten to paint the instrument, but he admired its construction and its electronic features.

"The T-60 was a tank, but there wasn't anything cheap about it," he said. "It was very solid and well-built. There were people who probably didn't understand the coil roll-off circuit, but it was so good and worked so well (that) it was one of the best features of the guitar, if not *the* best feature. The guitar also played well, and I usually used mine for slide."

An October 1977 crash of a chartered airplane had taken the lives of three members of Lynyrd Skynyrd, including Ronnie Van Zant, as well as three other persons. The group would disband, and guitarists Allen Collins and Gary Rossington would form the Rossington-Collins Band in 1979.

However, just prior to the formation of the ex-Lynyrd Skynyrd guitarists' new musical aggregation, .38 Special and Molly Hatchet performed at the Civic Auditorium in Jacksonville. Collins and Rossington sat in with .38, and Carlisi played slide on his T-60.

"It was a year to a year and a half after the plane crash," Carlisi remembered. "It was great to let everyone know the guys were alive and well, and we got them to play a song. It was a jam-type song; maybe 'T for Texas' or 'Statesboro Blues'."

1979: Carlisi plays slide on his T-60 onstage with Allen Collins, left, and Gary Rossington, right. *Jeff Carlisi*

Carlisi summarized his experience with his T-60 by noting that he regretted having parted with it.

"It was one of the most interesting guitars I've ever had, and I'd give anything to have it back," he said.

Jeff also remembered that .38 bassist Larry Junstrom was a longtime user of Peavey basses and bass amps.

Two unique examples of the T-60 were made and presented to Hartley and Chip. They had bodies of

American black walnut and controls that loaded through a rear cavity in the body; i.e., there was no pickguard. The necks were made of figured bird's-eye maple. Hartley's guitar (serial #00000001) was in a matte finish, and Chip's (#00000002) was in a glossy finish. Todd later made a walnut neck for his guitar, installing the bird's eye neck on a T-60 that Hartley had given Todd's daughter.

And Hartley and Chip would later communicate about those two instruments in the early Nineties, when Chip's guitar was stolen.

Hartley's walnut-body satin-finished T-60, with rear-load controls, serial #00000001 *Willie G. Moseley*

Over their time in the marketplace, the T-60 and T-40 would receive a few refinements—larger toggle switches would replace the mini-toggles, pickup blades would be exposed, and the nut would change from aluminum to a plastic composite that was later marketed as "Graphlon."

Later version of the T-60 — solid color, with exposed pickups blades. *Heritage Auctions*

Later version of T-40 in solid color, with exposed-blade pickups, and rosewood fretboard. *Heritage Auctions*

Peavey's original groundbreaking T-60 guitar and T-40 bass would finally finish their commendable run ca. early 1988, and were last marketed in a black finish only.

Not surprisingly, plans had been tentatively broached for additional models of Peavey guitars even before the sales results of the T-60 and T-40 validated such expansion. Todd had been considering the idea of developing a student model called the T-15, and was also thinking about a single-pickup bass, but wasn't pursuing those projects aggressively.

"I was in kind of an idling mode, designing end plates for an electric piano, speaker boxes, and monitor cabinets," he remembered.

Then Todd was contacted by representatives of the CBS/Fender conglomerate about going to work for the California guitar builder. Chip informed Hartley that CBS/Fender had offered him a job in California at considerably more than Peavey was paying him.

Hartley maintains that he tried to warn Chip of the dangers of working for a giant conglomerate ("I knew what they were up to," Hartley said), and his admonition to Todd compelled the guitar designer to bargain for a three-year contract with CBS/Fender.

The fact that Hartley and Chip held patents together had the potential to boost any tension that may have (subliminally) manifested itself.

"Hartley didn't make a big thing of it," Chip said, "but he sent around a memo telling everybody that I was going to work on a competitor, and not to discuss plans with me. I wasn't surprised, and I didn't have any bad feelings about that."

Chip Todd departed from Peavey Electronics Company in early 1981. Charley Gressett also left Peavey for Fender at the same time.

Hartley and Chip would stay in touch over the decades, but the initial separation, with Todd going to work for a competitor, was obviously awkward for both of them.

Todd would work for Fender for only the duration of his three-year contract.

"Fender was, obviously, wanting to hire me to pick my mind about how Peavey did things," he said, with 20/20 hindsight. "I *did* get in a change at Fender in the method of fretting, and a few other improvements, without doing anything like we had done at Peavey, and I suppose that's why Hartley and I are still friends. [Fender] even wanted me to tell them how Peavey covered amps and speakers with one piece of material."

Hartley and Chip continued to communicate on a fairly regular basis after Todd had left Fender. Hartley also took an interest in mentoring Chip's son, Skip.

"We talked over the phone every couple of months, and passed interesting 'FYIs' back and forth by e-mail," Chip said. "Hartley also sent articles that he thought Skip might be interested in. Neither Skip nor I can ever thank him enough for his interest in Skip's education."

CHAPTER 6

The advent of the Mike Powers era

While in Chicago for a NAMM show, Hartley and his wife Melia stopped by a local guitar shop, during an intense snowstorm, as the Peavey founder recalls. The repairman/luthier on the premises was named Mike Powers, and he established an immediately-positive relationship with the visitors from the Deep South.

Originally from the Windy City, Michael V. Powers (1950-2013) had been interested in old guitars as a youngster. His first acoustic instrument was a $22 Sears guitar, and his first electric was a Sears Silvertone 1446 hollowbody thinline, which had a slight resemblance to a Gretsch hollowbody guitar, but was made by the Harmony company, a gigantic Chicago manufacturer of budget instruments.

"I couldn't afford a real Gretsch like (the Beatles') George Harrison used," he recalled. "I later used that guitar as my 'guinea pig' for my first try at re-finishing, by stripping for the black finish and spray-painting it with red Krylon, or something like that."

Powers owned and played numerous classic guitars as he was coming of age, but ultimately settled into live performance as a bassist, so he acquired several classic basses as well. He played on the same circuit as Cheap Trick, Rufus, and Styx, and also did live-in-the-studio radio work with deejay Steve Dahl.

All the while, however, Mike was honing his repair skills. Among the craftsmen he spent time with was the legendary guitar repair icon Dan Erlewine, and he ultimately decided to concentrate on repair and design rather than a performance career.

"It was pretty clear to me by 1980 that I wasn't a rock star," he said, "but I had a lot of time invested in repair—a good area to work in, and I had a large customer base, so it seemed much more stable than risking everything at that time just to play."

Powers had done consulting work with other manufacturers, and Hartley was impressed with Powers' knowledge and guitar-repair acumen…even though the new prospect wasn't a good ol' boy.

Negotiations quickly resulted in Powers touring the Meridian facilities. One employee recalled seeing "…some skinny little dude with a big Afro for a white guy walking through the factory with Hartley."

Powers was hired, and began making plans to relocate to Meridian, but he actually began working with Peavey prototype instruments in his Chicago shop prior to the move.

"They called anybody who came from north of Memphis a 'Yankee'," Powers said of his move to the Deep South. "I was finally raised to the rank of 'Damn Yankee'—that's a northerner who refuses to leave. I was honored!"

The Chicago transplant would prove to be a mercurial individual, according to Hartley, but Powers would oversee the introduction of dozens of Peavey guitar and bass models for a number of years.

"Mike was crazy, in a good way," Hollis Calvert remembered. "He had it together as a great bass player; he knew a lot about pickups, tone circuits, and instruments in general. He was perfect for us at that time."

Powers' initial involvement in Peavey products included helping to finish out designs of instruments such as the T-15 short-scale guitar and the T-45 bass, the development of which had been initiated by Chip Todd. Such models are considered somewhat "transitional," as they had features that both Todd and Powers interpolated.

As an aspiring player in the early Sixties, Hartley had been intrigued by Sears Silvertone amp-in-the-case guitar models, made by a company in New Jersey called Danelectro (In 1964, an untold number of American teenagers would purchase such instruments after seeing the Beatles on "The Ed Sullivan Show").

Peavey opted to develop two smaller, budget-priced, short-scale models that were somewhat oriented towards students, but the quality of those instruments was on a par with the T-60 and T-40, since the manufacturing process was the same.

The T-15 debuted on an April, 1981 price list, and the T-30 followed by several months. The T-15 (two pickups, originally listing at $219.50 with blow-molded hardshell case) and T-30 (three pickups, with angled treble pickup, $259.50 with blow-molded hardshell case) had a scale of 23 1/2", as seen on the Gibson Byrdland, a classic thinline electric-acoustic guitar. The pickups were single-coil, and were the same on both models (only the housings were different).

Unlike the T-60, they had master volume and tone knobs. A three-way pickup toggle switch for the T-15 was located on its treble cutaway horn, while the T-30's five-way switch was near the master volume and tone controls. A newly-developed, smooth-looking bridge/tailpiece assembly with rounded corners still had individually-intonatable bridge saddles, and was installed at three points on the body. Strings loaded through the end of the bridge.

T-15 *Heritage Auctions*

T-30 *Heritage Auctions*

What's more, Peavey offered an "Electric Case" option for those models (Chip Todd had been involved with its design before he departed). Still in a blow-molded configuration, the case contained a ten-watt amplifier with a five-inch speaker. There was even an overdrive feature (cited as "pre- and post-gain controls") to evoke a distorted sound. The price list also noted a "special contour equalization control" on the Electric Case.

If included with a T-15 or T-30, an Electric Case was an extra $60. By itself, the case listed for $140.

(History needs to be note, however, that any inspiration/influence by Danelectro on Peavey products was peripheral or selective. Hartley resented his guitars and amps being compared to Danelectro and other cheaply-built products, and he also eschewed comparisons to early—and iconic—Fender instruments.

"It really bothers me when someone says my guitars are 'cheap'," he would growl in an early Nineties interview. "The T-60 makes a [Fender] Broadcaster look crude and cheap, so when somebody starts comparing our earlier instruments to early instruments from the Fifties and Sixties, I feel like I've been kicked in the butt.")

The T-15 and T-30 were introduced in a natural finish, although one Peavey veteran recalls a brownish-bronze metallic finish as an early, and apparently-not-publicized finish. It was estimated that the Electric Case option for T-15s and T-30s outpaced the regular case option by a two-to-one margin.

T-15: Early bronze metallic finish with Electric Case *Heritage Auctions*

Both instruments were later offered in a satin sunburst finish, which had a sort "root beer-ish" tint. Other woods besides ash were used for laminated bodies that had a finish other than natural; somewhat mis-matched graining usually worked fine under solid color or sunburst finishes. Poplar and basswood would prove to be the most popular of these alternate woods.

T-15: Sunburst finish *Heritage Auctions*

The T-15 was the more popular of the two models, and would later be marketed in red, black, and burgundy finishes (for a $50 step-up in price). It would last for about a half a decade after its introduction.

The T-30 was only around for about a year, and was only offered in a natural finish on price lists. However, other finishes also appeared on the model.

"I thought the old Gibson Byrdland scale [23 1/2"] looked pretty interesting, and that's what I put on the T-15 and the T-30," Hartley said of his company's effort. "Great idea...didn't sell! Many times, a guitar teacher would tell kids they needed a full-scale guitar to learn on, but my opinion was that they needed something to play, not something to grow into."

Guitar division employee Rusty Culpepper is shown in a forest of T-40 and T-15 necks

The T-45 bass, the other instrument that was in development when Todd left the company, would also appear in 1982. Initial reaction may have been that the T-45 was designed to hit a lower price point, but here's the historical rub: Throughout the half-decade or so that T-40s and T-45s were both offered, they always carried the same list price (all finishes and options being equal), with one exception (the natural-finished T-40s--$399.50 with a maple neck, $424.50 with a rosewood neck in '82).

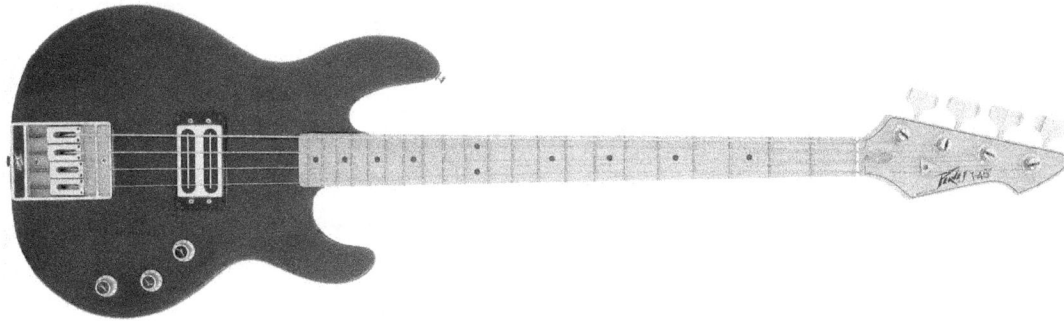

T-45: Heritage Auctions

The less-popular T-45 differed from the T-40 in a number of ways besides having one less pickup, so a side-by-side comparison is revelatory.

The T-45 had 21-frets, compared to 20-frets on the T-40. Most subsequent standard production, non-signature-model Peavey basses would also have 21 frets.

The single humbucker on the T-45 was the same as the two pickups found on the T-40, and it also had the same unique tone circuit. The bridge/tailpiece was also identical, and like the T-40, the T-45's strings loaded through the rear of the body.

However, the location of the T-45's "harmonically-placed" pickup differed from the placement of the T-40's pickups. Unlike some other brands, where a single pickup was in the same location on a bass where one of two pickups would be located on a similar two-pickup model, the T-45's pickup was located at a "nodal point," where the signal of a vibrating string would be the strongest.

And a quick glance at both bodies makes it obvious that a primary difference in the two earliest Peavey basses involved controls—the T-45's potentiometers were installed from a rear control cavity through the top of the body, with only the knobs exposed, negating the use of a pickguard for placement of such electronics. The T-45 was the first production Peavey instrument—guitar or bass—to have rear-loaded controls.

The T-45 didn't have a phase switch, since it was a single-pickup instrument. However, the T-45 had three knobs – volume, tone, and a "special mid-frequency rolloff control for maximum tonal flexibility," according to a November 1982 price list.

Curiously, one word was altered in the T-45's specs on price lists after '82; the third knob was referred to as a "special *low*-frequency rolloff control" (italics added).

While some early T-45s were made with a natural finish on an ash body (a la the original T-40s), that version didn't appear on price lists. Instead, the single-pickup basses were first offered in Black, White, Sunburst, Blood Red, and Royal Burgundy finishes with maple fretboards at a list price of $424.50, or with a rosewood fretboard as a $25 upgrade.

So the T-45, which was around for about five years, was not just a one-pickup version of the T-40. Rather, it had its own features and capabilities, and any perception that it was simply a cheaper version of the original is a misconception.

Years later, Powers was still maintaining that the T-45 was an underrated instrument. However, several new guitars and the T-20 bass were also in the works for an '82 debut, and those models exemplified even more of Powers' influence. Moreover, the Chicago transplant contributed a slew of innovations himself.

Peavey was attempting to diversify beyond the T-60 and T-40, which had been eagerly accepted in the marketplace, and the concepts, shapes, and versatility of the new instruments were impressive.

Three new guitar models, the T-25, T-26, and T-27, had a new and thinner body style, as well as new finish options. They had an intriguing 23-fret neck with a 24 3/4" scale; most guitar necks had 21 or 22 frets, and 24-fret/two-octave fretboards had begun to appear in the guitar marketplace about a decade earlier. All three had the same three-point bridge/tailpiece that had been introduced on the T-15 and T-30, and a hardshell case was included in their respective base prices (natural finish) when they were introduced.

Each of the three models had its own particular sonic attributes and abilities:

The T-25 was a basic two-humbucker guitar, with a variable pickup coil tap circuit and a three-way toggle switch like the T-60; however, it had exposed pickup coils. Controls differed from previous two-pickup models, consisting of a master volume control, and separate tone controls for each pickup.

T-25

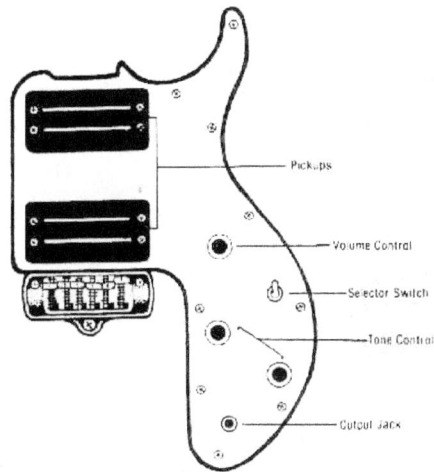

T-25 control layout from owner's manual

The T-26, with three single-coil pickups, also had a master volume and two tone controls, which controlled the neck pickup or the bridge pickup. It featured an innovative pickup switching system, and while the circuitry made sense, it had to be learned. Like most three-pickup guitars, the T-26 had a five position switch, and each position had a unique sonic signature. "By the numbers" in the owner's manual, the system worked as follows:

1. Neck pickup only
2. Neck and center pickup in a *humbucking* configuration
3. Center pickup only
4. Center and bridge pickup in a *humbucking* configuration
5. Bridge pickup only

The owner's manual emphasized that the tone controls were tonally inoperative in the #3 position (middle pickup only), but tone controls *would* work for that pickup when it was combined with another pickup, in either the #2 or #4 position.

T-26

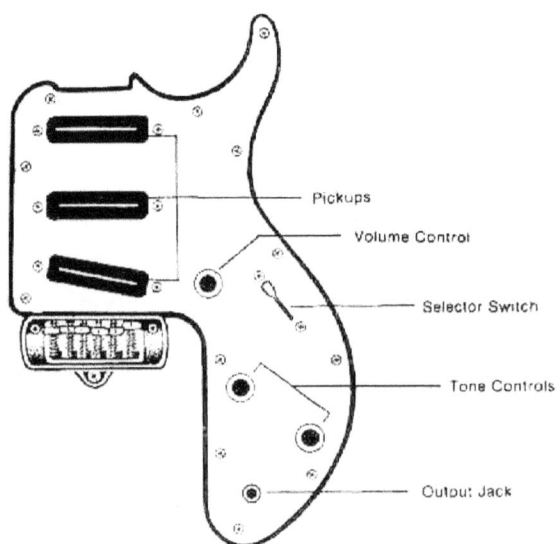

T-26 control layout from owner's manual

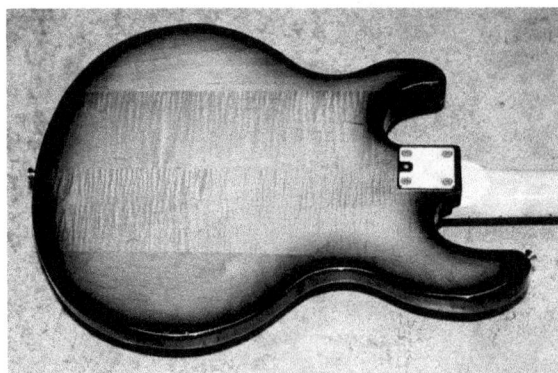

**This T-26 has a four-piece maple body, the two center portions of
which exhibit some noticeable "flame" graining** *Willie G. Moseley*

The T-27 was innovative as well, as it had a relatively early "single-single-humbucker" pickup layout (sometimes abbreviated as "S/S/HB" in guitar jargon), which would become a highly-sought configuration for many guitarists later in the Eighties (and beyond). Once again, the model had a master volume control and two tone controls, but on this model, all three pickups had tone circuits. One tone knob controlled the neck and middle pickup, while the other controlled the humbucking bridge pickup, offering, as expected, the coil roll-off circuit.

Positions #1 and #2 were the same as on the T-26, but the middle-pickup-only position (#3) did offer tone control for this model.

Position #4 brought the bridge humbucker into play, along with the center pickup, which meant that the roll-off could be utilized to get two single-coil sounds if desired. The fifth position was the bridge humbucker only, and the roll-off circuit was available on that setting as well, of course.

T-27

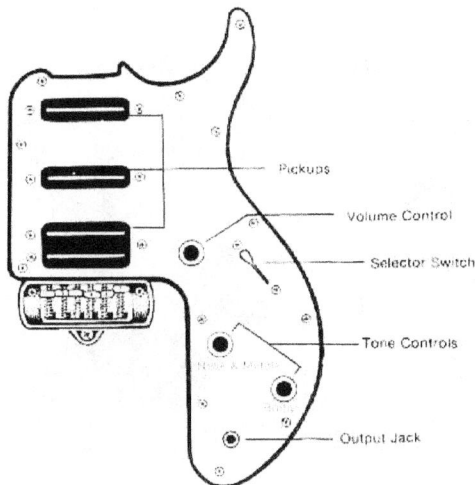

T-27 control layout from owner's manual and 1982 T-27 ad

Special editions based on the new models were available right at the outset—the T-25 Special, listing for $100 more than the T-25, appeared as a limited production model on a November '82 price list. It was touted as having the features of the T-25 as well as two higher output humbucking pickups with the variable coil tap circuit, upgrade 14:1 ratio tuning machines, and a black phenolic fretboard. The T-25 Special came in black only, and had a three-layer, black/white/black pickguard. A plush-lined hardshell case was included.

The T-27 Limited appeared on the same price list offering better-grade tuners and pickup switch and a rosewood fingerboard for $30 more than the basic T-27.

The new series also beget a prototype that never advanced beyond an embryonic status. An experimental version of the T-25, with a body made from a composite material called Sustanite, never made it to the production line.

T-25 prototype with composite body—front

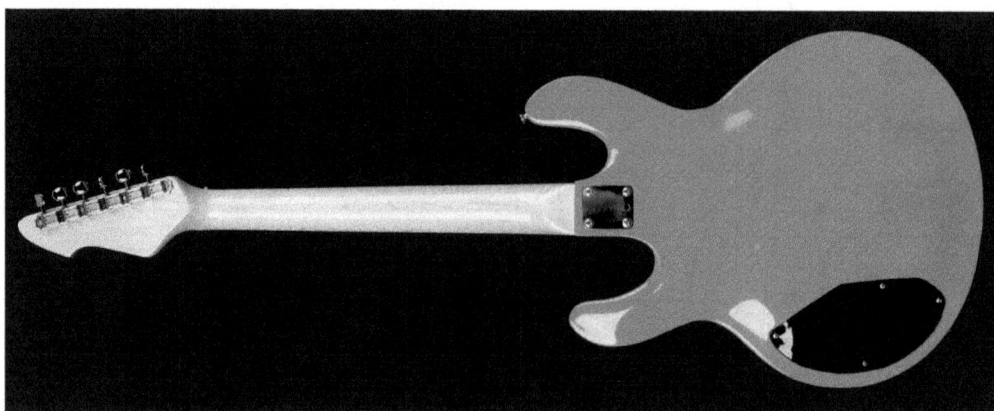

T-25 prototype with composite body—back

"That was one that never really took off," said second-generation Peavey employee Tim Litchfield. "We made two or three prototypes, but it was just too heavy. Just the body alone weighed ten or twelve pounds."

Litchfield's mother had begun working at Peavey in 1973, and her son joined the company in 1979. Tim, who had been playing guitar since age nine, moved to the guitar division in September, 1980, where he would remain for decades.

Peavey ultimately opted to publicize its variable coil-tap pickup innovation by advertising "The Circuit." A full-color ad displayed a sunburst T-27 with a rosewood fingerboard, but the model shown wasn't named—instead, all of the models with The Circuit were listed. The T-27 shown in the ad was still intriguing, however, as it had a laminated body, and changes in the wood pattern along joint lines could (barely) be seen.

"The Circuit" ad

Also introduced in 1982, Peavey's T-20 bass was definitely different from the T-40 and the T-45, and would also be pronounced to have been a Mike Powers project. The single-pickup model looked sleeker than its predecessors, and would push Peavey further into the bass market.

Also a 34" scale instrument, the T-20 was introduced with a "selected hardwood" body (according to a price list) and a 21-fret maple neck.

The body silhouette of the T-20 was different from the other two Peavey basses. To some observers, the T-40/T-45 body looked stodgy, and the T-20's slimmer, more traditional profile brought it more in line with most contemporary bass body silhouettes. Company literature also touted a laminated cream pickguard.

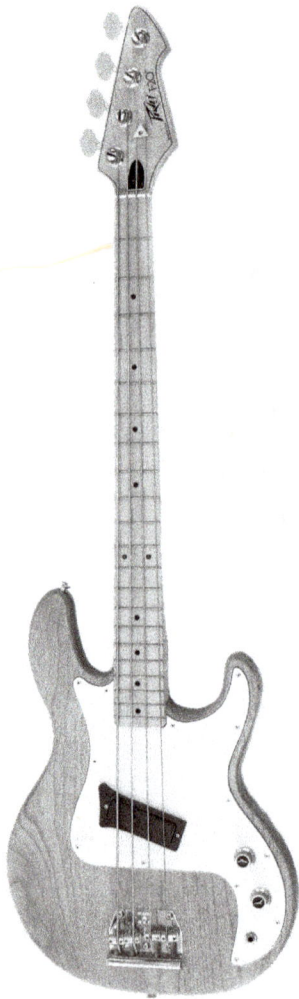

Early T-20: *Willie G. Moseley*   **T-20FL—lined fretless variant:** *Bill Ingalls Jr.*   **T-20—metallic finish:** *Bill Ingalls Jr.*

T-20—metallic finish with black pickguard: *Willie G. Moseley*

There were hardware differences as well. The tuning key ratio on the T-20 was described as 24:1, while the tuners on the other basses were 22:1. What's more, the T-20 had a new bridge instead of the die-cast monsters seen on the earlier twosome. The T-20's bridge was a lightweight "triple chrome plated" item, which had barrel-shaped saddles instead of the rectangular saddles found on the earlier bridge. Unlike the T-40 and T-45, strings loaded through the end of the bridge on the T-20.

The new electronics on the T-20 were obvious at first sight. A powerful new single-coil Super Ferrite pickup was installed at an angle, and the price list proclaimed that it, too, was "harmonically placed."

The pickup was surrounded by an "integral, mounting ring/thumb rest combination", according to factory literature, and the practical, asymmetrical item was yet another aesthetically-intriguing idea that probably caught the eye of many players.

Sporting "lightning bolt-P" knobs like all other Peavey guitars and basses of the time, the T-20 had a (less-complicated) "tone compensated volume control" and a "wide-range tone control" (since the pickup was single-coil, the variable coil tap circuit was not on this model).

The T-20 had two finishes noted on the April '82 price list, "Satin Sunburst" and "Gloss Sunburst". There's no mention of an satin natural finish, although such instruments were available right at the outset. The new bass model would quickly acquire the same finish options that were available with the three new T-series guitars. A lined fretless neck was also available.

The new, sleeker-looking Peavey bass proved to be popular, possibly because it was a simpler instrument, visually *and* sonically. It was balanced, easy to play, and the potent new pickup was bright and beefy.

Many rock bands already utilized Peavey sound gear, and as the lineup of Peavey guitars and basses began to diversify, more players were attracted to that facet of the Meridian manufacturer's products. Numerous bands began stopping by Peavey's facilities while they were on tour.

One of Hartley's earlier musician buddies who became an enthusiastic booster for Peavey gear was a bassist named Leon Medica, who hailed from the Deep South state just west of Mississippi.

Louisiana's LeRoux—the state being a part of the band's name for their first two albums—had broken onto the music scene in the late Seventies with a huge hit, "New Orleans Ladies", and would ultimately place several other songs on the charts. Some members of the band would also become ardent Peavey players and endorsers.

"We had a really good relationship with them," Medica (who co-wrote "New Orleans Ladies") recalled over a third of a century later. "The first contact we had with them about their instruments was when we were playing in Jackson (Mississippi), and they brought some guitars and a bass—a T-40—for us to try out. After that, we tried to stop by the factory in Meridian when we were out on the road and passing through. They always treated us nice, and if they asked me to do something like check out a new bass they were designing, I'd sit down and play while they monitored it on scopes. I was kind of a 'sounding board guy'."

Medica would be seen at LeRoux concerts holding down the bottom end with a T-40, and he later utilized a T-45, as well as more than one example of a T-20. He also did ads for the T-40 and the T-20.

Leon Medica appears in an ad for the T-40

Leon Medica onstage with a T-45...*laleroux.com*

...and a T-20: *jamesrobinson.biz*

"I really liked the way that thumbrest that was built in around the pickup," he said of the T-20.

The LeRoux bassist also noted that he didn't particularly have a favorite Peavey bass model, "...because I liked all of them. They each sounded a little different; they were all easy to play, and they held up on the road."

The fall of 1982 also saw the introduction of an important marketing tool for all Peavey products, as the first issue of *Monitor* magazine was published.

The cover story of that first issue profiled members of the John Cougar Band (the "Mellencamp" surname had yet to be interpolated). Therein, guitarist Larry Crane discussed his use of a T-25 Special, singing the praises of its phenolic fretboard, which, according to Crane, facilitated more precise playing due to its hardness.

Mike Wanchic, Cougar's other guitarist, detailed his use of a T-27, citing the versatility of The Circuit on that model.

As for the writers for *Monitor*, Hollis Calvert, Marty McCann, Jack Wilson, and other employees had been pressed into a journalism task for the company.

"I'd had no real previous experience, but it seemed to come naturally," Calvert said. "I really enjoyed the writing, and the personal relationship scene with the interviews."

John Cougar's two guitarists, seen in the first issue of *Monitor* magazine

The T-27—as well as Peavey's overall guitar program, for that matter—would get a huge boost in 1985, when Carl Perkins used a sunburst example with a rosewood fingerboard in his television special, which also featured musicians such as George Harrison, Eric Clapton, Ringo Starr, Dave Edmunds (who was the show's musical director), Earl Slick, Slim Jim Phantom, and Lee Rocker, among others. It was reportedly Harrison's first public performance in over a decade.

**Carl Perkins gives some onstage pointers to up-and-coming guitarists
Dave Edmunds and George Harrison.** *Sven Arnstein*

As noted earlier, Perkins was already a fan of Peavey, and had already been playing a T-60, but his use of a Peavey T-27 guitar in a one-time event among rock royalty (who were, of course, longtime fans of Perkins) was a memorable and important moment of visibility for the company's guitar program.

"I believe he was only trying out the T-27 at that time," said Calvert, "and I'm not sure if he went back to the T-60, but that may have been the way it happened. That TV special was great for the time, and we got tons of great reviews on our instruments because Carl played a Peavey on the show."

"That was pretty cool, and it got a lot of people excited around here." Litchfield averred.

The concert was later released as an 18-track album, and also marketed in more than one video format.

CHAPTER 7
Oddballs and icons

By 1983, Peavey was feeling its oats somewhat, regarding its guitar line. Price lists in that annum noted four new models—three guitars, one bass—and while the guitars were interesting (if not highly-successful), the bass would become a mainstay of Peavey's lineup for almost two decades.

Brandon Stolte, a "townie" in Urbana, Illinois (where the University of Illinois is located), was already familiar with Peavey gear—including the T-40—when he graduated with a degree in Industrial Design in May of 1982. He was actually more of a guitar player than a bassist, but as is sometimes the case with musicians, opportunities can manifest themselves with alternate instruments.

While still in high school, Stolte was playing a Gibson Les Paul Standard "…when some of my friends asked if I would consider playing in their band. The only catch was that they needed a bass player, not another guitarist. So I traded my Les Paul for a T-40 and a Peavey Century head with one 15-inch speaker cabinet, and I was a bass player. The T-40 had been introduced maybe a couple of years earlier, was American-made for the price of an import, and was capable of producing a wider range of sounds than a Fender P-Bass, which was the de-facto standard rock bass at the time."

Stolte relied on the T-40 during his college days, and found the potential employment road to be rough going when he graduated, due to a sluggish national economy.

"I sent out 75 résumés to different manufacturers and consulting firms without any luck," he recounted. "I sent a résumé to Peavey on a whim, really, based solely on the fact that I had used their equipment for years, and I thought highly of it. I was told that my résumé somehow got to Hartley, who decided that they could use someone with my particular set of skills."

While Mike Powers was also from Illinois, such a geographical association didn't really count for much when Stolte relocated to Mississippi to go to work for Peavey as a draftsman.

"Since I was going to be an 'at large' designer with assignments coming from any department that needed me, I don't know that an 'Illinois' connection' with Mike carried much weight," said Stolte. "We *did* often talk about making the adjustment to life in Mississippi, and what we missed about being away from home—mostly deep dish pizza, Italian beef sandwiches, and Chicago-style hot dogs."

And in his first job out of college, Stolte would be involved with the design of more than one memorable Peavey instrument.

The Horizon, Mystic, and Razer, all introduced in 1983, had the same pickup configuration and circuitry… and they even shared the same owner's manual.

The trio had two humbucking pickups with exposed blade coils, a master volume control, and two tone controls with coil roll-off circuitry. Like the T-25, T-26, and T-27, they had a 23-fret neck, and a 24 3/4" scale.

While the initial price list description referred to the models having a "polycarbonate" nut, the name of the plastic-type alloy was later marketed as "Graphlon," and that type of nut would ultimately appear on many Peavey stringed instrument models.

The three new models were originally shown with the smooth, rectangular bridge/tailpiece unit found on most T-series models, but many, if not most, examples of the Mystic and Razer that were "hardtails" (no vibrato system) actually had the earlier, square bridge/tailpiece unit as found on the T-60.

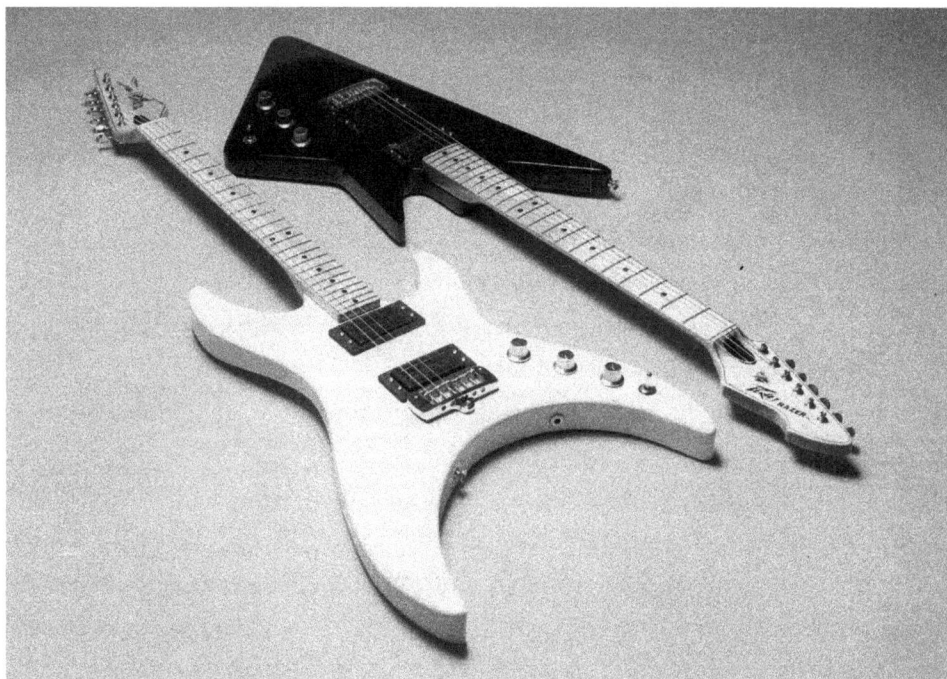

Photo from a Peavey ad showing early versions of the Mystic and Razer
with a smooth, rectangular bridge/tailpiece

The body of the Horizon followed a standard Peavey concept of ash for the natural-finished version, and an alternate wood such as poplar for the painted versions. The bodies of the Mystic and Razer were made from maple.

While the body silhouette of the T-25/T-26/T-27 series had seemed to be an improvement over the T-60, it was still a bit "stodgy," and the new Horizon went head-to-head with the T-25 with even more of a traditional double-cutaway solidbody shape.

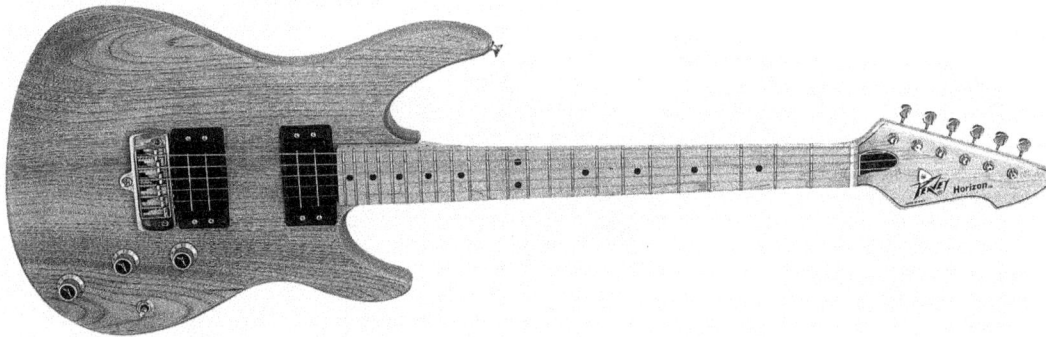

Horizon *Bill Ingalls Jr.*

"The T-25, -26 and -27 were considered too 'hippy,' and needed to be trimmed down and streamlined," Stolte detailed. "The Horizon was also the first Peavey guitar with no pickguard and a back-routed control pocket."

The Mystic and Razer were Peavey's first entries in the "modernistic shapes" segment of the guitar market, a.k.a. "pointy-headstock" guitars, although it needs to be noted that while the guitar bodies on the twosome were wild-looking, the headstock still had the traditional harpoon/barb Peavey silhouette. Some examples had a plainer-looking decoration, with the Peavey logo, the model name, and just two stripes underneath; i.e. no 1/16" pinstripe all the way around the front.

The body shapes of the Mystic and the Razer were radically different from other Peavey instruments, and even from each other, making them *extremely* fraternal twins.

"I wasn't present at any high-level meetings at that time," Stolte recalled, "but I have to imagine the Peavey retailers were asking for something to appeal to the MTV crowd—flashy instruments were seen as a growing segment of the market. Peavey was trying to broaden their appeal beyond the country and western base that they'd been identified with."

Hartley and Powers monitored the evolution of the new guitar designs, and Powers recalled that the Razer had been an attempt to design a guitar body in the shape of the company's "lightning bolt P" logo.

"On these particular models, Mike gave me a lot of leeway," said Stolte. "I remember sketching some body shapes for Mike, designing around existing necks, pickups and bridges used elsewhere in the product line. In particular, the Razer was a case of me wanting to develop a unique profile that could not be mistaken for anything else, even in silhouette. The Mystic was developed as a curvaceous counterpoint to the straight-edged Razer."

Razer in short-lived silver finish with T-60-style bridge/tailpiece unit. *Bill Ingalls Jr.*

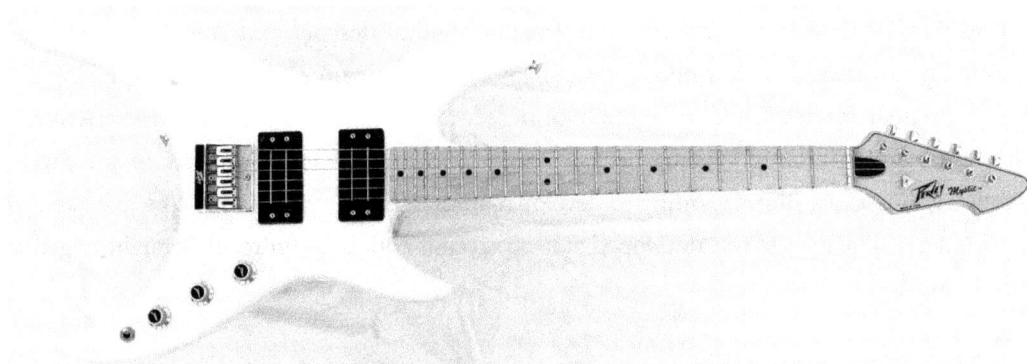

Mystic with T-60-style bridge/tailpiece unit. *Willie G. Moseley*

But the Mystic had aesthetic roots that dated back to 1958, when Hartley had sketched out his idea for a Bo Diddley-inspired solidbody guitar on butcher paper. Stolte doesn't remember being made aware of any comparisons between the late Fifties sketch and the Mystic at the time the Mystic was being developed, but recalled: "Hartley was always making suggestions about 'massaging' the shapes of guitar bodies, so maybe he was thinking of that old sketch when he guided me with the shaping of the Mystic."

While the Mystic seemed to have a bit of a scorpion-like look (and resembled the swooping guitar body silhouettes found on some models by other manufacturers), the Razer looked like nothing else, but ergonomically, they were both quite comfortable and balanced.

The Mystic and Razer were announced on an '83 price list as Peavey's first "special rock 'n' roll-shaped guitars." They were conjoined on the price list with a slash (i.e.; "Mystic/Razer"), and such a designation would always be the case, as they had the same specifications.

Among the few notable users of early modernistic Peaveys was Mark Farner of Grand Funk Railroad fame, who played a custom-made three pickup Mystic.

As for the Razer, Mississippi bluesman "T-Model" Ford performed with a black example, which was decked out with stick-on letters that read "T-Model Ford—The Tale Dragger." Ford died in 2013.

T-Model Ford plays the blues on his decorated Razer. *Courtland Bresner*

Interestingly, the Mystic and Razer were among the first Peaveys to acquire a vibrato system (and such a device was practically requisite in the hard-rock genres in which most modernistic guitars were found).

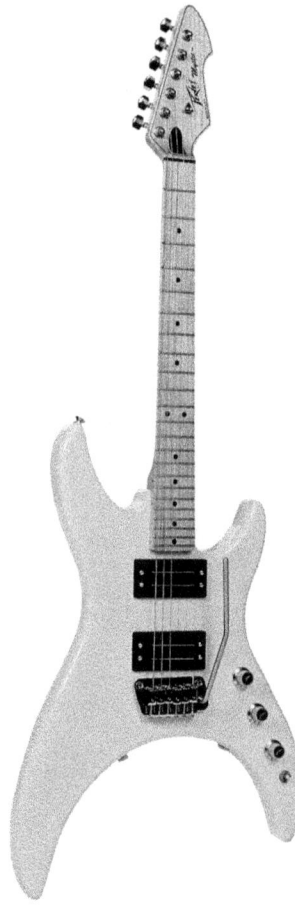

Mystic with vibrato. *Bill Ingalls Jr.*

"It was probably thought that the Razer and the Mystic wouldn't be big sellers for Peavey, so they gave this straight-outta-college Yankee in the drafting department more freedom to dream up wild shapes," Stolte summarized. "I got the feeling that the company wasn't real comfortable venturing into this market niche, so the product support seemed to be somewhat lackluster, at least from my perspective. Apparently the response from the market was something along the lines of 'This market is too important for Peavey to ignore completely, so it's nice that they are addressing it, but these models aren't going to set the world on fire'."

Peavey's first two modernistic guitars didn't hang around too long, fizzling out around 1987.

Around the same time the Horizon, Mystic, and Razer were initially marketed, Peavey introduced the Foundation Bass, a slim, balanced, two-pickup model that would prove to be a long-running mainstay in the company's bass lineup.

"That changed the whole 'tune'," said Tim Litchfield. "We'd had some comments about our [bass] necks being too big or too wide, but a lot of people really liked the feel of [the Foundation]."

The new Foundation Bass had Peavey's typical semi-arrowhead/harpoon four-on-a-side headstock, and a slim maple neck that was 1 1/2" wide at the nut, with 21 frets and a 34" scale. Fretboards were maple or rosewood. A lined fretless option on the rosewood 'board was available from the outset.

The first price list on which the Foundation appeared stated that the instrument had a maple body, and it was initially offered in natural, white, black, and sunburst finishes. However, some early examples had a more-typical-for-Peavey natural ash body.

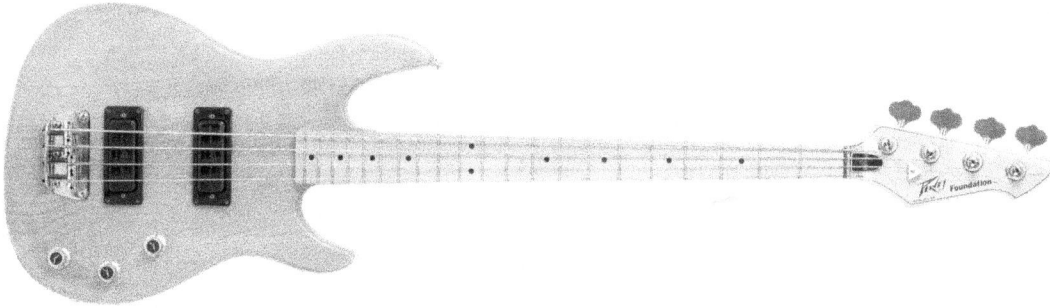

Early Foundation with natural body. *Bill Ingalls Jr.*

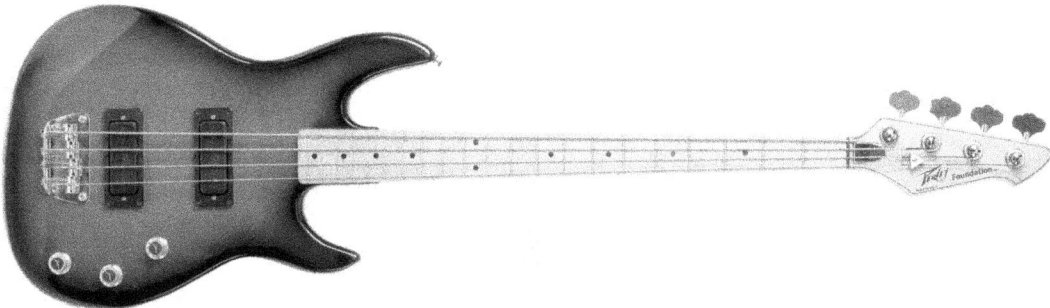

Foundation in sunburst finish *Bill Ingalls Jr.*

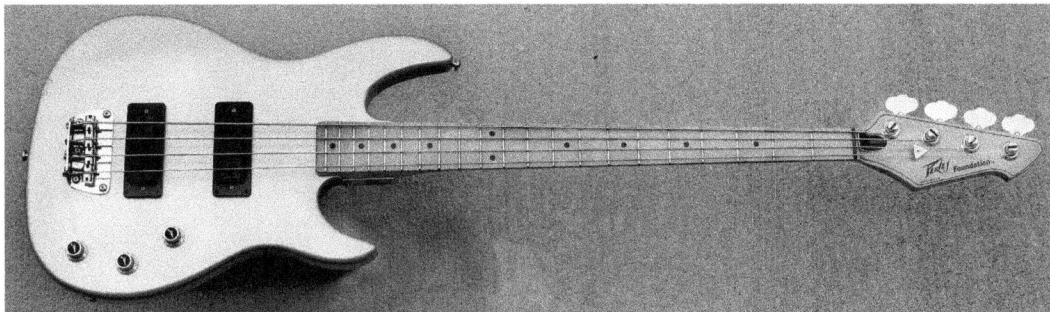

Foundation in short-lived silver finish. *Willie G. Moseley*

Hardware for Foundations included a new trapezoid-shaped bridge with large, cylindrical saddles that could be adjusted for height and intonation.

The Foundation was the first Peavey bass to feature two of the company's potent single-coil Super Ferrite pickups, and its controls consisted of two volume knobs and a master tone knob. When both pickups were turned on, they functioned in a humbucking mode.

The simple efficiency of the Foundation made it a hit among bass players in numerous musical genres. It would go through numerous configurations during its almost-20 year history, as well as variants such as the

Foundation Custom, which had matching headstock and a choice of several metallic or pearl finishes.

The Foundation Custom was introduced with a phenolic fretboard, but that high-grade plastic part was soon dropped. "Custom"-labeled variants with matching headstocks and special finishes would ultimately be an option on many other Peavey guitars and basses.

Foundation Custom (aftermarket graphics) *Bill Ingalls Jr.*

As the word spread about Peavey's new entry into the bass market, notable endorsers also lined up for the Foundation Bass, including Roger Glover of Deep Purple, and Kyle Henderson of the Producers, among others. Glover's primary Foundation bass was somewhat unique, as it actually had a white headstock with a "Fury" label (see next chapter RE: that model).

Roger Glover rocks out onstage with a Foundation that has a matching headstock that labels the instrument as a Fury model

Glover with the same instrument in a studio

"Beware of Rog," indeed…

Kyle Henderson endorsement ad

There was also a left-handed model called the Foundation LH. The Foundation S (P/J pickup configuration) came in active and passive versions, and garnered a positive review in *Guitar Player*. A five-string model was also proffered.

Foundation S, mid-Eighties

Foundation S Active, mid-Eighties

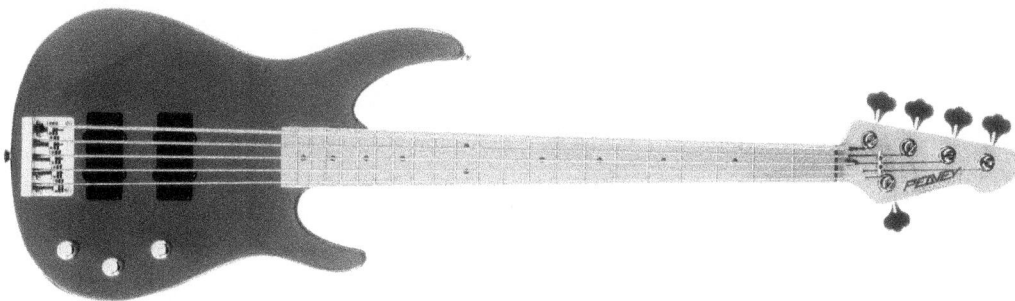

Foundation 5, ca. 1992

Towards the end of its days, the body silhouette of domestic models in the Foundation series would be reconfigured; its new shape had a longer, more streamlined upper cutaway horn for better balance.

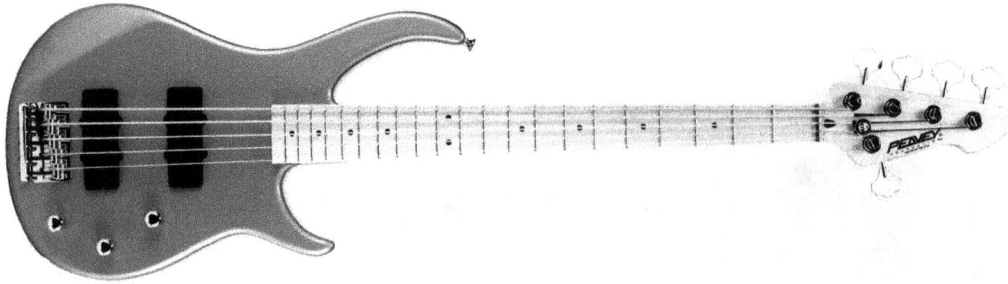

Foundation 5, late model

CHAPTER 8

Mid-Eighties Diversity—Double octaves, doublenecks, active circuitry, and more strings

1984 saw the introduction of a number of new and innovative models of basses and guitars that demonstrated Peavey was continuing to assert itself.

The January '84 price list announced the first Peavey models with vibratos, as the company committed itself to building instruments that could be made to "warble" by changing the pitch via the manipulation of a metal handle that stretched or slackened the guitar strings. Perhaps not surprisingly, Peavey's earliest vibratos were developed in-house, and were known as the Octave Plus and the Power Bend.

Such a gizmo would be (erroneously) referred to as a "tremolo" on price lists, but Peavey's opposing use of "vibrato" and "tremolo" wasn't the first time such terms were switched in the electric guitar marketplace.

The Horizon was apparently already outta there; its direct competitor, the T-25, remained, but there were also several new, somewhat-similar models that had sleeker body shapes (usually including pointier cutaway horns).

The Milestone was Peavey's first model with a full 24-fret/two-octave fingerboard. It had two humbucking pickups with the coil roll-off circuit as well as a phase switch, and an optional vibrato system added $50 to the list price. It had two "blade" humbucking pickups. Later examples had new powerful P-12 ceramic humbuckers (with polepieces), and/or more generic-looking knobs (instead of "lightning-bolt P" knobs). The Milestone was also available in a Custom version.

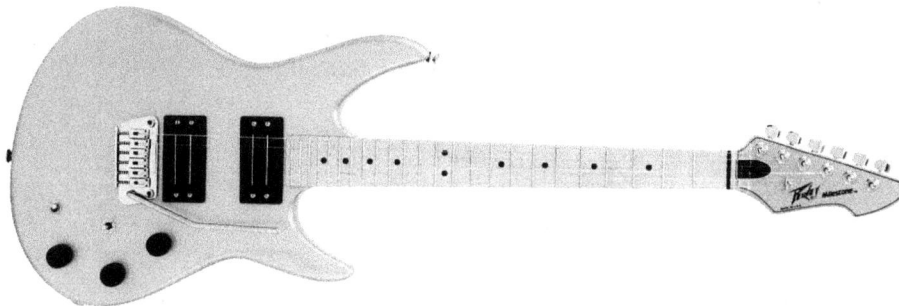

Milestone Custom

The no-frills Patriot had two single-coil pickups and an Electric Case option, but unlike the T-15 or T-30, the Patriot had a full, 24 3/4" scale. It did, however, have controls similar to the T-15, including master volume and tone controls, and a pickup toggle switch on the treble cutaway.

Some of the earlier Patriots had the same plainer headstocks that earlier Mystics and Razers had. More than one style of bridge/tailpiece assembly appeared on the model.

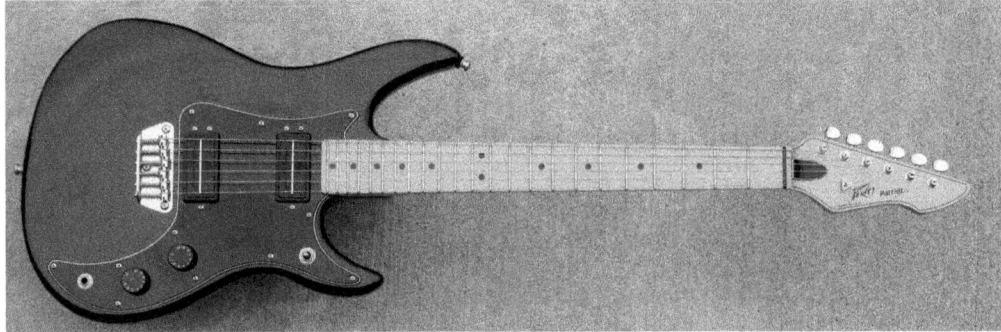

Patriot *Willie G. Moseley*

The Patriot later became available in a Custom version and a Natural variant (satin-finished mahogany). Another later model, the Patriot With Tremolo, had one traditional-style humbucking pickup, a volume control only, and a Power Bend vibrato; it was marketed as a straight-on rock-and-roll machine.

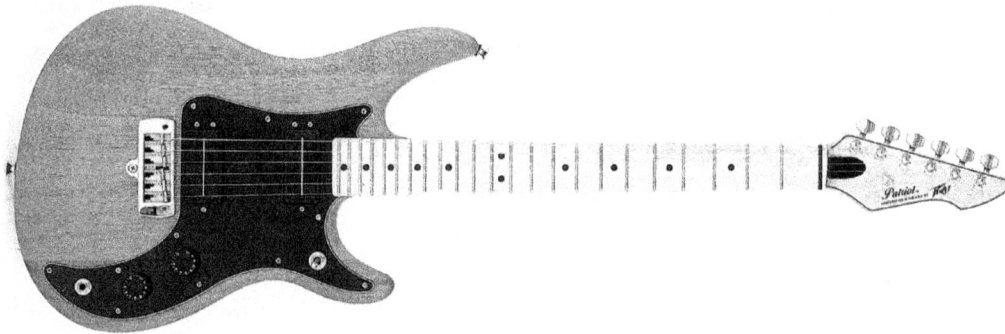

Patriot Natural *Heritage Auctions*

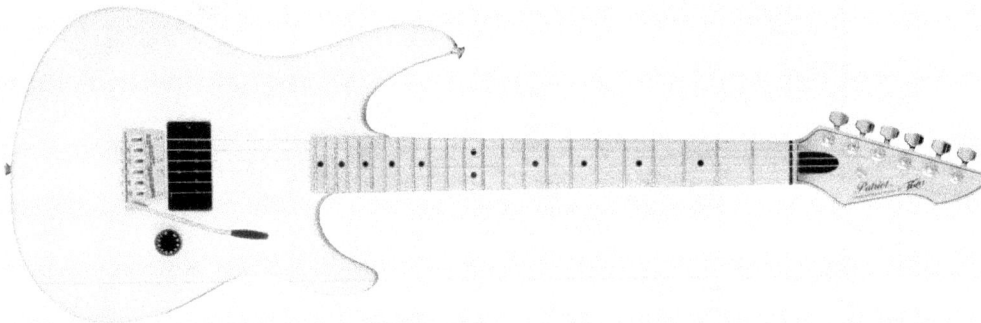

Patriot with Tremolo—white finish

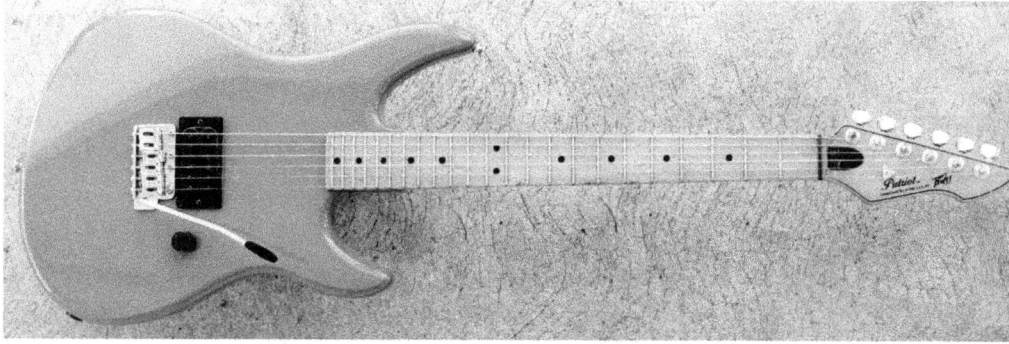

Patriot With Tremolo—teal finish *Willie G. Moseley*

The Horizon II was another two-octave instrument, but was perhaps more noteworthy because of its unusual humbucker/single-coil/humbucker (HB/S/HB) pickup configuration (all with exposed center "blades"), which meant the model had a corresponding innovative control system, including the variable coil-tap circuitry. Its two tone controls worked the bridge and neck humbucking pickups, as might be expected, but there were two toggle switches on the surface of the body. One three-way switch worked the bridge and neck pickups, but the other switch, also a three-way, controlled the middle single-coil pickup in a on/off/on function. In the "up" position, the middle pickup was on, and in phase with the other two pickups, and in the "down" position, the middle pickup was on, but was *out*-of-phase with the other two pickups, allowing for more unique tones.

Original style Horizon II

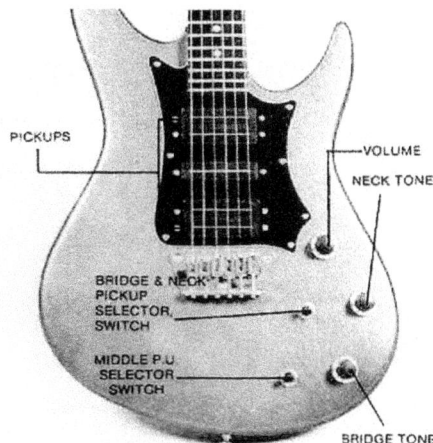

Line drawing for control operation from Peavey owner's manual

Closeup of front with original HB/S/HB pickup configuration

The Horizon II also came in a Custom variant. Some later examples of Horizon IIs had P-12 humbucking pickups with polepieces (the center pickup retained a blade).

Horizon II Custom—later configuration with P-12 humbucking pickups. *Jack Mason*

Closeup of later pickup configuration

When the January 1984 price list was published, the T-20 bass was missing…or was it?

The only new bass listed at the outset of that annum was the Fury. Not only did the Fury look familiar, its description was almost identical to the T-20. However, literature also referred to the Fury's "select hardwood Naturalite body design" and "Graphlon top nut." This time, the pickguard was noted as a black/white/black laminate, instead of a cream-colored scratchplate being cited.

"Naturalite" was a code word for Peavey's program that used unique and lighter-weight woods for instruments (mostly basses). Multiple-laminated bodies, some using more than one type of wood, had been constructed with incredible precision from the inception of Peavey's guitar manufacturing effort. On natural-finish instruments, seam lines between two pieces of wood were extraordinarily smooth, and were barely visible. Some Peavey bodies were made from as many as six different pieces of wood, and the company experimented with numerous other woods to supplant the northern ash originally used for the earliest T-60s and T-40s.

Mike Powers recounted that the company began using hackberry and experimented with gum, walnut, light mahogany (on Patriot guitars and basses), and even cottonwood. Solid color bodies were usually made from poplar.

"Hackberry is a form of swamp ash," he explained, "and it had more grey streaks and knots, but it sure was lighter and easier to work with."

A close perusal of a first edition Fury indicates that differences between that model and a T-20 include an even-sleeker body shape (cutaway horns that are more pointed), a narrower pickguard that conforms to the body silhouette, and a trapezoid-shaped bridge, as found on the Foundation.

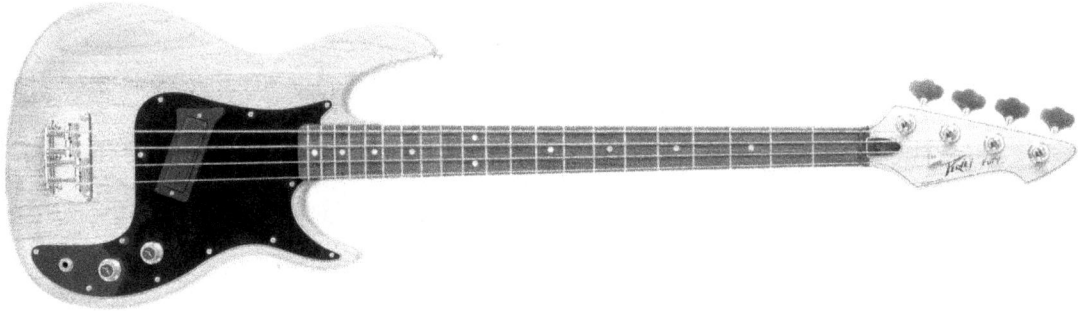

Fury—original configuration *Bill Ingalls Jr.*

Fury—metallic finish with blow-molded case *Willie G. Moseley*

The T-20ish configuration of the Fury would last until sometime in 1986, but the Fury moniker would subsequently be placed on an instrument that had a split-humbucker P-style pickup and traditional-style knobs. It underwent further changes to the silhouettes of its body and headstock in the ensuing years. The American-made version of the Fury was made until the late Nineties, when it was supplanted by an imported model.

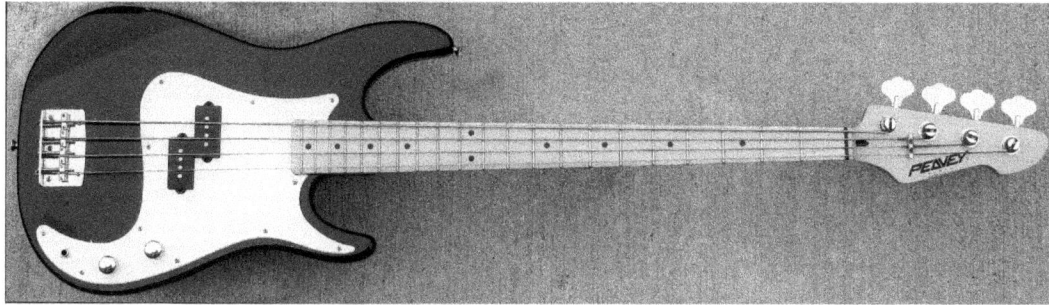

Comparison invited: A close examination of the ca.
1987 Fury bass, top, and the ca. 1994 Fury bass, bottom, validates the
ongoing evolution of the model. Differences include the headstock silhouette, logo,
tuners, string tree, truss rod access on the headstock, body silhouette, knobs,
knob placement, pickguard screw placement, pickguard layers,
and jack placement. *Willie G. Moseley*

A May '84 price list added the Hydra, Peavey's first doubleneck instrument. Like the majority of two-fer guitars, it had a twelve-string neck on top, and a six-string neck on the bottom. It, too, would begin its existence with "blade" pickups, and would later be marketed with P-12 pickups. Given the weight of such instruments, Peavey's "Naturalite" program obviously came into play with the Hydra, which was available on a custom-order basis.

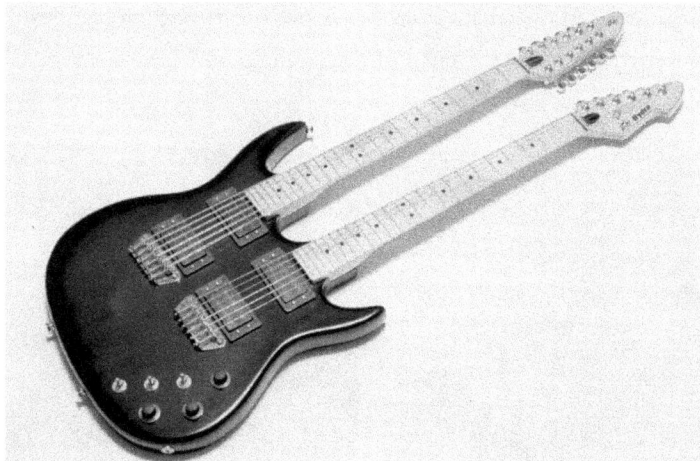

Hydra with original blade pickups

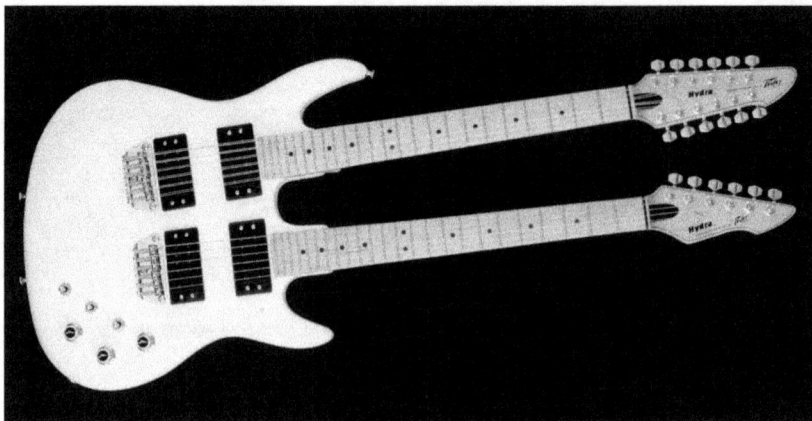

Hydra—later example with P-12 pickups

Brandon Stolte credited Powers with the development of the doubleneck model.

"The Hydra doubleneck was Mike's brainchild," he recalled, "and I think it was produced 'because we can'. It was a sort of 'halo product' meant to show the world that Peavey really was a full-line instrument manufacturer."

The May price list also introduced the Patriot Bass. Like its guitar counterpart, it was a budget, no-frills instrument; Powers noted that the Patriot Bass exemplified Peavey's efforts of trying to hit decent price points with decent instruments. Tim Litchfield fondly recalls the Patriot Bass as "…a fine little bass."

And like the Fury, the Patriot Bass featured one Super Ferrite pickup, albeit in a perpendicular-to-the-strings/standard configuration. The pickup was located closer to the bridge than might have been expected (and not surprisingly, the Patriot Bass's pickup was also advertised as being "harmonically placed").

The Fury and Foundation basses didn't have guitar siblings like the Patriot Bass, and the new single-pickup bass actually differed cosmetically from the other two Peavey basses that also sported Super Ferrite pickups—the Patriot Bass had a different body with longer horns, and earlier examples had a neck that was 1 3/4" wide at the nut. Like the Patriot guitar, some earlier Patriot Bass headstocks featured two stripes under the brand logo and model name instead of the pinstripe along the edge of the headstock.

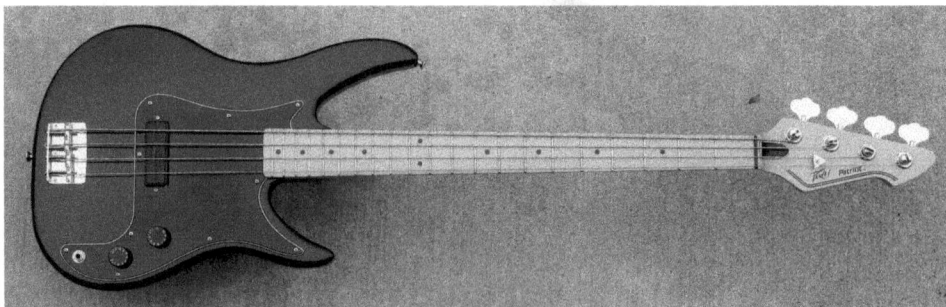

Patriot Bass—original style *Willie G. Moseley*

Later examples of Patriot Basses conformed more to Peavey construction and aesthetics, with a 1 1/2" neck width at the nut, and a standard-looking headstock. It, too, became available in a satin mahogany finish, but that variant wasn't marketed on price lists as a separate "Patriot Natural Bass."

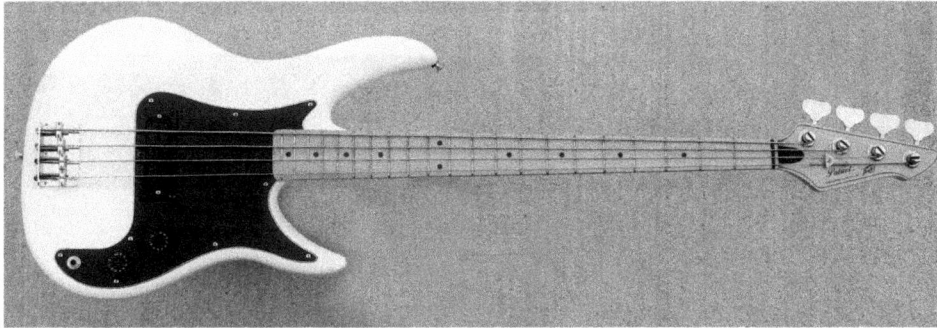

Patriot Bass—later standard style with narrower neck and different tuners *Willie G. Moseley*

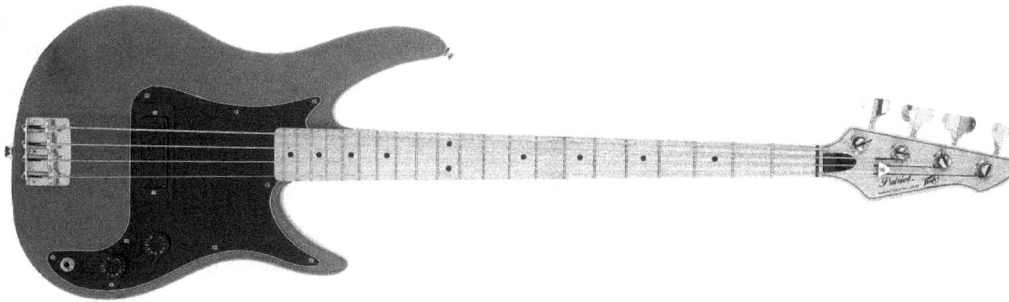

Patriot Bass—"Natural" variant *Heritage Auctions*

And since mahogany was fairly lightweight, that version of the Patriot Bass was slightly neck-heavy to some players. The usual remedy was to move the strap button at the end of the body upwards by at least a couple of inches for a different and more-body-centric balance.

P

Peavey's May 1984 price list was soon supplanted by another list. As a marketing ploy, the new price list divided guitars and basses into three categories—the Technology Series (T-40, T-45, T-60, T-15, T-25 Special, T-26, T-27, and T-27 Limited), the Contemporary Series (Mystic, Razer, Mantis), and the Impact Series (Patriot, Milestone, Milestone Custom, Milestone LH, Horizon II, Horizon II Custom, Hydra, Fury, Foundation, Foundation Custom, Foundation LH, Patriot Bass).

New additions on the June '84 price list included the southpaw Milestone LH, and the Mantis, a one-pickup modernistic sibling of the Mystic and Razer. It had somewhat of an X-shaped body (also made of maple, like its two older siblings). Its shape wasn't quite as cutting-edge as the silhouettes of the Razer or Mystic, and it was equipped with a vibrato as standard equipment. Just like its two modernistic predecessors (and the Patriot guitar and bass) the plainer two-stripe headstock was sometimes seen on this model. Like the Milestone, Horizon II, and Hydra, later examples had a P-12 pickup.

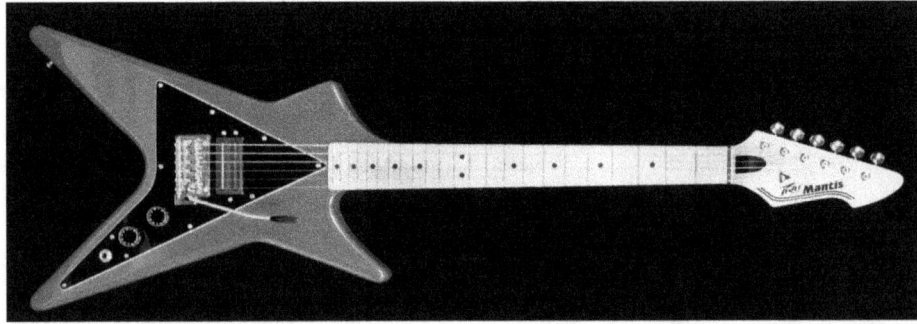

Mantis

Stolte: "The Mantis was created to answer those who wanted a more 'traditional radical' guitar, which certainly seems like a contradiction in terms. My contribution was limited to shaping the pickguard."

The Technology/Contemporary/Impact notion was discontinued in less than a year, and by mid-1985, T-series instruments were gradually being phased out, as was the pickup variable coil-tap circuit, which appeared to have run its course ("I just don't think rock players 'got it'," one Peavey veteran said of the most unique electronic idea that original Peavey guitars had introduced).

The Mantis now came in an "LT" version, which featured a licensed Kahler Flyer vibrato system. All three Peavey "rock n' roll-shaped" guitars would be featured in a full color ad that showed each member of the trio sporting a vibrato.

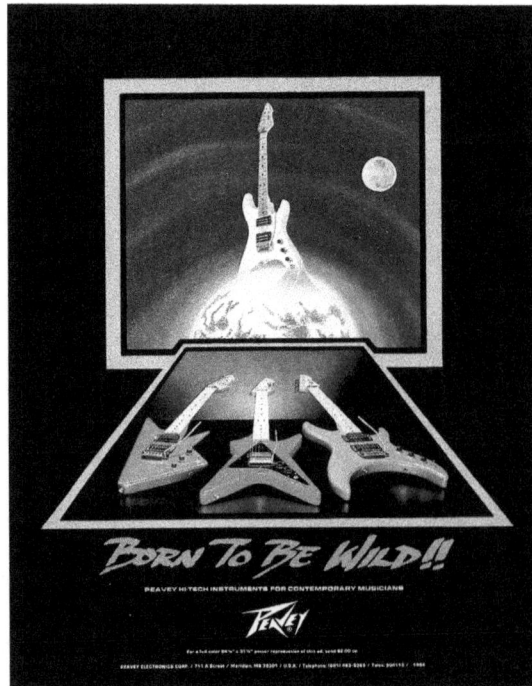

And the Patriot actually had a short-lived big brother—the original version of the Predator, also introduced in 1985, proffered a similar look, but sported new P-12 humbucking pickups and a Kahler vibrato. The pickups had coil roll-off circuitry (through a *master* tone control), but interest in that innovation was on the wane. A rosewood fretboard and matching headstock were available for a $50 step-up price, but that version was not referred as a "Custom" variant. The original Predator lasted until mid-1988.

Predator

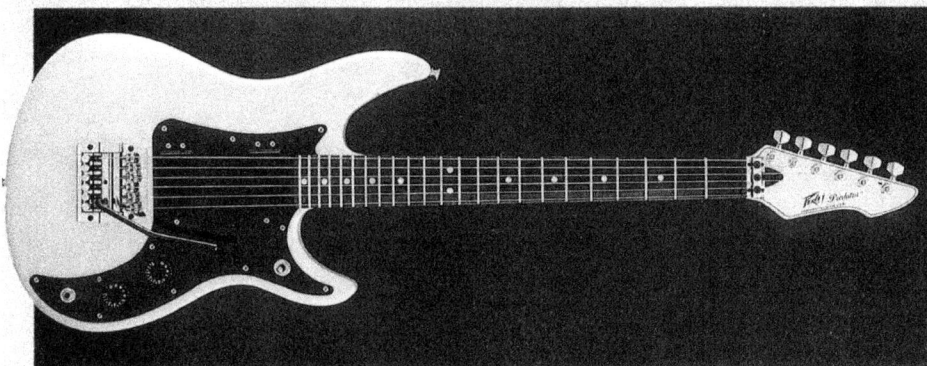

Predator—upgrade variant

Peavey's first signature model was introduced in late 1985. Jeff Cook, lead guitarist for the mega-successful country band Alabama, authorized a special variant of the Hydra, which had a Kahler vibrato on the six-string neck and a special Pearl Heather color. It was available only by special order, and was promoted with phrases like "extremely limited production."

Jeff Cook onstage with his signature Hydra

The Milestone 12 twelve-string was developed around the same time as the Jeff Cook signature Hydra, as Peavey also sought to penetrate the market niche of twelve-string electric guitars with a single-neck instrument.

Milestone 12

1985 also saw Peavey expanding and promoting its colors and finishes on instruments. Some hues had been around for quite some time, and not all finishes were available on all guitars and basses, but the Winter 1985-86 issue of *Monitor* displayed a sample palette of fifteen colors. In alphabetical order, they were Banana Yellow, Black, Fluorescent Pink, Fluorescent Red, Frost Blue, Metallic Charcoal, Natural, Pearl Heather, Pearl Rose, Pearl White, Raging Red, Sunburst, Sunfire Red, Transparent Red, and White.

The Winter 1985-86 issue of *Monitor* also heralded the new Dyna-Bass, Peavey's first instrument with active circuitry. Using the successful Foundation as its, er, foundation, the Dyna-Bass had battery-powered circuitry that was sensible, as well as an easy-to-understand and easy-to-manipulate control layout. According to Hartley, the new bass was actually named after the company's first bass amplifier (i.e., the company had already registered the name many years earlier).

And Hartley referenced the Dyna-Bass as an example of Peavey's diversification in the mid-Eighties, noting, "When we did the 'T' series, it was fashionable to have big, heavy bodies. Then, there seemed to be a shortage of basses that were not P-Bass or J-Bass copies. While I would be the first to admit that our T-40 was kinda clunky, I believe our Dyna-Bass was a step in the right direction."

The original Dyna-Bass configuration had a bolt-on maple neck that was offered in two neck widths, "Wide" (1 11/16") or "Narrow" (1 1/2"). It had two Super Ferrite pickups, as found on the original Foundation.

Hardware, including a bridge made by Schaller, was black on all colors (which included some brief finishes like Bermuda Coral and Teal Blue), except for Pearl White and Sunfire Red, which had gold hardware.

Dyna-Bass *Bill Ingalls Jr.*

Dyna-Bass—short-lived "Bermuda Coral" finish with original hang tags. *Willie G. Moseley*

The controls of the Dyna-Bass included a master volume and a rotary pickup pan control with center detent. The three equalization controls—Low, Mid, and High—were also sensible, and also had center detent.

The two-way mini-toggle switch was an active/passive switch to conserve the battery...or, according to the owner's manual, "...to allow the player to conveniently switch to the passive mode in the event of battery malfunction or failure."

Soon after its introduction, the Dyna-Bass would be offered with a Kahler bass vibrato option, and by spring 1987, a five-string version was available.

Dyna-Bass five-string—original configuration with 4 + 1 headstock

The Dyna-Bass was indeed a dynamic entry into the active instrument portion of the guitar and bass market. Early users included Pete Sears of Jefferson Starship, Jay Davis of Rod Stewart's backing band, Chris "Johnny Turbo" Campbell with Bob Seger's Silver Bullet Band, and Leon Wilkeson (1952-2001) of Lynyrd Skynyrd, who played a Pearl White Dyna-Bass on the band's 1987 reunion tour.

Pete Sears

Leon Wilkeson

A Limited version of the Dyna-Bass, introduced in late 1988, was a neck-through model with a flame maple body in transparent colors, oval fretboard markers, gold hardware, and a P/J pickup layout; it would be in the lineup for around two years. A review of the Limited in *Guitar Player* praised its versatility, noting "The passive mode is as good as any out there, thanks to excellent humbucking pickup design and construction. The P/J setup contains a full sonic spectrum that gets the most out of this instrument. The active mode is no slouch, either. A flip of the switch kicks in the preamp, boosting sensitivity and power, and making this a truly fine bass for rock and roll..."

Dyna-Bass Limited

The Dyna-Bass would go through several changes (including control layout, pickups, and cosmetics) during its time in the Peavey lineup, which lasted until the mid-Nineties. It would also be available in a "Unity" neck-through variant.

Dyna-Bass—1992 version with different headstock "block" logo, and alternate control configuration

Dyna-Bass five string—ca. 1990 variant with 3 + 2 headstock, "lightning-bolt" logo, alternate control configuration, and black hardware

Dyna-Bass five string—ca. 1992 variant with "block" logo

By mid-'86, Peavey had introduced Impact and Vortex guitar models, which were somewhat different in aesthetics, but attempted to follow developing trends in the electric guitar business.

The Impact 1 and Impact 2 were the first Peavey models to venture into a genre/niche that had a body silhouette that was a bit sleeker/more pointed than traditional double-cutaway solidbody electrics. Such instruments usually had three pickups, laid out in a single-coil/single-coil/humbucking (S/S/HB) style. Most guitars of that style also had a high-tech vibrato system.

The Impacts had a maple body and a 25 1/2" scale on a 22-fret neck, the back of which was painted the same color as the body instead of having a natural finish. Headstocks were also painted. Controls included master volume and tone knobs, with three mini-toggle switches to switch pickups on and off. The system was simple and logical, as were the differences in the "1" and the "2"—the Impact 1 had an ebony fretboard and a Kahler vibrato system; its hardware was black with the exception of Pearl White examples, which had gold hardware. The Impact 2 had a rosewood fretboard, chrome hardware, and a Kahler fine-tune non-vibrato tailpiece.

Impact 1

Impact 2

A 1987 review of the Impact 1 in *Guitar Player*, written by luthier Harvey Citron, was a boost, and included comments like, "This entire instrument is impeccably crafted with a flawless finish, and its set-up is well done", "…these pickups sound great. They're bright and clear", and "The Impact 1's sound is really impressive. I think that this is a very viable professional electric guitar at a reasonable price."

Not surprisingly, the review was reprinted in *Monitor* with *Guitar Player*'s permission.

Mark Farner was also a fan of the Impact, and he used two Impact 2s—one red, one white—during his solo career. Venturing into the Christian rock field in the mid-Eighties after Grand Funk Railroad had tapered down and out (again), Farner installed decorative crosses on the upper cutaways of his guitars. The idea of separate pickup toggle switches appealed to the veteran player.

"That ability to choose on, off, and out of phase was how I got a great sound," Farner remembered. "The wood was solid, the necks straight and true."

And Farner also noticed differences in his two Impacts.

"Even though they were the same axes electronically, and had the same pickup configuration, they were uniquely different in sound," he recounted. "The red Impact was a little louder, and didn't break up as quickly as the white one."

Mark Farner with one of this two mid-Eighties Impact 2s

Mid-Eighties generic Peavey guitar ad featuring an Impact 1 with black hardware

Attempting to be even bolder statements in the "pointy headstock" guitar market, the Vortex 1 and Vortex 2 were modernistic guitars that were as radical as the Mystic and Razer, if not more so. Like Peavey's original angular twosome, the Vortex 1 and 2 would be marketed like fraternal twins. They featured a phenolic fretboard ("Polyglide polymer," according to a spec sheet) on a 25 1/2" scale, and like the Impact models, the entire neck was painted. Not surprisingly, a Kahler vibrato was standard, as were P-12 pickups.

Vortex 1

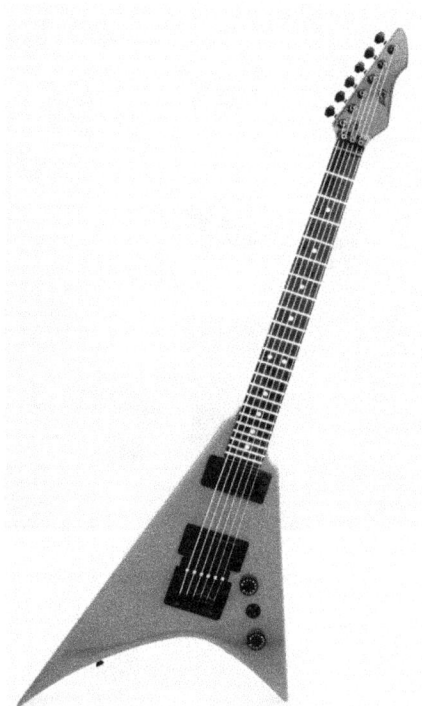

**Vortex 2—interestingly, this may be a prototype/pre-production example,
as there is no model name on the headstock**

There was, however, a contradiction to the aesthetic appeal that the Vortex sought, which was the ongoing use of the original "harpoon" headstock silhouette. While the body shapes of both Vortex models were most likely appealing to hair band members (and wanna-bes), it's possible that the headstock looked too traditional to some prospective players, particularly since it had been found on every other Peavey guitar model. While the Vortex looked quite flashy in a color like Fluorescent Pink, one might wonder if it would have fared any better had the headstock been as radically-shaped as the body.

VORTEX I
FLUORESCENT RED

VORTEX 2
PEARL WHITE

Vortex™

One look says it all: Peavey Vortex™ guitars were born to rock.

Twin P-12™ pickups deliver stunning power chords and fiery lead lines. The Kahler® locking tremolo system produces searing, dive-bombing effects at a touch. Optically enhanced colors and all-black hardware combine with knockout punch styling in purpose-built guitars with the hard-driving look and sound that defines rock'n'roll.

If you're the player who rides the tempest of today's high-energy rock, let a Peavey Vortex take you to the center of the storm.

	VORTEX 1	VORTEX 2
Body Wood	Select Western Maple	Select Western Maple
Neck	Bi-Laminated Rock Maple	Bi-Laminated Rock Maple
Fingerboard	Ebony (12" radius)*	Ebony (12" radius)*
No. Frets/Scale Length	22/25½"	22/25½"
Pickups	(2) P-12 Humbucker	(2) P-12 Humbucker
Controls	1-Vol., 1-Tone (1) 3 Pos. Toggle	1-Vol., 1-Tone (1) 3 Pos. Toggle
Bridge	Kahler Cam	Kahler Cam

*Early models were produced with Polyglide™ Finger Board.
See chart inside back cover for available finish options.

This ad for the Vortex models has a complete specifications list

CHAPTER 9
Further guitar and bass expansion

A late '86 price list announced the introduction of the Nitro I, which beget two other models in that series. All three variants had satin-finished necks, rosewood fretboards, black hardware, and Kahler vibratos. Bodies were made of poplar, except for maple bodies on sunburst-finished IIs and IIIs.

The Nitro I was an upgrade version of the Patriot With Tremolo, having one humbucking pickup, and a volume control (but no tone control). Peavey advertising text used the term "no-nonsense" to describe this model.

By the middle of the year, the Nitro II and Nitro III had joined the lineup. The Nitro II had two humbuckers, master volume and master tone knobs, and a three-way toggle switch. The Nitro III borrowed heavily from the Impact, with a S/S/HB pickup configuration, master volume and tone, and three mini-toggles for pickups.

Nitro I—original style

Nitro II—original style

Nitro III—original style

And perhaps Peavey did indeed learn a lesson regarding aesthetics from this time period. Sometime in '87, the Nitro's headstock evolved from the standard "harpoon" into a curved, pointed silhouette that looked like an eagle's beak. The forward edge of the headstock took on a three-tiered, sculpted, somewhat "stairstep" appearance that made its profile even more unique.

The '88 catalog featured even more Nitro models. The Nitro I Custom would replace the Nitro I during that annum; the new model sported a new headstock, a flatter 15" fretboard radius (compared to the Nitro I's 12" radius), and a different pickup.

Nitro I Custom

Nitro I Custom with original inspection tag. *Willie G. Moseley*

Yet another new one-pickup variant was the Nitro I Active, which was what its name implied; it was essentially a Nitro I Custom with active electronics and a tone control.

Nitro I Active

The Nitro II would be phased out fairly quickly. The Nitro III also received a "Custom" moniker, as it, too, received the new headstock, a different humbucking pickup, and a 15" fretboard radius.

Nitro III Custom

Peavey's most ambitious effort with the Nitro series was the Limited Neck-Thru (based on a Nitro III), which came along later in 1987, and was the company's first effort with a neck-through guitar. It was available only in Black Cherry Pearl, and had gold hardware.

Marketed as "Unity" construction, the neck-through concept would pick up steam for Peavey the next year.

Nitro Limited Neck-Thru

Notable players who were profiled in *Monitor* (sporting Nitros in accompanying photos) included *Nashville Now*'s Fred Newell, Chris Camozzi (who was backing Michael Bolton at the time), and Australian player Steve Grace.

Fred Newell

To its credit, Peavey also sought endorsements in the burgeoning Contemporary Christian Music field, as the company hooked up with God-rockin' aggregations such as White Heart, Petra, and Whitecross. Mylon LeFevre and Broken Heart would grace the cover of the Spring 1988 edition of *Monitor,* and inside, LeFevre (who grew up in a gospel family, had a modicum of success in the secular rock world, and was already a "Jesus rock" veteran) was shown playing a Nitro III.

Mylon LeFevre with a Nitro III

A few other Nitros would appear briefly in the early Nineties, as the model was being phased out.

Another late '86/early '87 debut was that of the Falcon, which had three single-coil pickups, and master volume and tone controls. It had a more traditional look, except for a Kahler locking vibrato.

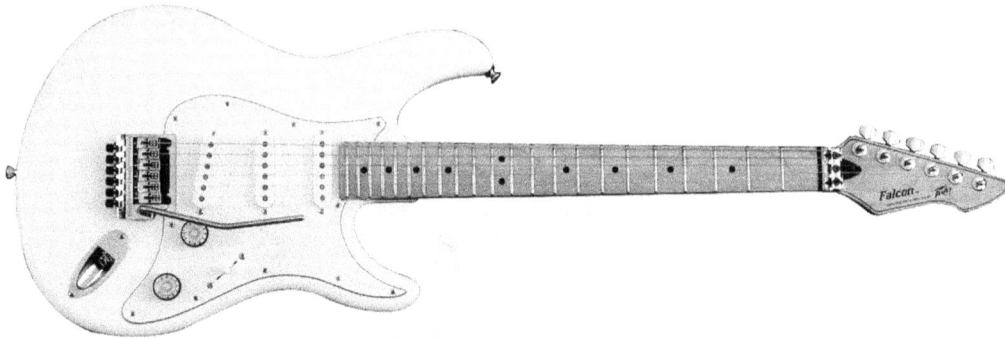

Falcon—original configuration

The Falcon also came in a Custom version with color-matched headstock (except on the sunburst finish). Later in '87, a Falcon Classic with a Peavey Power Bend vibrato would be introduced at a lower price point. By the spring of '88, a Falcon Active variant had joined the series.

Not long after its introduction, the Falcon series would be reconfigured to sport a new headstock shape that seemed to coordinate better with the traditional body silhouette, and the standard and Custom Falcons would get Peavey's new Power Bend II vibrato system.

The necks of some Falcons had noticeable "flame" graining.

Falcon Custom

Falcon Classic

Falcon Active

Among the users of the Falcon were Nashville studio icons Reggie Young and Brent Mason.

Pop and country icon Billy Joe Royal also played a Falcon, having been given one when the instrument debuted in the mid-Eighties.

"A guy from Peavey came to a show," Royal recalled in 2014, "and wanted me to try one of their instruments. I loved it, and I've been playing it ever since. I've got one of their amplifiers as well."

Royal appreciates the fact that his Falcon and other Peavey gear has been durable through his decades on the road. He continues to play it on several songs during his performances.

"I'm not that much of a guitar player," he said with a chuckle, "but it's held up, and it's a great guitar."

It's fair to opine that the Tracer series supplanted the Patriot series in mid-1988 as Peavey's lowest-priced/entry-level guitar series, but Tracers were more sleek-looking, and came in wilder finishes (in colors such as Rock-It Pink, Laser Red, and Express Blue, among others). Two different headstock silhouettes were seen on Tracers during the model's existence—one was the Nitro's curved and pointed headstock profile, and the other appeared to be a truncated version, without the sculpted "stairsteps."

"We had an amp called the Pacer, which is probably why we called the guitar series 'Tracer'," Hartley said.

The starting Tracer, listing for $299.99, was similar to the Patriot With Tremolo, with a single humbucking pickup (albeit a "high-output, distortion class" unit, to quote from the spec sheet). Like the Patriot With Tremolo, it also had a Peavey vibrato, but *unlike* the earlier model, the Tracer also had a tone control. Chrome hardware was standard.

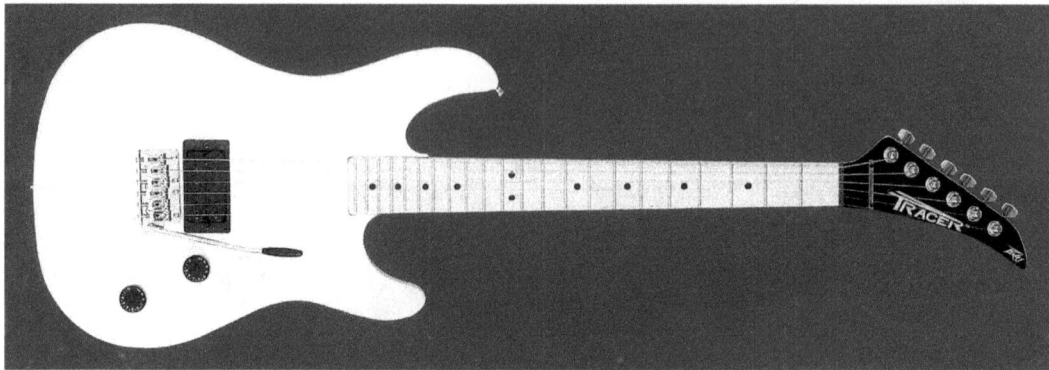

Tracer

Tracers in a 1988 ad

Interestingly, Fred Newell fell in love with a basic Tracer that he received from Peavey, and he had a wiring modification that interpolated a coil roll-off circuit (a la early Peavey guitars) installed by a luthier/technician in the Nashville area.

"I'd told Peavey 'Send me the cheapest guitar you've got'," Newell recalled, "and that little sucker was dynamite. I thought it sounded great. As a matter of fact, Glen Campbell heard it when I used it on 'Nashville Now', and borrowed it for some sessions."

The Tracer Deluxe added a single-coil pickup near the neck, and a high-tech vibrato. The Tracer Custom had a stereotypical S/S/HB configuration, but a five-way pickup switch was standard, instead of individual switches for each pickup. Black hardware was standard on both the Tracer Deluxe and the Tracer Custom, and the Custom was also offered in a left-handed version.

Tracer Deluxe

Tracer Custom

Interestingly, the price list indicated that the Tracer and Tracer Deluxe were only available with maple fretboards, while Tracer Customs were only proffered with rosewood 'boards.

The next year, numerous changes were appeared in the Tracer series. All models except for the Custom Lefthand now had 24-frets, according to a price list, and were offered with a standard or reverse headstock (again, not applicable to the southpaw variant).

A new model, the Tracer II, also debuted. It was a two-pickup model (emulating the Deluxe layout, but with a Peavey Powerbend vibrato) that came in even wilder colors, such as Multi-Chartreuse and '62 Blue, and such finishes had extra, er, "psychedelic splotches" in contrasting colors that were equally bright. It later settled into more subtle—but still flashy—finishes, and was offered with a standard or reverse headstock.

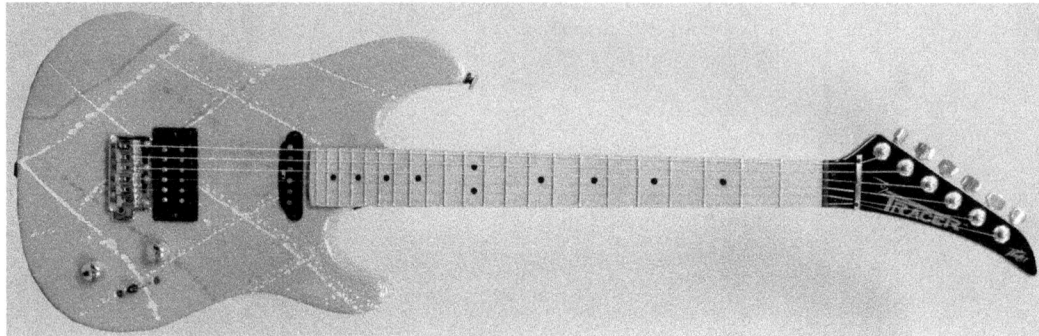

Tracer II

Curiously, the Tracer II's owner's manual shows an instrument with a 22-fret neck, and the fret count is indeed cited at that lower number in an introductory list of features.

Moreover, another owner's manual was printed for the "Tracer II 89," which shows a solid-color instrument (no decorations) and a 24-fret neck (also listed with that number in the features list).

And based on a referral from Fred Newell, Peavey reportedly sent Glen Campbell a two-pickup, 24-fret Tracer.

In 1990, almost all non-endorsement Peavey guitars and basses would be offered in a shiny "Eerie Dess" finish for a $25 upcharge. This looked particularly fancy on Peavey's hard rock-oriented guitars, including the Tracer series.

The number of models in the Tracer series tapered back, and it was offered (again) with its singular moniker but with a single/single/humbucker pickup configuration, chrome hardware, and a Powerbend vibrato as late as 1992.

Tracer—latter day variant

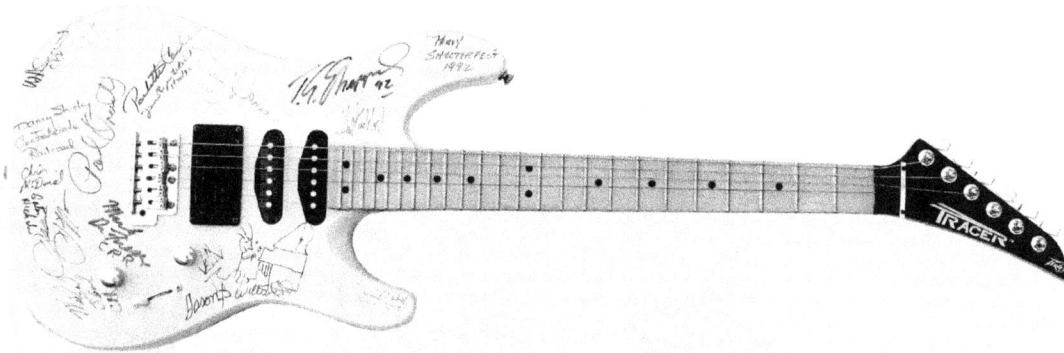

**This Tracer was autographed by participants in Peavey's 1992
"Shelterfest" benefit concert.** *Willie G. Moseley*

The last model of Tracer that was proffered was the Tracer LT. It was also an S/S/HB guitar, with a high-tech vibrato and rosewood fretboard. It was last seen in early 1993.

Tracer LT *Heritage Auctions*

The latter half of the Eighties saw Peavey emerge as a serious contender in the electric bass market, as the technology and sounds of electric basses had evolved to the point that it was no longer just a rhythm instrument designated to help a drummer maintain the beat/groove. Five-string basses and six-string basses began to be seen and heard more regularly as a combo's low-end stringed instrument came into its own.

And Peavey would go after the neck-through facet of the electric bass in a big way, ultimately creating numerous endorsement models with the input of famous bassists. First, however, the company created neck-through variants of models that were already in the Peavey lineup.

Neck-through configurations of the Dyna-Bass and a new version of the Impact 1 guitar were announced in the Winter 1988 edition of *Monitor* as the first examples of the manufacturer's "Unity Series." The text cited the use of koa, purpleheart, maple, poplar, and ebony in the construction of such instruments, concluding with a confident assertion of the instruments' "state-of-the-art feel and sound." Both of the instruments also had a new style of headstock with curved, recessed sculpting along the lower edge.

Fred Newell checks out a prototype neck-through Impact at a NAMM show. *Brooke Newell*

While the Impact 1 and the aforementioned Nitro Limited were commendable efforts, Peavey's neck-through basses ended up getting more attention, acclaim, and collaborations with famous bassists on endorsement models.

And in the same issue of *Monitor* in which the Unity Series was announced, a profile of David Sikes, bassist for the regrouped edition of the mega-rock band Boston, showed him with a new neck-through Dyna-Bass.

David Sikes with a Unity Dyna-Bass

Originally from Cambridge, England, David Sikes had immigrated to America with his family when he was a child. He began playing bass in high school, and majored in music in college. His earlier gigs of note were with Aldo Nova and Giuffria (and keyboard player Gregg Giuffria, the founder of the latter band, would figure into the Peavey guitar story in a unique way ca. 2005).

Sikes was offered an audition with Boston via Gary Pihl, a former bandmate with Aldo Nova. In addition to having to learn the songs for touring, Sikes would end up having to quickly learn how to adapt to a five-string bass.

"I recall talking with (Boston founder) Tom Scholz about some of the very low notes on the *Third Stage* album," Sikes recounted. "He mentioned that he had to tune down or vari-speed the recorder to get notes as low as B out of his four-string bass. We were discussing how to get those notes live, and I mentioned that I was aware of five string basses being available. I didn't know much about them, but some companies had started to offer them."

Sikes had seen a Peavey Dyna-Bass five-string bass in a local music store. It would become the first five-string bass he had ever played. He contacted Peavey with questions about their products, and was subsequently put in touch with their Artist Relations division.

"Learning to play the (five-string) bass was pretty easy for me," he remembered. "The only issue I had in the beginning was when I would let my guard down and forget that the low string was a B, not an E, as is standard on a four-string bass. I got pretty good at sliding to the correct note if it happened during a show; I remember getting some funny looks from Tom, though!"

Peavey supplied Sikes with four-string and five-string basses, and he was delighted with their playability and sound (as was Scholz). The bassist was particularly imbued with the rotary pan pot on the Dyna-Bass "…that blended the neck and bridge pickups like a balance control instead of on-or-off, like most instruments of the time."

Sikes first used the original bolt-on version of the Dyna-Bass, and later acquired a Unity/neck-through version of the model.

"I love neck-through designs, since they seem to sustain notes better than bolt-on necks," he said. "I also like the absence of the heel you have to deal with where bolt-on necks connect to the body."

CHAPTER 10
Signature instruments and set-necks

Another Chicago-area transplant joined Peavey's guitar R & D/custom shop in 1988. Jim DeCola, a native of Munster, Indiana, had worked for Mike Powers at the same Chicago-area music shop prior to Powers joining Peavey (and DeCola had taken over that shop).

DeCola had an opportunity to go to work for the Kahler vibrato company around the same time, but chose the company located in the Deep South.

"I decided Peavey would be the right choice, because it was a big company with a good reputation, and was very stable," DeCola remembered.

His original title was "engineering technician." Other personnel in the custom shop included Powers, whose responsibilities had been boosted to include supervising the entire guitar operation. He now monitored facets such as the wood shop and final assembly.

"He needed someone to kind of take over what he had been doing in R & D," DeCola detailed. "We also had Wilburn Moffett, who was one of the first employees that Hartley ever hired."

Some Peavey models underwent tweaks/fine-tuning after DeCola's arrival, and he would set about working on designs for new models. However, Peavey's first signature model that involved the actual design input of a notable guitarist was already underway.

P

While the aforementioned Winter 1988 issue of *Monitor* contained a profile of David Sikes, the cover story featured Whitesnake guitarist Adrian Vandenberg and bassist Rudy Sarzo.

To some critics (and cynics), Whitesnake epitomized the "hair band" phenomenon of the Eighties, but the lineup was composed of dedicated (and savvy) musicians that took full advantage of the now-*de riguer* video facet of popular music. The *Monitor* article hailed the band's formidable success onstage and on camera.

And within their mélange of brief comments, both artists alluded to upcoming Peavey signature model instruments. Vandenberg was actually shown with what appeared to be a black prototype of his signature model guitar, but the instrument didn't appear in Peavey's product listing section in the back of that issue of the magazine.

Sarzo was already endorsing Peavey amplifiers, but his signature bass took longer to develop, so the Vandenberg signature guitar debuted first.

P

Adrian Vandenberg's guitar appeared in the product listing of the Spring 1988 issue of *Monitor* (as noted earlier, Mylon LeFevre and Broken Heart were on the cover). It was the first Peavey signature instrument where the artist had collaborated with the company on an entirely new product.

"Adrian actually designed the body, as he was educated in graphic arts," DeCola remembered.

The initial version of the guitar had a reverse Nitro-style headstock with pearl dot inlay on an ebony fretboard that had 24 frets and a 24 3/4" scale. The neck was a bolt-on, and made of bilaminated maple. The body was made of poplar, and sported intriguing "violin"/"fiddle" notches. The first three colors were Gloss Black, Laser Red, and Rock-It Pink.

Its electronics consisted of a humbucking bridge pickup and a single-coil neck pickup, both set at an interesting "harmonically-placed" four-degree angle off of a perpendicular position in relation to the neck joint and high-tech bridge. The guitar had two volume controls (and no tone control), plus a three-way pickup toggle switch.

Early ad for Vandenberg Signature model

Initial reaction to (and sales of) the Vandenberg were encouraging, and by the next year the Vandenberg Custom had been developed and introduced. Differences included a mahogany body, which accommodated a maple neck in a "neck-through-bridge" configuration. Such construction wasn't quite fully-neck-through, but encompassed all of the parts along the path of the strings. The company hyped such a style's stability, as well as increased sustain. A different pickup was now found in the neck position.

Vandenberg Custom *Heritage Auctions*

One variant of the Vandenberg had puzzle graphics.

Vandenberg with a puzzle model of his signature Peavey guitar

Mike Powers and Adrian Vandenberg with signature instruments at a Peavey NAMM show exhibit

Somewhat of a contradiction (but still aesthetically interesting), the Vandenberg Quilt Top had, as its name indicates, more "traditional" construction (but the same silhouette and high-tech vibrato) when it was introduced in 1990. Its features included a figured maple top on a mahogany body, a mahogany set-neck (with a heelless juncture), rosewood fretboard with pearl bar inlays, gold hardware, and two humbucking pickups.

Vandenberg Quilt Top

By mid-1992, the starter Signature and top-end Quilt Top were the only Vandenberg models remaining on a Peavey price list. They would last until sometime in '93.

By early 1989, Peavey had introduced the Generation series (the first instruments that were DeCola designs), which was perceived as the company's modern high-end take on one of music's most traditional electric guitar forms.

The initial offerings, the S-1 and S-2, sported gold hardware, figured maple tops on contoured mahogany bodies, a 25 1/2" scale, a single-coil pickup in the neck position, and a humbucker in the bridge position (with a coil tap switch). Both models also had active electronics, and the S-2 had a high-tech vibrato.

Generation S-1

DeCola: "The body was more streamlined in terms of body perimeter, and it was a little bit smaller and ergonomic. Since we were going with a figured maple top, we wanted it to look upscale, so it didn't have a pickguard. It was different, but still traditional. Wilburn (Moffett) and I made about 20 prototypes to supply samples for the sales force."

Generation S-2

Generation ad

Jeff Carlisi played an early Generation S-1 on .38 Special's hit single "Second Chance," and also used it in the accompanying video. Comparing it to his T-60, the guitarist recalled: "It was apples and oranges; they were completely different guitars. The S-1 was lighter, obviously, and more user-friendly; there was that 'familiarity' and that 'comfort factor'. It was the first guitar I ever used with active pickups. It also had a shallow neck, which a lot of manufacturers were doing back then. When I used it on the recording, it was for the rhythm 'tick-tock' part, along with a Buscarino guitar."

By the second half of the year, the Generation Standard had come onboard as a plainer sibling at a much-lower price point. It had passive circuitry and two single-coil pickups. Fred Newell used more than one Generation on "Nashville Now" (including two in custom sparkle finishes from Peavey's R & D shop) but preferred the Generation Standard.

This *Monitor* spec sheet shows the Generation Standard and S-2

"They were experimenting with sparkle finishes on Generations," Newell said of Peavey, "but apparently they decided not to do it. I worked with Mike Powers and Jim DeCola. I tended to use Generations more than any other Peavey model, but they had also supplied me with Tracers, Falcons, and Nitros. Peavey was trying to compete with all of the 'pointy' guitars that were around back then, but I played all of those models on the show."

Fred Newell picks a Generation with a custom sparkle finish. *Jim Horner*

Another variant, the Generation Custom, made a brief appearance; it featured a poplar body, ebony fretboard, black hardware, and a vibrato.

The S-3 was added in early 1991. Unlike other Generation models, it had three passive pickups (which had hum-canceling circuitry) and a five-position pickup toggle switch, as well as a bookmatched maple top and an alder body "…with resonant, hollow tone chambers," according to the owner's manual. It was the only model in the Generation series to have a hollowed-out body.

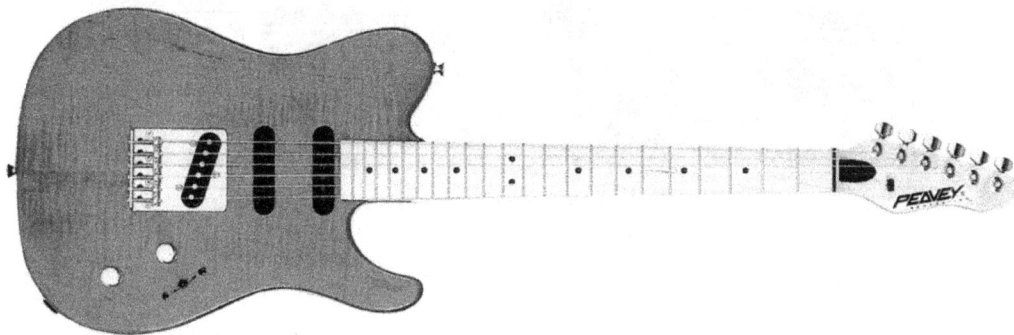

Generation S-3

127

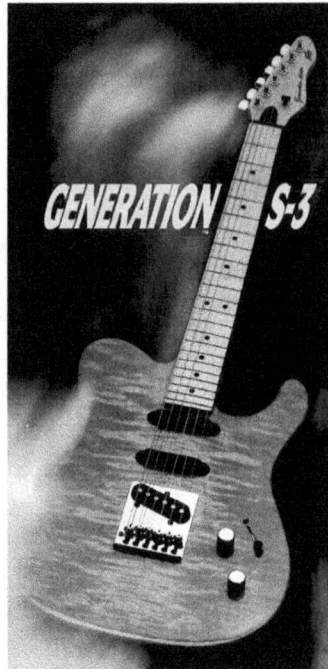

image of a Generation S-3 in a Peavey ad

Among the not-particularly-famous players of a Generation guitar was Peavey's own Hollis Calvert, who was by that time on the road as a sale rep for the company. The model suited his preferred playing style perfectly. He still owns and plays a blue Generation S-1.

Hollis Calvert, center, picks on his Generation S-1 at a steel guitar convention in the early 2000s. *Hollis Calvert*

The entire lineup of Generation models would be phased out in 1993, but the basic configuration would be resurrected a couple of years later as the signature model of Memphis icon Steve Cropper. A new series of imported Generations would crank up later.

Many music fans recall the twang of Steve Cropper's guitar on "Green Onions," an iconic instrumental by Booker T. & the MGs from the early Sixties, and he also contributed to numerous other Memphis soul hits on Stax, Volt and other labels in the ensuring years (Guess who's being cited when the exhortation "Play it, Steve!" is heard on "Soul Man").

Cropper also stayed in the public eye in later decades as a member of the Blues Brothers band. He ultimately became a fan of Peavey's Generation model, and played one as a frontline instrument for over a decade.

"Paul Robinson was our sales rep for the Nashville area, and several years earlier, he'd given his Generation prototype to Cropper," DeCola recounted. "(Cropper) had it for a year or two, and we hadn't heard anything from him, but then, he was getting ready to go out on the road—I think it was with Dave Edmunds—and he lined up all of his guitars to decide what he was going to take with him. He decided on the Generation, which happened to be the first prototype we'd made. So he had the first prototype of my first (Peavey) design. He played it for a number of years and really loved it."

Staying true to his southern roots, the Memphis picker collaborated with Peavey in the mid-Nineties on the Cropper Classic, perhaps the ultimate statement on a guitar of its type. By the time Cropper's efforts with Peavey's R & D staff cranked up, the Generation series had been discontinued, but old blueprints were dusted off and re-examined as Peavey created a guitar that featured Cropper's favorite aspects of the Generation series as well as new innovations.

Cropper's instrument, which debuted in 1995, had a traditional silhouette, and like the S-1 and S-2 Generation models, had a bookmatched maple top on a contoured mahogany body. The neck was satin-finished maple with a rosewood fretboard, and the neck juncture was a unique and patented "Maxcess" aluminum-reinforced joint, offering access to the highest frets.

The Cropper Classic was a passive instrument. Pickups included a dual-blade single-coil unit at the neck, and a four-blade humbucker (with coil tap) at the bridge.

Gold hardware was standard, and the Cropper Classic's colors had unique names, including Memphis Sun, Onion Green, Rhythm Blue, Gloss Black, Tiger Eye, Gold Top, and Harlequin Violet/Gold.

Cropper Classic—Gold Top finish

Cropper Classic—Memphis Sun finish

First year ad

The Cropper Classic would remain in Peavey's lineup into the new century.

"Working with Steve was a real pleasure," DeCola summarized. "I can't say enough good things about him."

**Cropper digs into his signature model Peavey onstage at the first James Burton
International Guitar Festival concert, presented in Shreveport, Louisiana's famed
Municipal Auditorium, 20 AUG 05.** *Mike Abene*

Peavey's first signature model bass was co-developed by Tim Landers, who had been shown with a Foundation Bass and a Combo 300 amplifier in a Peavey ad in early 1985 (Hartley credits former Peavey rep Jack Wilson, who was now working in Artist Relations, with recruiting several notable West Coast bass players).

1985: Tim Landers poses with a Foundation Custom bass and a Combo 300 amplifier

In 1989, Landers, primarily known for his session work, would earn a place in the house band on Pat Sajak's late night show (and Hollis Calvert recalls that bassist Randy Jackson had been in the running for the same gig). Around the same time, Landers also collaborated with Peavey in designing signature five-string and six-string basses.

Using a Dyna-Bass prototype instrument as a starting point, Landers worked with Mike Powers and Jack Wilson to craft a neck-through version of that model, followed by the TL-Five instrument, which debuted shortly before the TL-Six.

The TL-Five was an all-maple Unity/neck-through model with purple heart stripes in the figured bilaminated neck. The body was described as a "4-way radial contoured solid body" on the price list; it had "wings" made of matched Eastern maple, also figured. The bass had a 3 + 2 headstock, and a 24-fret ebony fingerboard.

The earliest examples of the TL-Five had active circuitry, Super Ferrite pickups, and a Dyna-Bass-like control system, but by 1991 the model had different pickups and an alternate control system with concentric equalization knobs. Gold hardware was standard.

The TL-Five was an immediate success among pro players. Noted bassists who used the model included Verdine White (Earth, Wind, and Fire), John B. Williams of *The Arsenio Hall Show,* Tony Hall (Neville Brothers), Paul Cullen (then in a brief tenure with Bad Company), and Jason Scheff (Chicago), among others.

TL-Five

The TL-Six was a more specialized model that debuted soon after the TL-Five. By its very name, it went a step further than a five-string's low B string, by adding a high C string, to create a stereotypical contrabass.

TL-Six

Obviously, Peavey's six-string bass had connections to its five-string progenitor, with Unity/neck-through construction, figured maple body wings, and an ebony fingerboard with 24 frets. Graphite rods reinforced the wide neck. The headstock was a 4 + 2 layout, and the unique bridge was made by Kahler.

While the TL-Six also had active circuitry, its two pickups differed from the TL-Five. The TL-Six pickups had what might have been termed a reverse P-Bass silhouette, with offset split-coil humbucking units that were "harmonically compensated" according to factory literature.

As is the case with any six-string bass, the TL-Six was a challenging, pro-grade instrument. It won a prestigious Music & Sound Award as the most innovative bass for 1991.

Tim Landers proudly shows off his signature Peavey instruments in 1990

Despite being cutting-edge and well-made instruments, both the TL-Five and TL- Six were gone from Peavey's lineup by mid-1997.

Mick Donner, an Iowa native, had been, like other Peavey employees, an aspiring musician, and had worked at Washburn Guitars in Illinois. He had been at Gibson's string manufacturing facility, also in the Land of Lincoln, for about a year when he was hired by Peavey.

"Mike Powers was trying to expand the R&D staff at Peavey and someone—I don't know who—recommended me to him while I was still at Washburn," Donner recounted. "Mike, Jack Wilson, and I had a covert meeting at the 1989 Summer NAMM show in Chicago. The Washburn and Peavey booths weren't far from each other, so we met in an office on the side of the Peavey booth that was out of sight of the Washburn booth. Jack and Mike both seemed impressed with my background, but were clear that the budget for another body in R & D hadn't been approved yet. I didn't hear anything more from them for over a year. In the meantime, I had left Washburn for Gibson. I got the call from Jack shortly after the 1990 'wake-on-the-lake' Summer NAMM show. He said that the budget was there and could I come down for an interview?"

Donner's initial introductions to Meridian, Hartley, and the Peavey company were similar to many others:

"At that point in time, the first impression everyone who came to Meridian was the last leg of the journey, on a little turbo-prop American Eagle aircraft. For most of us, it was our first time on a plane that small, and it was usually a 'white knuckle' ride.

"When I arrived, I was taken right to the hotel and then over to the old main office at 711 'A' Street. I went to Jack's office first, and hung out with him and Mike until Hartley was ready to see us.

"My first impression of Hartley is pretty much the same way I see him now—no B.S.; the 'good ol' boy' persona masking one of the smartest guys I've ever met. We talked, I showed him a guitar I'd built—a two-color sunburst with a matching headstock, ebony board, gold hardware, and pickguard, loaded with EMGs (pickups).

"Then it was off to Plant 2. I met Jimmy DeCola, who is still one of the most talented designers and builders I know, and [I met] some of the crew that was building TL-6 basses. After that, we went to the guitar production facility."

Donner was hired, and reported to work with Mike Powers as his supervisor.

Two DeCola-designed instruments that were quite different from each other hit the market at the end of the Eighties.

The Destiny was Peavey's ultimate statement in the Eighties hair band/hard rock market. It featured "neck-through-bridge" construction; i.e., the S/S/HB pickups and vibrato tailpiece were mounted on a very long tapered dowel that inserted into a very long slot in the (poplar) body. DeCola had first seen the concept on a no-frills, American-made brand.

"I got the inspiration from [short-lived American guitar company] S.D. Curlee," he said, "but I did it differently; I put a taper in the neck for more of a 'big dovetail' shape. It continued the taper of the fingerboard, extending it to the bridge so it could be inserted in a way that would basically lock it into place like a traditional dovetail. It was, of course, glued, and not bolted in."

The "neck-through-bridge" concept on the Destiny was later interpolated on variants of the Vandenberg when that signature model began to diversify. The original Vandenberg came first, but the "neck-through-bridge" construction was first found on the Destiny.

A rosewood fretboard (24 3/4" scale, 24-frets) and black hardware were standard on the Destiny. The circuit for the pickups was designed to provide hum-canceling operation regardless of what position the five-way toggle switch was placed.

A Destiny Custom featured a figured maple neck, ebony fingerboard with oval inlay, mahogany body with bookmatched, figured maple top, and gold hardware. It would be in the line until ca. 1994.

Destiny

Destiny Custom

Among the individuals who were seen with Peavey Destiny models was rapid-fire guitarist Tony MacAlpine, whose instrument had customized electronics.

Tony MacAlpine

The Odyssey was the antithesis of the Destiny. It had much more of a traditional vibe, including an easy-going, single-cutaway silhouette instead of swooping lines and angles. It also had a set-in neck that was heel-less, offering an incredibly smooth feel. The instrument had mahogany construction (body and neck) with a carved, bookmatched flame maple top. The "3 + 3" headstock and ebony fretboard had cream-colored binding, and the side of the body had a natural-finished maple section around it that resembled binding.

Electronics included two humbucking pickups with separate volume and tone controls for each pickup, and a pickup toggle switch on the upper bout. Modernistic additions included 24 frets, and a coil-splitter mini-switch. Gold hardware was standard, and the (separate) bridge and stop tailpiece referenced classic designs.

Odyssey

The Custom variant of the Odyssey (of which there was a 25th Anniversary version in 1990) had Tahitian black pearl and mother of pearl block fretboard inlay that had a "3-D" look, black hardware, and actual ivoroid body binding.

Odyssey Custom

Players shown with Odysseys included "player's players" Al Pitrelli and Lanny Cordola, and Kim Thayall of Soundgarden, a Seattle band associated with the "grunge" genre that was popular in the early Nineties. A very positive review in *Guitar Player* also helped to call attention to the model.

Kim Thayall of Soundgarden was featured in this ad for the Odyssey

Rudy Sarzo doesn't relate to being referred to as an "émigré" from Cuba.

"It's more like we were 'refugees'," he said. "The reality is that we left for political reasons."

Sarzo's family moved to the U.S. when Sarzo was eleven.

"I can remember when Castro came in, a lot of the American music was prohibited," he recalled, "and when I arrived in America in 1961, 'rock and roll' did not really exist on American radio. Elvis was in the Army, Buddy Holley had died, Little Richard was a minister, and Chuck Berry was in jail, so the airplay consisted of teen idols like Frankie Avalon and Pat Boone; the music was very 'vanilla'. It was right before the Beatles, and it wasn't until the British Invasion that rock and roll got back on the airwaves."

Once Sarzo became a player, he settled into being a bassist, and had already gigged with Quiet Riot and Ozzy Osbourne before joining Whitesnake in the spring of 1987. He remained in that aggregation until the fall of 1994, and that portion of the band's chronology was considered to have been Whitesnake's most successful era.

Sarzo had been familiar with Peavey sound reinforcement gear for a number of years.

"When I was living in Miami, and was a struggling musician, I was looking for the best deal," he remembered. "There was something about Peavey that meant it was reliable, unbreakable, and durable. And if you spent 500 bucks on an amp, you'd get twice the amp from Peavey. They were still 'building their brand'; some of the other brands were 'status symbols'. So quality-wise and money-wise, you got a better deal playing Peavey."

Sarzo did use other brands of amplifiers on tour, and had even endorsed another brand, when a 1983 incident while he was touring with Quiet Riot sold him on the brand from the Deep South.

"We were on the *Metal Health* tour, and had a performance booked in Puerto Rico," he recalled. "Back then, a lot of countries weren't set up to provide good gear for national bands that were touring. The promoter took my bass tech to a local music store, where he lined up some Peavey gear. I thought I'd use it just for one show, but I was blown away, to say the least, by the sound, the tone, and the quality. I had a blast playing that show!"

Sarzo's standard domestic touring rig did not come up to the tone of the Peavey rig that he had used in Puerto Rico, so he contacted Peavey, flew to Meridian, and met with Hollis Calvert. He's been playing through Peavey sound reinforcement gear ever since, and garnered a cover story in *Monitor* magazine in the summer of 1984.

"One of the things that's interesting about being a musician is that you originally spend a lot of time starving, and you can't afford anything," Sarzo said with a chuckle. "Then, when you become successful, everybody wants to endorse you."

Rudy Sarzo graces the cover of *Monitor* in 1984

He considered previous endorsement experiences with other brands of basses to have been an education, and one of the appealing facets of the proposed Peavey signature bass was that it would be built in the United States, where Sarzo could monitor the quality of production instruments.

"During the Eighties, all of the high-quality basses that were being sold in the market were neck-throughs," Sarzo detailed. "There were an emphasis on that high-end market, but I wanted the same kind of quality in a bass that would list for less than a thousand dollars."

Sarzo worked with Powers and DeCola closely, and the luthiers admired his intense focus on the new instrument. The bassist did not have a problem with the fact that the company was using CNC machines on bodies and necks.

"I appreciated the accuracy," he said. "To me, there's nothing better to be able to approve a prototype, and you're guaranteed that every single instrument of that type will come up to the same quality as your own prototype."

Product development of the Rudy Sarzo Signature Bass took about a year and a half, and the model debuted in mid-1989.

DeCola: "I had first met Rudy in January, 1982, when I did some work for Randy Rhoads; he and Rudy were with Ozzy Osbourne. I never thought I'd work with Rudy years later at Peavey. It was a great experience. Rudy and I collaborated on the body shape and pickups, which were basically T-40, dual-blade humbuckers in plastic covers, but they weren't the exact same wind [as original T-40 pickups], so they sounded different."

The Rudy Sarzo Signature Bass was constructed with Peavey's Unity neck-through style, utilizing a flame maple center piece with decorative purple heart stripes. The body wings were made of northern ash. The overall body silhouette had a longer upper cutaway horn for better balance. Sarzo also wanted decently-figured woods on the body, since most of the colors on the instrument were to be see-through/tinted finishes.

The ebony fingerboard had 24-frets, and the inlay was mother-of-pearl, in an oval-shaped pattern that was dubbed "Open Eye". Hardware was gold.

The controls were similar to a Dyna-Bass active system, but differed in that there were two volume controls instead of a master volume and a pan control. The instrument still had three controls for tone/equalization, and an active/passive switch. Sarzo said that he wanted such electronics to be as "ballsy" as the controls on higher-end (and usually neck-through) bass brands.

Rudy Sarzo Bass

Early publicity photo of the man and the bass

When the prototype was delivered for Sarzo's inspection, the bassist didn't have any major complaints.

"There was very little, if anything, we needed to do," he said.

Sarzo was bemused about the initial reception to the Peavey Rudy Sarzo Signature Bass.

"The reaction was interesting," he recounted. "I'd wanted it to be a versatile or 'universal' instrument, not just a heavy metal bass, and as it turned out, the first musicians that actually gravitated towards it were the *jazz* musicians, which, to me, was a compliment, because I really admire jazz. And Verdine White, from Earth, Wind, and Fire, played one for a while. It was fine for someone in a heavy metal band or rock band, like me, but it was just as much at home with a lounge band at a Holiday Inn or in a wedding band."

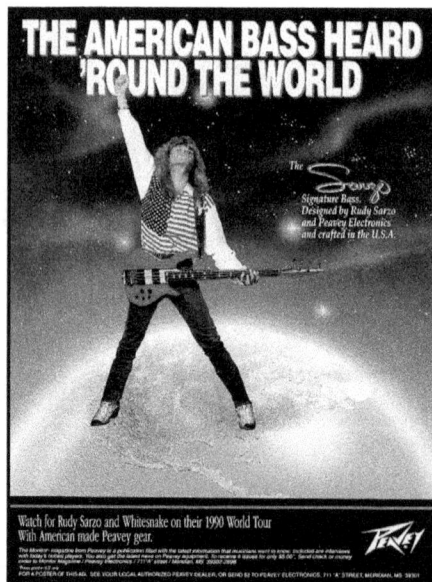

One of several ads for the Rudy Sarzo Bass

Several other noted bassists utilized a Peavey Sarzo. For example, Vail Johnson, who backed up reed player Kenny G., had a fretless example.

Sarzo summarized that his Peavey signature instrument was everything that his previous endorsement models by other manufacturers had not been.

"Peavey really delivered," he said, around a quarter-century after his bass debuted. "We really worked together as a team, and we came up with one hell of a bass. And it was all done in Meridian; it wasn't done overseas. As a matter of fact, if you look through the ratings on bass forums on the internet, it always gets five stars. I was incredibly proud of that instrument."

Sarzo rocks out onstage with his signature bass at a Whitesnake concert

Different instruments, different genres, mutual admiration: Fred Newell and Rudy Sarzo appear at a Peavey exhibit at a 1989 guitar show in Texas. Newell has one of his sparkle-finish Generation models, while Sarzo displays his signature model bass. *Brooke Newell*

At the advent of the Nineties, DeCola became the Guitar Design Engineering Supervisor, a position he held for the duration of his tenure at Peavey (until 2000). A few years later, guitar design and bass design separated, with DeCola in charge of guitars and Powers in charge of basses. Ed Pope, who had been with the company since 1987, transferred to the guitar division in 1996; Pope initially worked in Quality Control, and later got into engineering with DeCola. A few months after Pope arrived in R & D, Tim Litchfield replaced Mick Donner (who was assigned to be a production supervisor).

To say that his weekly appearance on "American Idol" was just the tip of the iceberg in the decades-long career of the ubiquitous Randy Jackson is an understatement.

The veteran bassist has played with and/or recorded with and/or produced musicians ranging from Jean Luc-Ponty to Bob Dylan to Jerry Garcia to Mariah Carey to Bruce Springsteen to Charlie Daniels…for starters (and the Daniels gig was at the Grand Ole Opry, no less).

However, many music fans probably recall a 1986 performance video of Journey's "Girl Can't Help It" as their first encounter with Randy Jackson, who had played on that band's *Raised on Radio* album (also released in '86) and was invited to tour with the band.

Jackson played a green bass decorated with gambling table graphics in those times, but a few years later, he collaborated with Peavey on a bass with logical utilitarian appointments.

RJ-IV *Bill Ingalls Jr.*

Curiously, more than one Peavey spec sheet referred to the model as the "RJ4" while "RJ-IV" was found on the headstock and the instruction manual.

The RJ-IV had several intriguing "what you don't see" facets. For example, its original stock "pearl burst" finishes made it impossible to tell that it was an all-maple instrument and had neck-through construction. Company literature also hyped the "…reduced body size with four-way radial contour."

The fingerboard was macassar ebony, and had fret markers that resembled icicles or golf tees.

Hardware was black, and the RJ-IV also came equipped with a Hipshot D-tuner flip lever for the E string. A separate set of instructions for setting up the tuner, signed by Hipshot's David Borisoff, was included.

Randy Jackson

As for its electronics and controls, the RJ-IV came off as practical and simple-to-operate...*on the surface*. Its P/J pickup configuration was active, and the control knobs were labeled "V" (volume), "B" (bass), "M" (midrange), and "T" (treble). Each of the three tone knobs had a center detent. Pickup selection was accomplished by a three-position mini-toggle switch.

The instruction manual noted that a player could access an eight-position DIP (dual in-line package) switch in the rear cavity, and by utilizing a small flathead screwdriver, an octet of sonic options could be pre-set by turning on the appropriate number(s) of switches. One wonders how many RJ-IV owners actually went to the trouble of changing the DIP switch from the pre-set configuration in which it was shipped from the factory.

An introductory ad for the RJ-IV appeared in the Summer 1990 issue of *Monitor*, which happened to be Peavey's 25th Anniversary issue. Inset photos showed the smooth back with no neck heel, and the Hipshot de-tune flip lever.

Not long after its introduction, an RJ-IV was also seen in the hands of Dana Strum, bassist for a hard rock band called Slaughter.

When Randy Jackson recorded in his instructional video, *Mastering the Groove*, in 1992, he appeared on the cover brandishing an RJ-IV.

Later, the RJ-IV was also available in solid colors. Some prototypes in natural finish koa were made also later in the model's existence and were shown in a catalog, but, according to DeCola, didn't go into full production (see Unity Series details in the next chapter). DeCola wishes that the koa variant *had* been produced:

"Sometimes we would show the prototypes at NAMM, and the sales force would voice their opinions about whether they thought they could or couldn't sell them. That was probably the case with the koa RJ-IV, since they had a hard time with the colors of the first RJ-IVs. It really wasn't fair, either. The koa RJ-IV could have really been a contender."

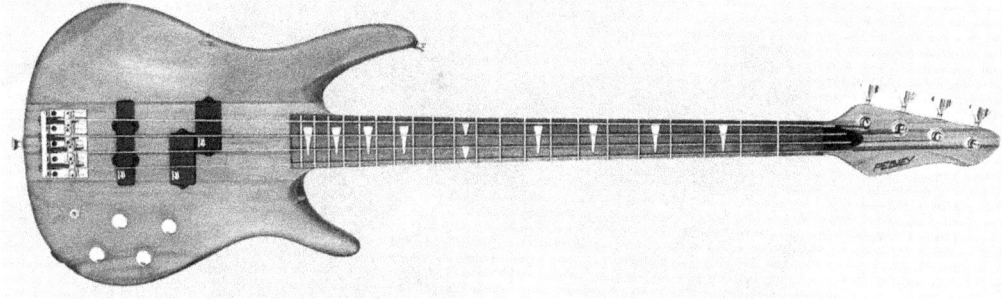

RJ-IV koa prototype

The RJ-IV bass was in the Peavey lineup for approximately four years.

A curious model called the RJ-B appeared briefly ca. 1993; apparently it was a passive RJ-IV style instrument with a bolt-on neck (which had a smooth heel) and a 2 + 2 headstock.

"I did an extended neck joint with kind of a 'scoop'—bolt-on with a reduced neck heel—which was coming into vogue with more than one manufacturer at the time," DeCola detailed. "That was our version."

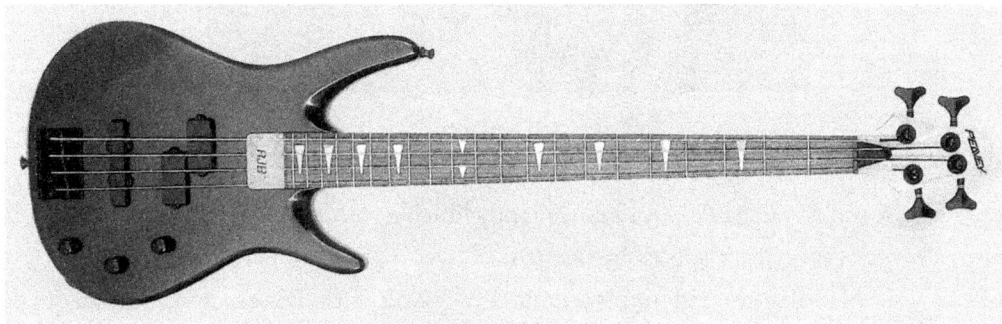

RJ-B

The highlight of the 1990 Atlanta Guitar Show (which Peavey co-sponsored) was an all-star jam session in which numerous guitar luminaries and "player's players" participated. Bassist Jeff Berlin, a respected and versatile musician who was known for his work in jazz and progressive rock, took the stage with the Dixie Dregs' Steve Morse and hyper-fast fingerpicker Scotty Anderson, and their romps through songs like "Wabash Cannonball" brought down the house.

"Scotty Anderson is probably the most brilliant country player I've ever had the privilege of playing with,"

Berlin said afterwards. "I found myself just wanting to play root-five, root-five, just so I would watch a master at work. Morse is another master. We ought to play or record together sometime, because our styles mesh so well."

And Berlin utilized a basic Peavey Foundation bass on his workout. Backstage, he praised its simplicity, sound, and playability to an inquiring reporter.

"It's all I need," he said succinctly.

Berlin also amazed music fans at Peavey's 25th anniversary concert in Meridian several weeks later.

Jeff Berlin

The veteran bassist was already a Peavey endorser and clinician, but at the time of those shows, he was deep into a collaboration with Peavey on a special instrument.

Berlin would visit Meridian at least once a month, working with Powers and DeCola in developing a production bass that actually referenced his "parts" bass, a no-frills instrument that he had meticulously assembled over the years.

By March of '91, the prototype had been completed, and Berlin was using it for clinics at music stores as Peavey geared up for production. The model didn't yet have a name when he commented, prior to presenting a clinic at a store in Montgomery, Alabama, that he didn't want the instrument to be known as the "Jeff Berlin Signature Model."

"I'd be embarrassed if my name was placed on a specific model of instrument," he said. "You see, we musicians sometimes tend to be pretty full of ourselves, and it seems like bass players can lead the pack. I think it's pompous to name an instrument after a musician. Now, if they wanted to say 'designed with the input of Jeff Berlin' or 'endorsed by Jeff Berlin', or maybe 'built to the specifications of Jeff Berlin', I wouldn't have a problem with that."

The new instrument would be marketed as the Palaedium, because Berlin thought the name was "elegant."

Palaedium

The bass had a slim maple neck (with graphite rods inserted for stability), and an ebony fretboard with mother-of-pearl inlays. The treble cutaway joined the body at the 19th fret. Its alder body was offered in Transparent Amber, Transparent Violet, and Transparent Red. Hardware, including a flush-mounted Leo Quan bridge, was gold. The pickups were high-output humbuckers in a "quad coil design."

The Palaedium was basically a sonically-high-end bass in a plainer-looking (therefore more economical) package, which was exactly what Berlin was seeking, as he proclaimed it was created to compete with custom-made basses that cost twice as much.

In spite of a good review in *Bass Player* by Tom Mulhern, in which it was described as "a terrific instrument" and "first-rate," the Palaedium only lasted until some time in '94.

**1993: Famed Memphis bassist Donald "Duck" Dunn
(Booker T. & the MGs, the Blues Brothers) checks out a Palaedium at a
product preview event in Anaheim**

Hartley and Chip Todd got back into regular contact with each other after Chip's house was broken into in November of 1990. Todd was still residing in California, but was no longer with the Fender company. Among the items stolen was his presentation walnut-body T-60, although it now sported a walnut neck (Todd had placed the bird's-eye maple #00000002 neck on another instrument owned by his daughter).

Todd contacted Hartley and Charley Gressett, asking what dollar amount should be submitted to the insurance company as the value of the guitar. Both responded with a suggested value of $2000.

Soon after Todd conversed with Hartley, he received a large package from Meridian.

"The doorbell rang, and some company had left Hartley's #1 [guitar] on my front porch," Chip recalled. "When I read his note, I was too choked up to call my wife."

Peavey notified its dealer base to be on the lookout for the unique instrument, but "…if a young girl came in with a maroon T-60 and a #00000002 neck, that was my daughter and her guitar," Todd recounted.

Five years later, the walnut T-60 was recovered in a sting operation in California. By then, Todd was living in Austin, Texas, and when the walnut instrument was shipped to him, he photographed it with the #00000001 guitar and wrote an article titled "The Case of the Wandering T-60" for *Monitor*. Then, he returned the #00000001 guitar to Hartley.

"I sent the #1 back, as I felt that it would have been selfish to keep it after Hartley had so warmly sent it to me," Todd said. "It wasn't that I didn't want it; it was just respect for what he had done for me when I was low. It belonged in his museum."

CHAPTER 11

Early Nineties (non-signature) innovations, transformations, and transitions

Peavey's 25th anniversary celebration in 1990 was organized by Hartley's wife Melia, and scores of dealers were invited. The events included a huge concert in Meridian (starring Kenny Loggins, Jeff Berlin, and others), held at the local high school football stadium.

"That was the only place big enough," Hartley remembered. "We had so many fireworks I thought we were going to set the damn high school on fire."

Not surprisingly, the event also included an effort to make dealers and players aware of recent innovations in the company's merchandise, including guitar models. New instruments were introduced, as other models were slated to be phased out and/or underwent transitions that resembled previous versions in name only.

Longtime Peavey sales representative Roy Rogers had joined the company's Audio Media Research division the previous year, and switched to Peavey sales in the spring of 1990, just in time to work the Atlanta Guitar Show. His recollections of the company's 25th anniversary bash in the summer of the same year underlined how impressive the celebration was to dealers, employees, and other attendees:

"The 25th anniversary concert kicked off with Jeff Berlin playing the National Anthem all alone on bass; it was beautiful. Scotty Anderson played one of our new Ecoustic guitar models that had an acoustic piezo pickup in the bridge—first guitar I ever saw with electric & acoustic sounds. It was a great guitar and a great performance by one of the most underrated guitar players ever. Gary Morris sang 'Wind Beneath My Wings', Melia's favorite song. Jeff Hannah from the Nitty Gritty Dirt Band performed, and Kenny Loggins killed as the main attraction. The Naval Air Station supplied four jets to do a tree top "fly-by" just as Hartley was introduced—perfect timing!"

Hartley: "It was a big deal. We had several parties, and I probably lost some of my retina because of all the camera flashes going off! It was probably the biggest gathering we've had in Meridian since some of the old-time 'Jimmie Rodgers Day' events back in the Fifties."

Rogers: "I seem to recall that we had rented 40 buses to transport the dealers from hotels to the various promotion venues. The Peavey museum was the biggest surprise, because Hartley had no idea that it existed."

Melia had been working secretly to convert an older building in north Meridian into a Peavey museum without her husband's knowledge, and Hartley was indeed surprised when the facility was announced at the 25th anniversary event.

The museum was located in an industrial park on U.S. Highway 45. The building had originally been a Department of Agriculture center constructed by the Works Progress Administration. Completely renovated (with Melia supervising), it housed numerous early and/or prototype instruments and amplifiers, along with other memorabilia such as Hartley's original basement workbench (meticulously reassembled, with old electronics magazines haphazardly decorating the layout), the original drawing of the Peavey "lightning bolt" logo Hartley had sketched when he was a senior in high school, and the company's first delivery van.

Autographed guitars and concert photos of Peavey endorsers were found throughout the museum. The outside grounds offered a series of bronze plaques with Hartley's favorite quotes.

Two instruments that heralded the new decade were the B-90/B-Ninety bass and the G-90/G-Ninety guitar. The bass is noted here first because it showed up on a price list before the guitar.

The working title of the B-90/B-Ninety was "Rock Bass", according to Jim DeCola. It was a more streamlined model with sharper cutaway horns and contoured "scoops" in the cutaways. It had black hardware, a black headstock (some examples had white pinstriping around the edge), and two split-coil humbucking pickups laid out in a P/J configuration. Its controls consisted of two volume knobs and a master tone knob. The bass was also available in an active version.

B-90/B-Ninety

B-90/B-Ninety Active

Seeking the same market segment, the G-90/G-Ninety's body silhouette matched that of the Destiny, but it also had contoured cutaway scoops like its bass sibling, as well as a bound neck. It also had a reversed sculpted headstock and a S/S/HB pickup configuration with a recessed vibrato.

G-90/G-Ninety

Around this time, Peavey also opted to introduce a Unity Series bass with exactly that model name. It came in painted versions with matching headstocks and black hardware. Bodies on the standard Unity models had a maple neck-through construction with poplar "wings".

An upgrade all-koa version was offered; it featured purple heart strips on the neck and a hand-rubbed oil finish, as well as gold hardware. Both variants were passive, with basic P/J pickup configurations and a two volume/master tone control system.

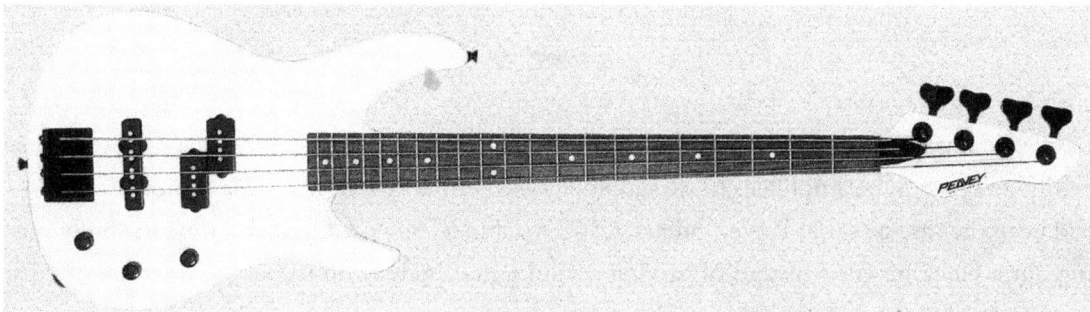

Unity bass

Unity bass, koa *Heritage Auctions*

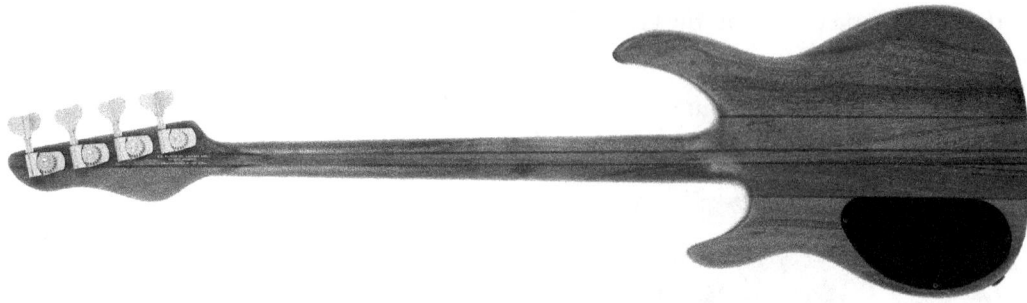

Unity bass, koa—back *Heritage Auctions*

Bass Player Magazine had been founded in 1989, and its founding editor, Jim Roberts, has pleasant memories of most Peavey products.

"The first Peavey bass that we reviewed at *BP* was the Unity," he recalled, "in the March/April 1991 issue. I wrote the review myself, calling it a 'superb value'."

Not long after the Nineties began, a new logo began appearing on the headstocks of some Peavey guitars. It was dubbed the "block" logo, as that was the style of the lettering of the company name. The "A" in "Peavey" was styled in a delta shape.

The Ecoustic was, as its moniker hints, Peavey's first attempt at an acoustic instrument, albeit in a style that was primarily designed to be amplified. Its development was primarily a Jim DeCola project.

As had been the case on other Peavey guitars, CNC machines were used, but this time the body was created by routing out a block of wood instead of carving a solid guitar body from it; i.e. the sides and the back were actually one piece of hollowed-out mahogany.

"Hartley wanted us to get into the acoustic thing, and that's a pretty big endeavor," DeCola recalled. "The hollowed-out chamber idea meant that we didn't have to bend anything or glue anything on the sides or back. We started with a cedar top with spruce braces in an X-pattern; we thought that since [the instrument] had a smaller profile, cedar might get a better tone. Obviously, we were intending to use a piezo pickup anyway, and we knew the bulk of the sound was going to come from the piezo, but the top was still moving, and *did* convey an acoustic sound."

The Ecoustic had a maple neck with a rosewood fretboard that had 22 frets and a 25 1/2" scale. Its piezo system had a volume control and three-band equalization controls.

Ecoustic

Peavey's new idea in electro-acoustic instrument debuted in 1990. Looking back, Hollis Calvert opined that the Ecoustic was a fine instrument, but its specialized production, including costs, troubled it from the outset.

DeCola agreed with Calvert's perspective: "It was an 'awakening' for manufacturing, and for us, too. If you develop something in R & D and then give it to production, you take things for granted. For example, cedar was soft, and it had to be sanded differently from maple or mahogany. (The Ecoustic) had a lot of potential, but there was a big 'learning curve'."

That being said, the model stayed in Peavey's lineup some eight years. It had begun with a 3 + 3 headstock, but later variants had a six on a side headstock.

One of those later models was the even-more-innovative Ecoustic ATS (Acoustic Tremolo System), which had a working vibrato. Attempting to exploit the trend of electric players to switch to acoustic instruments (re: "Unplugged" albums), a '95 Peavey ad touted the Ecoustic ATS as having "…the first (and only) patented tremolo system for acoustic guitar allowing the expression of electric while preserving the tone of acoustic."

Among the users of Ecoustics were Canadian country chanteuse Michelle Wright and Bret Michaels, front man for Poison.

Michelle Wright

One particular Ecoustic was custom-decorated like an American flag and presented to President George Bush when he visited the Peavey manufacturing facilities on December 3, 1991 (by this time, Peavey had 19 U.S. plants).

"He was trying to re-elected at the time," Hartley said, "and he made two stops that day. The first was at an orange juice factory in Florida."

Hartley was fascinated by the advance work that federal officials did prior to the visit:

"They sent an 'away team' down here that did background checks on me and everybody else. When he flew in, they had a communication center set up, and snipers on rooftops. The President was just as gracious as he could be."

Bush was given a tour of more than one factory line, spent some private time with Hartley and Melia, and gave a speech to employees who were assembled in Plant 3.

Hartley was slated to introduce Bush, but was momentarily struck dumb.

"I walked out on the stage," he recalled with a chuckle, "and there were seven or eight cameras from CBS, CNN, NBC, ABC, and a wad of microphones. I thought to myself 'Holy ****, I'm about to introduce the

President of the United States!' I'm used to public speaking, but to put it mildly, I was at a loss for words. I saw it later on TV, and I guess my introduction came off okay."

Bush praised the company for its ongoing competitiveness in an increasingly-international market, and after his remarks, the President was presented with the custom Ecoustic, which had been named "The Chief."

President George Bush shows off his new Peavey Ecoustic guitar, which was presented to him by Melia and Hartley.

As for the preparation of that particular guitar, DeCola remembered, "(Mike) Powers told me that the Human Resources department had informed him that George Bush was coming to the factory, and we needed to do something, and I said that we needed to make a guitar for him. We thought about an Ecoustic, because they were starting to come through production, and it made sense to give him an acoustic instead of an electric and an amp. It was a perfect opportunity."

DeCola didn't make the special Ecoustic, but oversaw its creation through manufacturing and monitored the application of its custom graphics.

After the President's visit, numerous photos and other memorabilia were placed on display in the Peavey museum.

The Peaveys and the President would cross paths again the next year, when Peavey Electronics Corporation was honored at the White House as the first corporation to receive a National Literacy Honors Award for their efforts to educate employees.

After Bush left the White House, he and Hartley still communicated, and Peavey flew the Bushes from Houston to Sea Island, Georgia for an event surrounding the fiftieth wedding anniversary of the former President and his wife Barbara. From Sea Island, the Bushes were flown to Nashville for a concert that featured the Oak Ridge Boys, Lee Greenwood, and the Gatlin Brothers.

At the opposite end of the concept of the Ecoustic was the Midibase, Peavey's effort in the stringed instrument facet of the MIDI (Musical Instrument Digital Interface) market. Obviously, such a venture was complex, and would necessitate hiring an Australian music electronics expert named Steve Chick.

DeCola recalled designing the body and neck, then tapped Mick Donner to work with Chick in getting the instrument into production. Ideally, the aesthetics of the MIDI bass were to be unique, compared to standard basses, to visually hint at its high-tech capabilities.

"Steve was brought in, and I was the design engineer assigned to him," said Donner. "This was a project *way* beyond anything the Guitar Division had ever done before. It was going to take a team made up of guys from Guitar and Digital to make it happen."

Donner believes he was probably chosen to work in the development of a MIDI bass because he was already familiar with Chick's system, having consulted with another manufacturer on the installation of the electronics (prior to being hired by Peavey), but that initiative by the other company never came to fruition.

"As a result, I had already played a bass with Steve's system installed," said Donner. "I understood the theory behind the system, but had no idea how much work it was going to be."

"Our intention with that first [MIDI bass] was to make it look different," said DeCola. "We wanted it to be a little more futuristic, and I put a chamfer on the top edge, so people who were standing up and playing it could see the readout."

A description in a 1992 catalog hyped the Midibase's "unprecedented triggering speed and accuracy," "two mono MIDI modes," "three 'poly' MIDI modes," " 'Finger', 'Pick', and right hand 'Tap' modes," "Fret-actuated program change and editing," "On-board bass and MIDI mixing capability," "Unique pitch bend mechanism," and "Digital readout."

The actual style of the "instrument" the company manufactured was a bass-to-MIDI controller. It could indeed be played as a straight-on, standard electric bass, but its description on a 1993 price list cited "…immediate fret sensing pitch detection, quad piezo pickups for velocity and sustain information, incredibly fast and accurate tracking, 24 performance preset locations, individual program change per string, fully programmable from fingerboard, four-character 16-segment LED system exclusive bulk dump and recall, two internally active humbucking pickups, 17" neck radius, maple neck, rosewood fingerboard with lexan overlays, black nickel hardware, one U rack mountable interface and power supply with sustain/modulation footswitch input, 20' eight-pin heavy duty cable, hardshell case."

The body was made of alder.

Midibase

Numerous bassists, including Victor Wooten and Dave LaRue, checked out the Midibase when it debuted at a NAMM show. The high-tech instrument also had fans in the music journalism world, including *Bass Player*'s Jim Roberts.

Mick Donner and Victor Wooten *Mick Donner*

Dave LaRue and Mick Donner *Mick Donner*

The futuristic version of Peavey's MIDI bass lasted for about a year.

"We got some feedback from players that indicated they wanted a more traditional-looking bass, so we redesigned it as the Cyber Bass," DeCola said.

The second edition came in solid colors and had a pearloid pickguard, but in spite of Peavey-sponsored clinics that featured Will Lee, bassist for the house band on David Letterman's late night show, the Cyber Bass also didn't catch hold in the marketplace. By the mid-Nineties, Peavey had exited the stringed instrument MIDI market, as had most other manufacturers that had ventured into that complicated sonic opportunity.

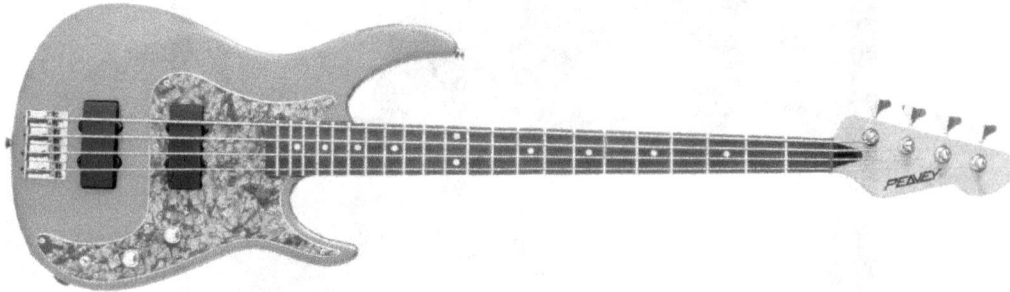

Cyber Bass

Mick Donner speaks at a Cyber Bass clinic while Will Lee demos the stringed Peavey digital product *Mick Donner*

Some Peavey guitar models that had been around for several years were phased out in the early Nineties, but some of them underwent radical transformations before they were discontinued. Moreover, one model name that had been in stasis was revived for a completely new instrument, signaling some significant changes in Peavey's guitar-making strategy.

The Nitro's final incarnation was as the Nitro C2 (humbucking-single-humbucking pickup layout) and the Nitro C3 (S/S/HB pickup layout). They were touted as having a new, sculpted body "…with thinner edge for improved comfort," according to a January 1991 price list (which was reportedly the only price list on which they appeared).

The Falcon went out in a very different design, compared to its original style. Two models, the Falcon H (HB/S/HB) and the Falcon S (three single-coil pickups) were seen in a 1993 catalog. They had alder bodies with "resonant sound chambers" and bookmatched figured maple tops. Each model had a vibrato, as well as a smaller pickguard, on which only the pickups were mounted.

Falcon H

Falcon S

One harbinger of Peavey's future guitar marketing and manufacturing direction happened in the early Nineties, when the company began importing guitar bodies to create a value-priced guitar that referenced a traditional design. Peavey resurrected the Predator moniker for the model. Necks were still made in Meridian, and since the body, neck, and other parts were assembled in Meridian, Peavey could still legitimately claim that such instruments were "Made in the U.S.A." or "Crafted in the U.S.A." (and other large guitar companies have done the same thing). The Predator went through several different headstock designs in its time, but its overall look had a classic style.

Predator early headstock with script name and lightning-bolt logo *Steve Forehand*

Predator—ca. 1992 with block logo

Predator—ca. 1994 with "sharper"/quasi-"harpoon" headstock silhouette *Willie G. Moseley*

DeCola noted that the company had strong requirements about parts that were imported.

"We wouldn't just buy bodies," he emphasized. "They had to be made to our specs."

The Reactor model soon followed the Predator. It, too, had a classic style, and was initially built in the same manner.

Reactor *Willie G. Moseley*

Reactor with "sharper"/quasi-retro headstock silhouette *Gbase*

Reactor—pickguard embossed with Alabama band logo; body signed by band members *Willie G. Moseley*

Reactor ad

Both the Predator and Reactor had upgrade "AX" variants, with rosewood fretboards.

The Predator AX had an extra pickup near the bridge, which could be switched to single-coil, double-coil, or "turbo" settings via a three-way mini-toggle. The "turbo" selection turned on both coils of the bridge pickup, regardless of the position of the standard/traditional five-way pickup switch.

The Reactor AX came in classic-style finishes such as Powder Blue, Sea Green, and a three-tone sunburst, and had a fancier pearloid or tortoiseshell pickguard, as well as pickups with two exposed blades.

Predator AX

Reactor AX *Heritage Auctions*

One unique marketing idea that utilized Peavey's Reactor involved Jeff Carlisi, who departed from .38 Special in the mid-Nineties.

Carlisi went into a unique guitar-marketing venture, forming a partnership with entrepreneur Dan Lipson, who owned licensing rights to NASCAR automobile racing memorabilia. Their collaboration resulted in the marketing of electric guitars decorated with NASCAR automobile racing team color schemes, numbers and autographs; the instruments were hand-painted by noted artist Wayne Jarrett of Greensboro, North Carolina. Their guitar of choice was the Peavey Reactor.

"It was an American-made guitar that had a lot of flat area for Wayne to do his work," Carlisi detailed. "The drivers would autograph them individually, with a paint pen."

NASCAR Reactor—Jeff Gordon *Jeff Carlisi*

NASCAR Reactor—Rusty Wallace *Jeff Carlisi*

The venture of Carlisi and Lipson caused other guitar companies to take notice, and limited edition series of other electric guitars authorized by other NASCAR drivers appeared in the marketplace.

"As far as I know, we were the originals," Carlisi recalled. "If someone had done guitars like these before, I never saw them. Later, I saw several offshoot companies marketing such instruments at a NAMM show after we'd been the groundbreaking company, but those were NASCAR guitars; they weren't 'driver' guitars"—you have to get NASCAR licensing, and if you want to deal with a driver, you have to get that licensing as well."

Carlisi and Lipson carried on with the NASCAR guitars until Lipson sold his licensing catalog.

ℱ

Predators and Reactors were made in Meridian for several years. Eventually, those two models and other classic configurations of electric guitars and basses would be made completely overseas and imported as "International Series" instruments. In the ensuing years, other imported models, designated as EXP and BXP instruments (among other monikers) would be introduced.

"The dealers' reaction to importing guitars was disappointment, mostly, but they were understanding," said Roy Rogers. "As long as the quality was there, they were okay. There were plenty of imported guitars already being sold."

CHAPTER 12
The EVH Wolfgang

Musicians everywhere had been aware of electric guitar virtuoso Edward Van Halen since the group bearing his last name broke out in the late Seventies. Peavey had scored a coup in the Eighties by collaborating with the guitarist on the redoubtable (and loud) 5150 amplifier, and ultimately, the company got a chance to work with him on a signature guitar.

Peavey had gotten some initial inquiries about a guitar from Van Halen's management, when the guitarist's endorsement deal with the Ernie Ball/Music Man company was about to expire.

"I called Sterling Ball, who's Ernie's son, and a friend," said Hartley. "I made sure that it was okay with Sterling to pursue a deal with Eddie on a guitar."

Jim DeCola had actually designed the body of what became the Van Halen signature guitar before Peavey and the guitarist finalized their business agreement, recalling "I'd been working on another guitar on the side—just for myself—and it was one of those things where I was thinking 'Well, maybe one of these days I can use this with Hartley.' It had an asymmetrical body shape for improved balance, but you still had total access to all the frets."

Peavey acquired an example of Van Halen's previous endorsement guitar, and at the behest of Len McRae, then-Artist Relations director for the company, the R & D staff originally replaced the neck with one of their own necks, "…just to show Eddie that we were capable of making that kind of guitar," said DeCola. "I ended up building an exact copy of the entire guitar, and I put an aluminum reinforced neck joint on it. It had a bird's-eye maple neck, just like his, with a standard Peavey six-in-a-line peghead. It had a basswood body and a quilted maple top. I still have that prototype."

Peavey representatives journeyed to Pensacola, Florida, where Van Halen—the band—was rehearsing for a tour to support the *Balance* album, released in January of 1995. Van Halen—the guitarist—checked out the prototype and, according to DeCola, approved working with Peavey on a signature model at that time.

Returning to Meridian, DeCola was advised that the birthday of Wolfgang Van Halen, Edward's son, was pending.

"I thought 'I'm gonna make a three-quarter-size guitar for Wolfgang, that will look like how I'd like to see the [endorsement] guitar made'," he recalled. "That way, it would butter up his old man! I got the body done with that asymmetrical shape, and was finishing the neck, when Eddie came to Meridian. I showed what I had started on, and told him I had wanted it to be a surprise for him and Wolfie. He loved it, and told me to make [the endorsement guitar] full-size. So that's how the body came about."

And the instrument would ultimately be named the EVH Wolfgang.

"Jim's crowning achievement here was the Eddie Van Halen guitar," Hartley said.

Development of the instrument proved to be arduous and meticulous, which was probably expected from working with a musician of Edward Van Halen's stature and talent. Input from Van Halen sometimes consisted of hand drawings submitted to the R & D shop, and DeCola recalled taking the drawings to the company's drafting department to get such sketches refined and digitized. Hartley monitored the development of the model, admonishing his employees to avoid any similarity in the style of the instrument to the guitarist's previous endorsement model.

It may seem like a bizarre analogy, but as was the case with the T-60 almost 20 years earlier, the peghead of the new endorsement model garnered a perhaps-inordinate amount of attention and development. Van Halen didn't care for the traditional Peavey headstock silhouette, and he showed the R & D luthiers a drawing of a small 3 + 3 headstock that resembled the peghead on a Gibson Flying V model. The guitarist was advised that it was too close to the Gibson style, even though it was smaller, according to DeCola. A second sketch by Van Halen was too close to a Washburn headstock design.

So while the guitarist was in the R & D shop, DeCola improvised a variant of a V-shaped peghead, designing it with offset 3 + 3 tuners, and routing in a "scoop", using a spindle sander. He proposed a black peghead, with a natural-finish scoop, and both Edward and Hartley were amenable to the look.

The electronics for the instrument also generated some debates and negotiations. DeCola recalled that Van Halen wanted the pickup toggle switch on the lower cutaway horn, which had been the location of that control on his previous endorsement model.

"It was better on the upper cutaway because we'd talked [Van Halen] into adding a tone control, so there were now two knobs below," said DeCola. "The way we presented it to him was 'Here's the jack, the tone [control], the volume [control], and the [pickup] switch, all in a straight line, complementing the asymmetry of the body.' We finally decided that if the toggle switch stayed up there, it would need to be wired in reverse; the 'down' position was for rhythm, and 'up' was for his lead breaks."

The pickups were two Peavey humbuckers, wound to Van Halen's specifications. The high-tech vibrato included a 'Drop D' mechanism to allow instant tuning changes.

The bodies on the original series of EVH Wolfgangs were made of basswood, and had a contoured top with binding. The necks were bolt-on, and were single-piece bird's-eye maple, with 22 frets and a 25 1/2" scale.

And while bird's-eye maple is eye-catching, it can be undependable, due to its uneven grain structure.

"The only way we found to make it 'stable' was to use two rectangular graphite/epoxy 'pulltrusions' on each side of the truss rod," Hartley detailed. "This was a costly but necessary technique that we had experimented with before."

In another construction first for Peavey, the truss rod was adjusted at the neck joint instead of at the headstock. DeCola recalled that a previous Edward Van Halen signature model "…had a wheel adjustment at the neck joint, but it protruded out of the neck into the body intersecting the neck pocket and neck pickup cavity. I felt this would possibly cause 'break out' when the body was machined and potentially weaken the neck joint. On the Wolfgang, the wheel was recessed into the neck yet still made contact at the base of the neck to the front of the neck pocket (on all side of the neck). Incidentally, the wheel style of adjustment had been used by various companies since the 60's, but ours was the first to recess it into the neck."

Overall, the creation of the EVH Wolfgang took approximately a year, and production began in mid-1996.

"Jim did the engineering, and I pretty much built prototypes," Ed Pope recalled, "and I did a lot of setup of prototypes to send to Eddie."

In sort of a variant of the "Technology/Contemporary/Impact" price list notion from over decade earlier, the July 1996 price list divided Peavey electric and (imported) acoustic guitars, basses and amplifiers into "Level 1", "Level 2" and "Level 3" instruments. The four models of the new EVH Wolfgang series were the only instruments in Level 3; all other Peavey electric guitars, including the Cropper Classic and Ecoustic, were in Level 1. There were no Level 2 instruments listed.

The "entry level version" of the four EVH Wolfgang instruments had a stop tailpiece and intonatable bridge, and came in solid colors. The next model added a Floyd Rose-licensed vibrato system. The third variant saw the addition of a figured maple cap on the body, which was proffered in transparent colors, and the top end model was the third model with the vibrato added.

It was a simple and logical lineup, with progressive steps of $100 each in the respective list prices of each model. Reportedly, stop tailpiece versions of the EVH Wolfgang were not produced for an extended time; i.e., instruments produced in the early production runs of the guitar all had vibratos.

The initial buzz about the EVH Wolfgang was encouraging. One advance promotion had involved a summer 1995 collage of photos that chronicled the efforts of Edward Van Halen and Hartley working on a prototype instrument. The text of the "A Guitar is Born" story stated "After an intensive period of designing, experimenting, specifying, band-sawing, routing, shaping, measuring, assembling, sanding, polishing, tweaking, and second-guessing each other, the determined duo and the Peavey guitar design team created a working model of a workingman's axe."

The final photo show Van Halen and Hartley standing by Peavey's G IV jet, displaying the unfinished prototype before Edward headed back to Los Angeles.

An allocation policy had to be introduced at the outset of the EVH Wolfgang's distribution, with the Peavey sales reps getting the first examples.

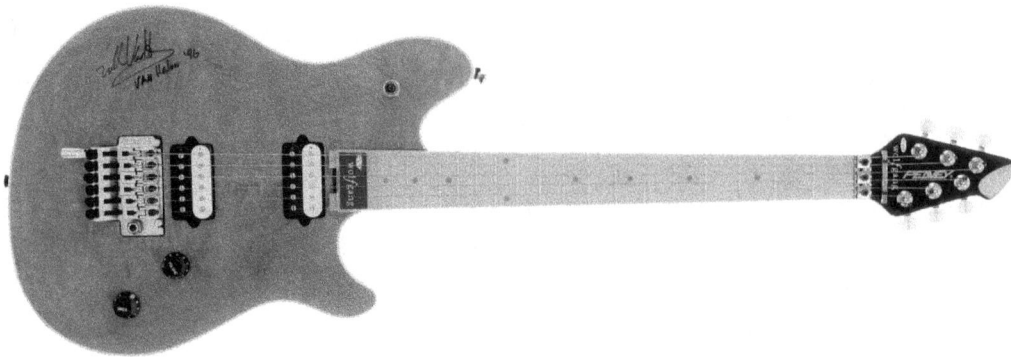

**EVH Wolfgang, signed first-year example. It still has
the slip-in fretboard shipping protector.** *Heritage Auctions*

**Provenance: Edward Van Halen displays the signed
EVH Wolfgang seen here.** *Heritage Auctions*

"The Van Halen years were very valuable to Peavey," said Roy Rogers. "The guitar was very unique, and very cool. The drop 'D' tuner was great. Players were lined up to see one, buy one…and sometimes, more than one! The demand for the guitar drove customers into the stores. It had the potential of a Les Paul but it also had more versatility. By having the neck designed to sit further back in the body it made playing much easier. It felt like a short scale but it was a 25 1/2" scale. It was very comfortable to reach every fret."

Edward Van Halen digs into his signature Peavey guitar onstage

For most of its existence, the Peavey Wolfgang was built in a second factory in Leakesville, located about 80 miles south of Meridian. Leakesville, which has a population of around 1,000, is the county seat of Greene County, one of the most impoverished counties in Mississippi. Peavey had gotten a number of economic incentives to locate a plant there, and Hartley was willing to support his home state in such a manner.

"We kept running out of space," Hartley remembered. "My general manager at the time, Willie Hatcher, who was one of the smartest people I know, and his idea was to go out and find buildings that we could convert, because we didn't have time to construct them. Building a building is the correct way to do it, but it's also a huge pain in the ass, and it takes a long time. He had found this old factory in Leakesville, out in the middle of nowhere. They basically gave us the building."

The transition to Leakesville also reportedly contributed to the aforementioned Wolfgang allocation policy.

"That happened around the same time as the Van Halen project," Jim DeCola said. "[The Leakesville factory] opened in late '96. It had a lot of good potential, but it was difficult to monitor the production, particularly of new models, from Meridian. We had vans and buses taking manufacturing and engineering personnel back and forth on a daily basis. I would go down there two or three times a week."

Peavey had gotten into the drum business, and those percussion instruments were also created at the Leakesville plant.

Mike Powers and Tim Litchfield actually stayed in Leakesville for a number of weeks, in an effort to train the new work force to make quality instruments.

At the time, Greene County had one of the highest unemployment rates in the state, and the work force proved difficult to monitor. DeCola recalled that too many local workers "…weren't used to a regular 'day gig'. To have a manufacturing job with regular hours proved to be a learning experience for them. The first year, we went down there when deer season started, and a lot of the workers were missing; they were out hunting deer. They were so used to deer hunting to provide for their families that it was understood that they'd take off to hunt deer."

"My favorite story about Leakesville involved a big ol' double-sided sanding machine called a Timesaver," Hartley recalled. "It had a sanding belt on the top and another on the bottom, and if you put a body blank on a conveyor, when it came out it'd be sanded on both sides. I walked in there one day, and there were two guys in there with a table that was three or four feet square, and they had glued this huge sheet of sandpaper on top. One guy would push a body blank one way—*Sssksh*—and the other guy would push it back the other way—*Sssksh*."

I stood there in awe for a moment, then said, 'Guys, what the hell are you doing?!?' They said 'We're sanding this guitar', I said, 'I see that, but why the hell are you doing it that way? That Timesaver right there could do it in two seconds, and you guys are taking two days!'

They said, 'Well, this is the way we were shown', and I just buried my head in my hands and said 'Oh, dear God…' I went to the plant manager and said 'Are you out of your frickin' mind?' He said 'They know about [the Timesaver]', and I said, 'Well obviously, they didn't!'"

P

August 1997 saw guitars, basses, and other instruments, as well as amplifiers, being divided once again into "levels" on Peavey's master price list. Level 1 guitars on the first listing included three new Firenza models with "TBA" pricing (see next chapter). There was no "Level 2" for electric guitars, and Level 3 consisted of EVH Wolfgangs, including two new models in a "Vintage Gold" color (one with a stop tailpiece, the other with a vibrato), priced the same as the maple top/transparent colors models.

This ad promoted both the EVH Wolfgang guitar and the 5150 amplifier

By January of 1998, another variant of the EVH Wolfgang had been introduced. The EVH Wolfgang Special, was, according the company literature, "…the result of an ongoing collaboration between Peavey and Edward Van Halen…many of the critical features of the EVH Wolfgang have been incorporated into this exciting and affordable instrument."

The Special had a flat-top basswood body, and sported a volume knob only (as had been the case on other brands and models Edward Van Halen had used). The company brochure described the placement of just a volume control as "In keeping with the straightforward approach."

A plus for the Special was that it had a base price under $1000, and it won several industry awards.

The award-winning EVH Wolfgang Special was hyped in this ad

Van Halen displays a black version of the EVH Wolfgang Special

A July 1999 price list still had listings of instruments in "levels", and while the Ecoustic was gone from Level 1, the EVH Wolfgang Special was the only entry in Level 2, while the other Wolfgangs were still in Level 3. The entire EVH Wolfgang line had experienced a price increase of approximately $100, but a case was now included with each instrument.

Van Halen onstage with an EVH Wolfgang Special

A year later, the EVH Special Flame Top, with a figured maple cap and "hand detailed flame body binding" appeared in Level 2, as did a new lowest-price variant, the Special ST, which had a recessed bridge and tailpiece

Optional rosewood fretboards debuted in EVH Wolfgangs at all levels on a summer 2001 price list. Fourteen different versions of Peavey's frontline guitar were now being touted. By the fall of the same year, it appeared that number had been cut in half to seven, but rosewood fretboards had merely been interpolated to instrument descriptions as an option, instead of being listed as a separate instrument.

EVH Wolfgang Special with rosewood fingerboard *Heritage Auctions*

The Leakesville factory proved too difficult to maintain and monitor because of distance factors, and it was closed in 2002. Production of models that had been made there was shifted back to Meridian.

Two unique EVH Wolfgangs were seen on the Peavey price list by 2003. The American-made "7.5" had a downsized scale of 22 3/4". Sometimes referred to as the "Wolfgang Junior" or "three-quarter" size Wolfgang, approximately ten prototypes were made. The model was displayed at a 2003 NAMM show, but there was not enough interest from dealers to allow Peavey to commit to full production.

A rare EVH Wolfgang 7.5 guitar beside a standard size EVH Wolfgang. *Geoff Knapp*

The other new Wolfgang model on the '03 price list was the Quilt Top Special XP, an imported model listing for about half of the price of its U.S.-made counterpart. Its introduction reflected a trend that was gaining ground within the company's guitar and bass lineup, as well as in the guitar industry in general.

Numerous one-of-a-kind Wolfgangs would also be made, and Peavey would outsource the unique paint jobs and/or fretboard inlay that appeared on such instruments.

The last EVH Wolfgangs were marketed in 2004, and curiously, the EXP variant was missing from a price list that was effective on July 15th of that year. Edward Van Halen and the Peavey organization reportedly parted ways amicably.

And by mid-2004, other American-made Peavey guitars and basses had other associations with other names.

CHAPTER 13
Other mid-Nineties instruments

Around late 1993, Peavey opted to create what was perceived to be a "budget" version of the Rudy Sarzo signature model bass. Also an active instrument, the RSB had a poplar body that had the same silhouette as the Sarzo, but its construction differed from the original, in that it had a heel-less (therefore comfortable) bolt-on maple neck. Its two VFL ("Vertical Flux Loading") pickups were different from the pickups found on the original Sarzo. Instead of its three knobs functioning in an expected two-volume/one-tone layout, the controls were a master volume, master tone, and pan knob with center detent.

A black finish and gold hardware were standard, and an upgrade version with an oil-finished koa body and pao ferro fingerboard was available.

Sarzo recounted that he had no input or affiliation with the model, but acknowledged that Peavey was trying to make an even more affordable bass similar to his signature model. The RSB was short-lived, and soon after its introduction, Sarzo's endorsement deal with Peavey expired, but he continued to use Peavey gear.

RSB — koa body

Jim DeCola said that the RSB was designed and built around the time guitar and bass responsibilities were split.

"That was actually the last bass I was involved with," he recalled. "We were just trying to come up with something more affordable, and since it wasn't neck-through, I did the same bolt-on with smooth neck heel design that we'd done with the RJ-B, which was built around the same time."

Another experimental instrument from the same era was the Resolite, Peavey's attempt at a chambered/reduced-weight bass. It had a maple neck with a 2 + 2 headstock, an alder body "...with resonant sound chambers" (said the catalog), and a maple top. There was one slash-shaped hole above the P/J pickup layout. The instrument had chrome hardware.

Resolite basses—reportedly, only four were made

"I was thinking the Resolite would be a cool instrument," DeCola recalled. "Since we had done a chambered guitar with the Generation S-3, it would be a natural to have a chambered bass, just to give it a deeper sound. I was used to doing four-in-a-row headstocks, but for whatever reason, I was into two-and-twos that year!"

The Resolite was catalogued, but never went into production. DeCola recalls making a total of four, two of which went to Europe and two of which stayed in the U.S.

Peavey's Axcelerator series, an upscale, sharper-looking lineup based on traditional styles, was introduced in the early Nineties.

Mick Donner: "The whole Axcelerator line was in response to a lot of the stuff that the West Coast boutique guys were building at the time—alder & swamp ash bodies with great finishes. The idea was to make that sort of boutique look and feel affordable."

The basic Axcelerator guitar had a poplar body, and its 22-fret maple neck was offered with rosewood or maple fingerboard options. Its pickups were three dual-blade single-coil units, set up with a hum-canceling circuit, and a Peavey basic vibrato.

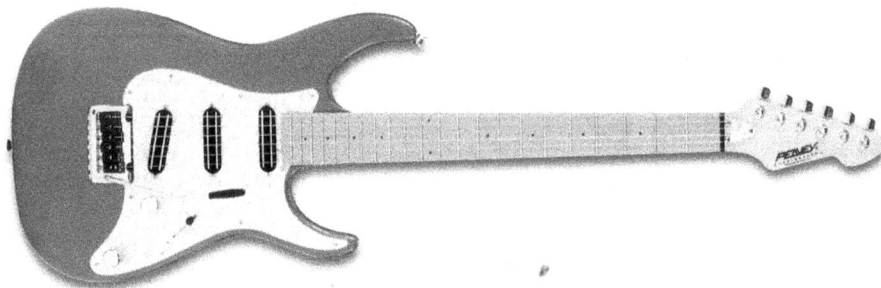

Axcelerator

1993: Ten-year-old Australian prodigy Nathan Cavaleri rocks out on an Axcelerator at a NAMM show

The Axcelerator AX had upgrades that included a swamp ash body, a four-blade humbucker in the bridge position, a fancier pickguard (tortoiseshell or pearloid, depending on the finish), gold hardware, and a high-tech vibrato. It also featured the same "turbo" switch as found on the Predator AX.

Axcelerator AX *en.audiofanzine.com*

The apparently-short-lived Axcelerator F was an Axcelerator AX sans turbo switch.

Volume 11, Issue 2 of *Monitor* (spring 1993) featured a "Product Focus" article written by DeCola that profiled Peavey's new versions of Impact guitars, but those models resembled the original Impact series in name only. Both of the new models had all mahogany construction with a set-in neck and a 3 + 3 headstock. The 24-fret Brazilian rosewood fretboard had binding. While the features listing noted nickel hardware, some examples were seen with gold hardware.

The models had two humbucking pickups were controlled by master volume and tone knobs and a *five*-way pickup switch. DeCola's article noted that the tone knob was "…actually a center-detented hi/low pass tone control." The centered setting operated the instrument "…the same as having a normal tone control wide open for maxium brilliance and output." Rotating the control clockwise would not only boost treble, it would also cut bass frequencies. The reverse was true when the control was rotated counter-clockwise.

To some observers, the toggle switch may have seemed to recall the company's innovative pickup switching ideas on the T-26 and T-27 models about a decade earlier. However, the setup of the Impacts was touted has having the "most requested switching combinations" without a plethora of switches, and was controlled as follows:

Position 1 (all the way down): bridge pickup only
Position 2: both humbuckers
Position 3: neck pickup
Position 4: both pickups in single-coil mode, wired as a hum-canceling circuit
Position 5: neck pickup only in single-coil mode

Once again, Peavey's circuitry on the new Impacts was innovative, but it had to be learned. The Impact 1 was now the lesser-frills model, with a separate intonatable bridge and stop-type tailpiece. The Impact 2 had a Peavey vibrato. Both models were very short-lived.

Impact 1

Impact 2

Impact 2 with matching headstock *99 Guitars*

DeCola recalled that he was trying to come up with something different.

"If you look at the body shape on those models, it's similar to the Randy Jackson (RJ-IV) bass," he said, "but I shortened that bottom horn. We also did chamfering and 'scoops'."

The mid-Nineties would subsequently see the "Impact" and "Firenza" monikers being transitioned in an overlapping manner.

The mid-Nineties Detonator series of guitars didn't start off with that moniker. The basic model and a step-up "F" model were originally catalogued as the "Defender" series, and while that moniker may have come about because of Peavey's then-raging battle with imported electric guitars, from a marketing point of view, "defender" might have sounded…well, defensive. There was also the fact that the last 75% of the model's moniker was the name of a competitor, so the Defender quickly became known as the Detonator.

The entry level Defender/Detonator had a poplar body, 24-frets on a rosewood 'board, humbucker/single-coil/humbucker (HB/S/HB) pickup layout, and a high-tech vibrato.

Defender

The Defender F begat the Detonator AX, as both guitars were similar, with alder bodies and fancier finishes. Price list text for the Detonator AX touted a single-piece maple neck with an "exclusive bi-directional heel-less neck joint", as well as a pearloid pickguard.

Defender F

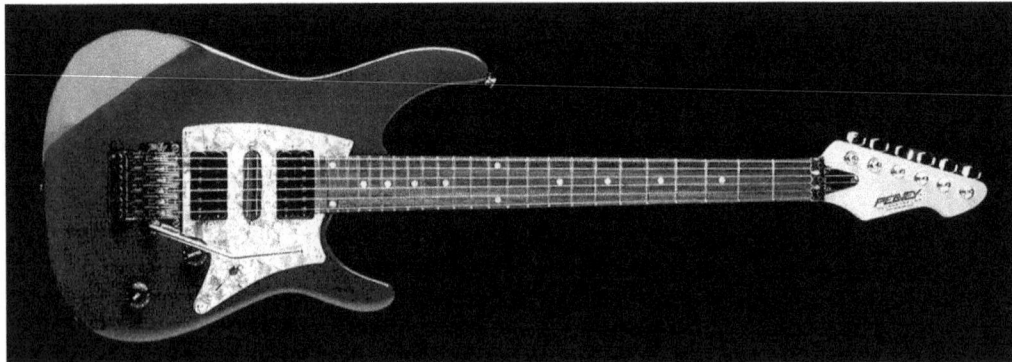

Detonator AX

A later variant was the Detonator JX, which had a single/single/humbucker pickup configuration. Some of those models had binding on the top edge of the body.

Detonator JX, front of body *guitar-museum.com*

Ed Pope recalled setting up some guitars with "Defender" on the headstock, so apparently such instruments with that model name did have a brief life in the retail market.

Axcelerator basses followed a slightly different path from their six-sting siblings. Even the basic model had active electronics, powering two VFL pickups. The neck pickup was mounted on the pickguard, as were the controls, and the bridge pickup was mounted on the body. Controls included a master volume, pickup pan knob with center detent, and stacked bass and treble controls. The Axcelerator Bass had a poplar body, maple neck with rosewood fretboard, and was also available in a fretless version. Five-string and six-string variants were later marketed.

Axcelerator 4

Axcelerator 5

Axcelerator 6

Like the Axcelerator AX guitar, the Axcelerator Plus stepped up to a swamp ash body, a tortoiseshell or pearloid pickguard (depending on the finish), and gold hardware.

Axcelerator Plus, sunburst with tortoise-shell pickguard *Music-Go-Round*

Axcelerator Plus, with pearloid pickguard and original inspection tag *Willie G. Moseley*

When the original lineup of Grand Funk Railroad reunited in 1996 and toured for three years, bassist Mel Schacher was presented with a Peavey Axcelerator Plus by the company. Mark Farner played his red Impact, although spinal surgery would later compel him to switch a very lightweight instrument. Grand Funk also used a backup musician, Howard Eddy, onstage; the keyboard player/guitarist/backing vocalist played Farner's white Impact guitar.

Mel Schacher plays an Axcelerator Plus onstage with Grand Funk Railroad in the mid-Nineties. Guitarist Mark Farner is shown with his mid-Eighties red Impact 2. *David Staats*

Circa 1996, the Axcelerator 2-T debuted, following the design of a standard Axcelerator bass, but sporting an aftermarket 2-Tek bridge. The innovative part was thick and heavy, and ran through the entire depth of the bass body. Its construction isolated the vibrations of individual strings, in a manner that negated sonic interference from the other strings. 2-Tek bridges could make a bass sound almost like a piano.

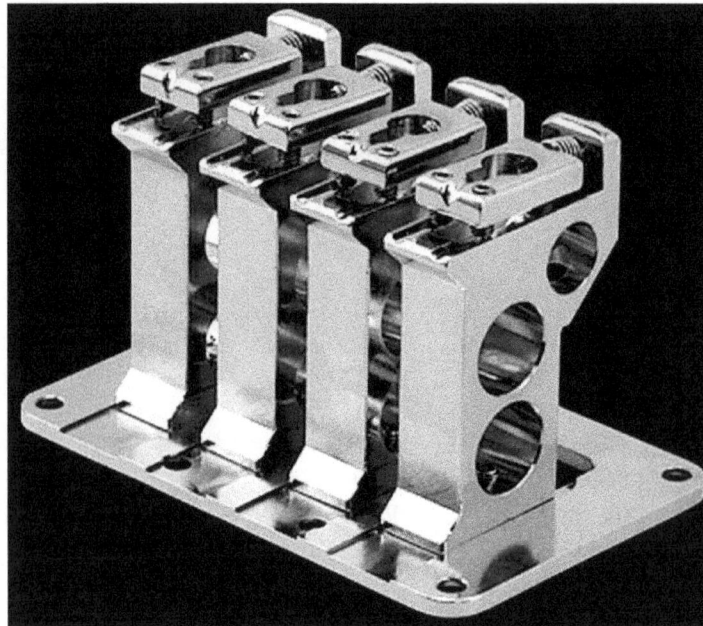

2-Tek bridge *Google Images*

2-Tek bridge installed on Axcelerator bass *Elderly Instruments*

Mick Donner fondly recalled the genesis of the collaboration between Peavey and 2-Tek:

"The 2-Tek variant came about after a meeting with 2-Tek's Jeff Hornbeck at a NAMM show. This was after I had moved from R&D into a product manager position for the Guitar Division.

"I used to get a *lot* of mail from inventors and smaller companies wanting to hitch their wagon to the very successful 'Peavey machine'. Most of it was either too ridiculous to consider, or just a rehash of an old idea.

"But when I got the prospectus from 2-Tek and read their claims, it really seemed like something new and different, so I decided to give them some time at the show.

"I went to their booth. Jeff started the meeting playing a bass that had been fitted with one of their bridges; Jeff hit the B string and turned the volume on the bass all the way down. He spent the next 10 or 15 minutes explaining how the 2-Tek bridge worked, and what effect that had on the way the bass strings reacted to each other. At the end of his talk he turned the volume back up on the bass. The B string was still ringing. I was sold."

Donner believes that Peavey was one of only two companies to interpolate 2-Tek bridges into production models.

Jim Roberts noted Axcelerator basses in issues of *Bass Player*, declaring the four-string model had "…intelligent design and solid construction," and citing the five-string to be "…as impressive as the 4-string," adding that the Axcelerator 5 "…delivers so much performance for so little money."

And in his 2003 book *American Basses*, Roberts was on target when he described another Peavey bass lineup that surfaced in the mid-Nineties, the Forum series, to be "meat and potatoes" instruments.

"Earlier, the Axcelerator and Forum AX had been included in our 'Amazing Bargains' issue of December 1995," the *BP* founding editor detailed, "and the Forum was in a 'Four-Strings Under $500' shootout in September 1996, where it got a five-out-of-five value rating."

The original version of the Forum debuted in 1993, with a P/J pickup configuration (in the same one-pickup-on-the-pickguard, one-pickup-on-the-body style as the Axcelerator bass), and a two-volume, master tone control configuration. The body's forearm and ribcage/belly contouring were "extra deep," according to factory literature, and the body was a bit more streamlined. An active variant, the Forum Plus, premiered in the same annum.

Forum bass—original configuration

1995 saw instruments bearing the Forum moniker undergoing radical changes. The basic Forum changed to a single-pickup, active instrument with separate bass and treble controls (with center detent) mounted in a pickguard with a different silhouette from its predecessor. As for the solitary pickup, the owner's manual stated, "The Forum's wide aperture humbucking pickup provides high output and wide frequency response. The pickup has been harmonically placed on the instrument, allowing greater harmonic and fundamental response to be obtained from each string."

The large, rectangular pickup was Peavey's new and powerful VFL Plus active unit (which had originally been designed as a passive model).

Forum bass—later configuration *Bill Ingalls Jr.*

The new two-pickup model, the Forum AX, was a sonic monster, with two harmonically-placed VFL Plus pickups, and appropriate controls—master volume, a rotary pickup blend control with center detent, and concentric bass and treble controls, each with center detent.

Unlike previous Forum models, the Forum AX's controls were mounted in a chrome plate. Pickguards on both models were usually three-layer, black/white/black.

Forum AX *Bill Ingalls Jr.*

The circuitry in the revised Forum basses was analog, according to Mike Powers. It was powered by two 9-volt batteries, and was described in owner manuals as "an active high/low pass shelving circuit."

The bridges on the second-edition Forum and the Forum AX were also different—the single-pickup bass still had a standard-looking bridge, while the two-pickup model's bridge was a hefty and aesthetically-sharp item.

"The massive ABM bridge on the Forum AX is machined from a solid block of brass for maximum sustain, and offers the ultimate in adjustability," the owner's manual stated. "String height, intonation, and spacing may be adjusted to fit literally any playing style."

A five-string model with a low B string, the Forum 5, was also offered in the new configuration. It had a 4+1 headstock silhouette, and was otherwise a five-string version of the Forum AX.

Forum 5

The same 1994 catalog that proffered the short-lived "Defender" models also cited several new Impacts. The Impact 1 and 2 were already gone, and the new "starter" model was the Impact Firenza, which featured the body silhouette of the Impact 1 and 2, but with a bolt-on maple neck, which had a six-on-a-side headstock. The body was poplar, and the 22-fret fretboard was rosewood. Pick ups were laid out in a S/S/HB configuration, with master volume and tone knobs and a five-way pickup switch. A Peavey Powerbend III vibrato ("with steel bridge saddles") was standard.

Impact Firenza

The pickup switching was yet another innovative/had-to-be-learned idea, but was a bit simpler, and was explained in a reverse numerical order from DeCola's earlier article on the Impact 1 and 2:

Position 1: Neck pickup only

Position 2: Neck and center pickup

Position 3: Center pickup only (reverse wound/reverse polarity/hum-canceling)

Position 4: Center and bridge pickups (single coil for bridge)

Position 5: Bridge pickup only (humbucking)

Perhaps not surprisingly, the Impact Firenza was also offered in an AX step-up model, with an ash body, fancier finishes, fancier pickguards, and upgrade tuners and bridge saddles.

The Impact Milano had a mahogany body with a figured maple cap, and a maple neck with a 24-fret rosewood fingerboard. Its electronics and controls consisted of two humbuckers, master volume and tone controls, five-way pickup switch, and a vibrato.

Impact Milano

According to the owner's manual, pickup switching was as follows:

Position 1: Neck pickup only (humbucking)
Position 2: Neck pickup only (single-coil, hum-reducing)
Position 3: Both pickups (humbucking)
Position 4: Both pickups (single-coil, hum-reducing)
Position 5: Bridge pickup only (humbucking)

Impact Torinos (of which there were two variants) were even fancier. Like the Impact Milano, the body was also mahogany with a maple top, and the electronics (and pickup switching) were the same. However, the neck was mahogany, with set-in construction. The 24-fret rosewood fretboard had sharp-looking "3D"/"shadow box" block inlays.

Impact Torino I

Impact Torino II

"3-D" block inlay on Impact Torino fretboard

The Torino I had a separate intonatable bridge and stop tailpiece, while the Torino II had a Powerbend III vibrato ("with Graph Tech String Saver bridge saddles"; Peavey had upgraded from steel saddles with its own trademarked alloy).

Axcelerators, Detonators, and Italian-referenced Impacts were outta there by the end of 1997; Forum basses were gone a year later.

The Firenza moniker would be continued on a trio of guitars made in Leakesville. Production on the latter Firenzas began in 1997, soon after the new southern factory opened.

The models had the same body silhouette as their recently-discontinued Impact predecessors, but interestingly, the body wood was different on all three models. All three models had bolt-on maple necks with contoured heels, and 22-fret rosewood fretboards. Their headstocks had a stubby, offset 3 + 3 silhouette that was somewhat similar to the Wolfgang's headstock, without the scoop. The outline has been dubbed as an "elf hat" look by some wags.

The Leakesville Firenzas had several parts that were imported. "Crafted/Handcrafted/Made in the U.S.A." wasn't found on their headstocks; the brand and "Firenza" (no differentiation about a particular model) were all that appeared, enabling the neck to be used on any of the three styles. The trio was usually advertised together, and "Handmade in U.S.A." was seen in at least one such ad. The unique attributes of each variant were emphasized in the marketing campaign.

Ad for the Leakesville Firenza trio

The "basic" Firenza lived up to its name—it was a no-frills, dependable instrument with a mahogany body, with two large, imported single-coil pickups (sometimes called "soapbars," a term applied to vintage pickups of that style). The model had a intonatable bridge and stop tailpiece, both of which were recessed, creating a smoother look and feel on the top of the instrument. One wonders why such a comfortable layout hadn't been seen earlier, even on other brands and models.

Firenza

This custom-painted Firenza body was signed by Hartley

The Firenza AX had two open-face humbucking pickups. Its body was swamp ash. The five-way pickup switch operated the pickups in the same manner as the Impact Milano/Torino, and the AX also had a vibrato.

Firenza AX

One of the more unique configurations for an electric guitar of its time, the Firenza JX had three pickups laid out in a standard S/S/HB configuration, but did not have a vibrato—its strings loaded through the rear of the (basswood) body. The five-way pickup switch operated in an easier-to-understand manner:

Position 1: Neck pickup only

Position 2: Neck and middle pickups

Position 3: Middle pickup only

Position 4: Middle and bridge pickups

Position 5: Bridge pickup only

The Firenza JX's middle pickup was wound in reverse, to evoke hum-canceling in the #2 and #4 positions.

Firenza JX

The production of Firenzas was terminated when the Leakesville factory closed in 2002.

Perhaps the most striking instruments ever produced by Peavey were the B-Quad 4 and B-Quad 5 basses, introduced in 1993. The bass was the design of veteran musician Brian Bromberg, a remarkably diverse player who excelled on both acoustic bass and electric bass in both the studio and in concert. Among the musicians with whom the bassist has performed are legends such as Dizzy Gillespie, Dave Grusin, Billy Cobham, Herbie Hancock, Gerry Mulligan, Michel LeGrand, and Michael Bublé. He opined that the most unusual gig he's ever done was playing the National Anthem on his acoustic bass at center court in Key Arena in Seattle for a Supersonics NBA playoff game.

Bromberg's first solo album had been released in 1986, and the title track of his sophomore effort, 1988's *Basses Loaded* (with its start-and-stop solo riffing) has the reputation of having been a breakout tune of sorts.

The versatile bassist had envisioned a versatile instrument, and owned the rights to its design. Bromberg began collaborating with Peavey—and with Mick Donner in particular—in the early Nineties. Donner was the project's design engineer, and he quickly discovered that putting the (patented) design of a professional musician into production was a challenge.

"That shape goes back over 30 years with Brian," Donner said.

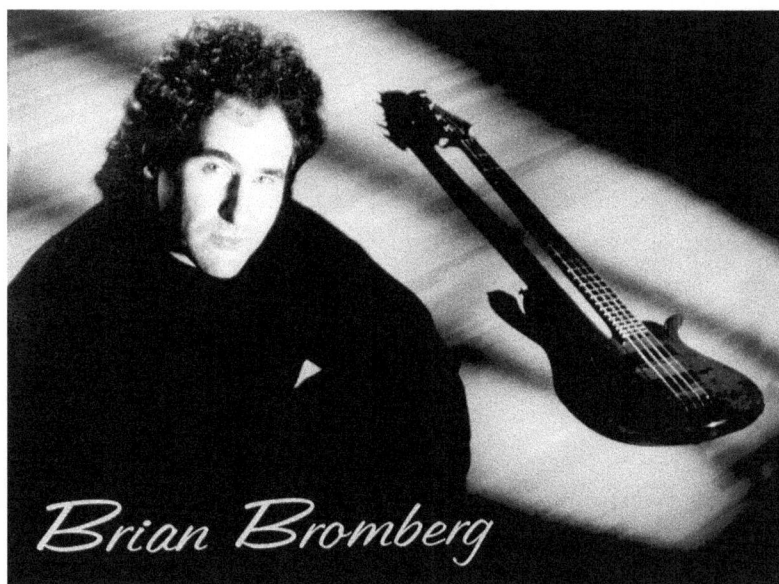

One of the unique features of his original design was what appeared to be a very long upper cutaway horn. According to Bromberg, it's a bit of an optical illusion.

"There are two reasons why it's like that," he said in a 2006 interview. "First, it removes a lot of wood that would normally be there, so the instrument's lighter and more comfortable. Second, the reason it looks longer is because of how deep the cutaway is; [the cutaway horn] is actually *not* longer than a traditional electric bass. The strap button is hanging out around the twelfth fret, so that's the balance point. It seems 'long' because I didn't want to lose the integrity of the balance. I don't like to play an instrument where someone designed the body specifically for aesthetics. It's extremely important that anything I design or play is as ergonomic as it is attractive. If it's comfortable for me, then it's comfortable for another bass player."

B-Quad 5

Another unique facet for the Bromberg collaboration with Peavey was the use of a neck made by Modulus Graphite, which had a phenolic fretboard with 24-frets. The B-Quad 4 had a 34" scale, while the B-Quad 5 had a 35" scale, and both models were available as fretless instruments. The body was made of figured maple.

The electronics were somewhat complicated, but made sense. Donner had to work with Peavey's digital and mixer departments in getting the proper setup.

Standard pickups were two active VFL humbuckers, but there were also four piezo transducers built into the bridge (to facilitate an acoustic sound). Donner recalls that the bridge was a Wilkinson model, which Peavey modified in-house with the transducers.

Controls included stacked volume controls for the standard pickups, a "tone network" knob (detailed in the owner's manual as "an active high/low-pass shelving circuit."), a solitary volume and tone control for the transducers, and a master volume control. A stereo/mono switch was also installed, as were two jacks.

The bridge was made from milled aluminum, and had steel saddles.

Bass Player's Jim Roberts remembered Bromberg's enthusiasm for the new Peavey product, recalling, "Brian was very excited about the B-Quad, and went out of his way to make sure we knew about it and how he was using it."

The B-Quad models were ambitious, and were around until late 1997. About eight years afterward, Bromberg had some 20/20 hindsight about his collaboration with Peavey.

"It was way ahead of its time in most ways," he recalled. "Had I known then what I know now, it could have had some other things incorporated into it, and I personally feel it would have been one of the most successful and one of the best unique, modern instruments to come out. I didn't know enough about designs, wood, materials, and pickups at that point for it to do what its true potential was. Considering what it was back then, including its price, it was a remarkable instrument. When it came out, there was nothing on the market that was even close to it…but I wanted to revamp the instrument, and it never happened."

CHAPTER 14
End of the century

The last few years of the Nineties and the first few years of the new millineum saw Peavey increasing its numbers regarding imported instruments, but the company was still endeavoring to develop viable, American-made guitars and basses.

Hartley experienced more than one personal tragedy when his wife Melia died in March of 1997, and his parents died within seven weeks of each other in early 1998. The experiences ultimately made him determined to carry on, guiding the company into new sonic opportunities.

He would be introduced to a Dallas real estate businesswoman named Mary Gray in 1999. Gray was also a Mississippi native and a Mississippi State graduate, but she and Hartley had not known each other previously. They would marry in December of 2000, and the new Mrs. Peavey brought her business savvy and enthusiasm to Peavey Electronics Corporation, becoming heavily involved with numerous facets of the company.

After the endorsement contract with Adrian Vandenberg expired, Peavey reintroduced the look of his erstwhile signature model as the "V-Type series." A U.S.-made V-Type was briefly included, and had a plainer reverse headstock compared to the stair-step version found on the original Vandenberg signature model. Some U.S.-made V-type examples were notable for the fingerboard inlay, which was only found on the twelfth fret—the pearl inlay was a mirror-image silhouette of a reclining, buxom female, an iconic symbol found on the mudflaps of an untold number of tractor-trailer rigs.

V-type

V-type headstock

Twelfth fret marker

The first new domestic electric lineup from Peavey in the new century had reportedly been originally designated as the Essex aggregation, but was known as the Limited series when it debuted in 2001. The guitars had a classic silhouette on an ash body, with a bound maple top. The neck was a new five-bolt configuration with a smooth heel (the fretboard was rosewood) and the headstock had a 3 + 3 layout, with a now-in-vogue straight pull on the strings. All models had a Hipshot brand vibrato with stainless steel bridge saddles.

Limited models were differentiated by their pickup layout and the wood pattern on the body cap:

HB: Two humbuckers, flame maple top
ST: Two single coil pickups plus bridge humbucker, flame maple top
VT: Three single coil pickups, flame maple top

Limited ad

A step-up called the Quilt Top (with a fancier cap of that type of figured maple) was available for each of the three models. Two imported Limited models were also introduced.

The pickup switching for the HB was, once again, five-position and unique, and actually referred to "inside" and "outside" pickup coils. The owner's manual cited the order of the switching as follows:

1. (towards neck) Neck pickup only
2. Two outside coils
3. Both pickups
4. Two inside coils
5. Bridge pickup only

VT and ST models had the following pickup control system:

1. (towards neck) Neck pickup only
2. Neck and middle pickups
3. Middle pickup only
4. Middle and bridge pickups
5. Bridge pickup only

Limited VT Quilt Top *Music Zoo*

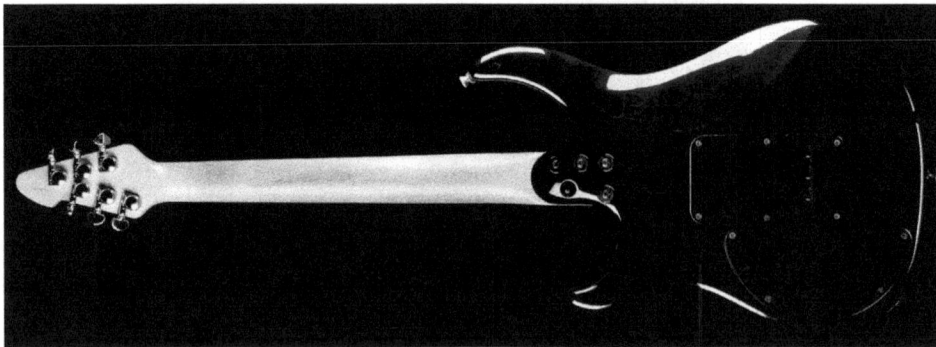

Limited VT Quilt Top back, showing five-bolt neck joint with smooth heel *Music Zoo*

Within two years, the Limited Standard was also offered, with two humbuckers and a single-coil pickup in between.

Limited Standard

Mississippi native Jim Beaugez joined the Peavey company in 2002 as a copywriter/editor. He'd grown up in Ocean Springs, and had been familiar with Peavey from a young age:

"I had an art class assignment in the sixth grade—I don't remember what it was—but I drew myself onstage rocking out with a band—you guessed it, with Peavey logos on the speaker cabinets."

For a long time, however, Beaugez did not know that the company was located in his home state.

"It was just that big and ubiquitous," he recalled. "That really speaks to the power of the brand."

Beaugez worked his way up the internal media ladder with the company.

"It was mostly trial by fire," he said, "but Mary Peavey was very encouraging and believed in me. To this day, I can say that. Peavey has always been a place of opportunity for people with the right skills and drive."

Edward Van Halen "dwarfed much of the artist roster" in those years, according to Beaugez. The company continued its presence in the Christian music scene as well.

1997 saw a strong effort cranking up in Peavey's bass division, as the G-Bass and Cirrus basses were announced in the middle of that year. Like the Leakesville Firenzas, which debuted on the same price list, the G-Bass (Level 1) and Cirrus series (Level 2, available in four- five-or six-string configurations) had "TBA" instead of a suggested list price.

The G-Bass was an active instrument with a single VFL pickup. Its controls were consisted of a volume control and a three-band (bass/midrange/treble) tone control system. Its sleek-looking body (with an extended upper cutaway horn) was made of basswood, and the neck had a pao ferro fretboard.

Reflecting a newer trend among basses, the G-Bass had a 35" scale instead of a standard 34". It was a regular-production instrument (as opposed to a signature model) with a graphite/carbon composite neck for optimum durability. The black neck and headstock had an industrial/stealth/semi-see-through look that underlined, at least visually, the strength and viability of composite necks. Its hardware included a Gotoh bridge.

The G-Bass was introduced at a list price of $799, and an early magazine ad for the model hyped the price point with a "No Way!" tag line, advising a reader that the equalization/preamp circuitry was "studio class," and also promoting the bass's light weight ("Under 8 lbs., under $800"). It was proffered in hip-looking holoflake and pearl finishes.

G-Bass ad

By mid-1999, the G-5, with a lower B-string and two pickups, had joined its single-pickup, four-string sibling. It had an alder body instead of basswood.

G-5

Both instruments lasted until around the end of 2002, but the body and electronics of the G-Bass would appear again a few years later, sporting a different neck and a different model name.

The Cirrus bass series was one for which the company appeared to have pulled out all the stops. The instruments were developed by Mike Powers and Tim Litchfield, and the 1997 price list promised four-, five-, and six-string variants (at Level 2). The instruments had multi-laminate neck-through construction (with graphite rods installed) and 24-frets on a 35" scale. The fretboard on most models was pao ferro, and a fretless neck was available at no extra charge.

Electronics were two active VFL pickups with a master volume control, pickup blend control, and a three-band boost-and-cut equalization system, powered by two nine-volt batteries.

The heavy-gauge ABM bridge and die-cast tuners were gold-plated.

Litchfield built the first prototypes.

An impressive 20-page catalog was published in 1998. Its extensive text and high-quality photography touted the numerous features of the Cirrus, beginning with a paean to its stunning looks at an impressive price point:

The Peavey Cirrus bass is the culmination of over 22 years of experience crafting guitars and basses for working musicians everywhere. We've learned a lot in the last two decades. The Cirrus is our idea of the ultimate neck-through bass. The Cirrus bass is, in its essence, a composite of fine toned woods and cutting-edge electronics combined with superb craftsmanship and attention to detail. Every part of the Cirrus—the shape, the electronics, the materials— contributes to something that is so leading-edge we had a hard time deciding on whether or not to put a pricey tag on it like other manufacturers. But for 34 years, the name Peavey has become synonymous with value, and we're not about to change that.

Powers, Litchfield, and Kay Moss were shown in a photo collage with Cirrus models in various stages of completion.

Other portions of the text detailed the bass's construction (including the use of CNC machinery). The Cirrus's 35" scale (instead of the standard 34" scale) was cited as a nod to the evolution of a low B-string on five-string basses, and the placement of tuners and a graphite overlay on the headstock were noted as contributing to sustain and the elimination of dead spots.

A lengthy explanation of Peavey's VFL pickup technology was also included.

Woods listed included walnut, maple, purple heart, wenge, bugbinga, and redwood. However, specific woods were cited on instruments with four, five, or six strings, with various comments about what kind of tone could be evoked by such woods:

• The Cirrus 4-String had a maple cap on an alder body with a maple neck, or a bubinga cap on a walnut back with a walnut neck.

• The 5-String model had a wenge cap on a walnut back with a walnut neck.

• The 6-String had a redwood cap on an alder body with a maple neck.

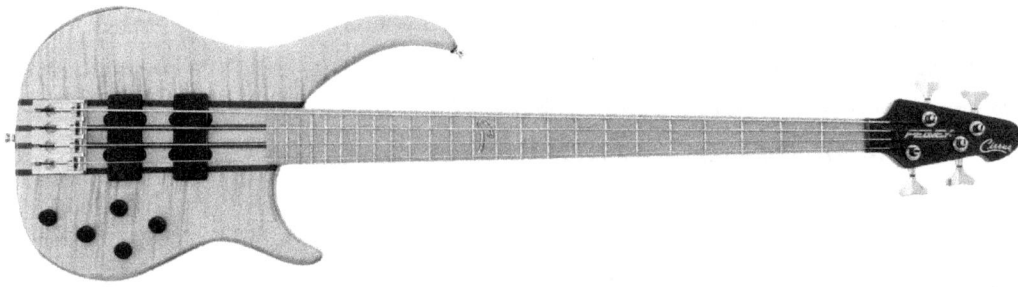

Cirrus 4—maple *Willie G. Moseley*

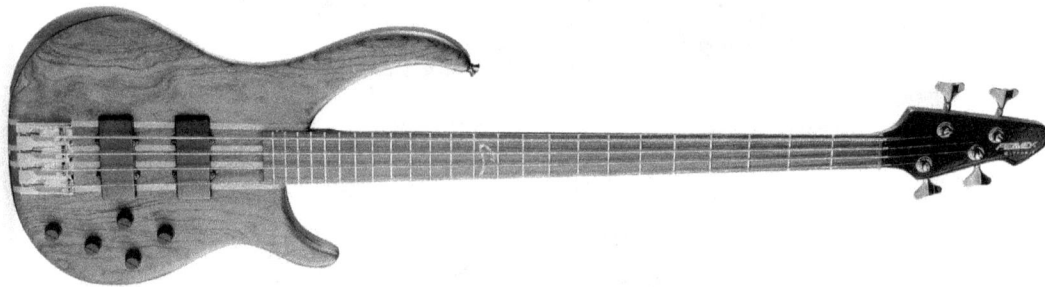

Cirrus 4—bubinga

Cirrus 5 *Willie G. Moseley*

1998 Cirrus ad

By the summer of 1999, a price list noted that other woods were being offered on four-, five-, and six-string models. A year later, Cirrus models came in three six-string variants, while the five-string and four-string models had four variants. The fanciest (and most expensive) finish was Claro Walnut. Gloss finishes ("w/ multi-process hand staining") also debuted in Peacock Blue and Ruby Red.

Toto's Mike Porcaro (1955-2015) onstage with a Cirrus 5-String... *Mark Reggeman*

...and posing with a Cirrus 6-String

Summer of 2001 saw the addition of a gorgeous Cirrus variant with a highly-figured tiger eye top and ebony fretboard. The new model was also expensive—the Cirrus 4 Quilt Top Tiger Eye listed for $250 more than the Cirrus 6 Claro Walnut.

By 2003, Cirrus five-string and four-string models began to be offered with bolt-on necks (five-bolt) that had a 34" scale, and by the next year, some Cirrus models were imported.

The Cirrus series was a decent competitor, and stayed in the lineup until Peavey's domestic solidbody guitar production was suspended.

"The Cirrus was a home run," said Roy Rogers. "It was sexy looking, great balance, beautiful woods, great price, 18-volt electronics for active pickups & EQ. An all-around amazing instrument."

P

The Millennium series was introduced (appropriately) in 2000. The development of the lineup was under the aegis of Tim Litchfield (Powers was in China).

"For some reason, a lot of people wanted a bolt-on [neck]," Litchfield remembered. "I wanted to use a lot of the features of the Cirrus, but a different look, and we experimented a lot of different kinds of woods."

The Millennium had a slightly-skinnier body silhouette, and the headstock had four-in-a-row tuners (a four-string Cirrus had 2 + 2 tuners; the five-string variants in both series had 3 + 2 tuners).

Millenium

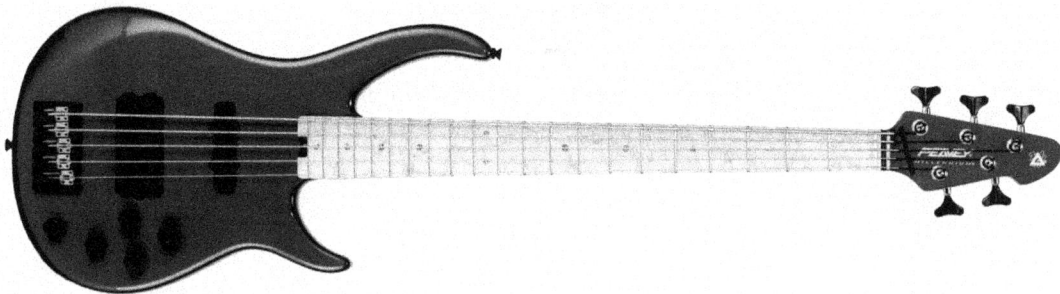

Millenium 5

Bodies were alder, and the bolt-on maple neck had a 35-scale and a pao ferro fingerboard with, interestingly, maple dot position markers. A bird's-eye maple neck with paua abalone dot position markers was optional.

The pickups were still active VFLs, but were styled differently (a "J-style" pickup near the neck, and a "MM-style" pickup near the bridge). The controls were similar to the Cirrus, with one notable exception—the midrange control had two concentric knobs, and was actually more versatile (or "shiftable," to quote a Peavey price list). The inside knob offered "variable" midrange, while the outside knob controlled midrange "sweep."

The headstock had lightweight Hipshot tuners (some variants included a Hipshot D-tuner), and the bridge was a Hipshot "Quadrajust" unit made of milled aluminum, with steel saddles. Strings could be loaded through the bridge or through the body.

One of the unique cosmetic aspects of the Millennium series was that it was offered in seventeen different colors.

The step-up Millennium Plus added a figured maple cap to the body and a Hipshot D-tuner to the headstock.

Twelve different versions were introduced on the July 2000 price list, but as was the case with certain EVH Wolfgang models at one point in that guitar's history, the only difference in several listings was a maple fretboard or a paò ferro fretboard.

By late 2001, the Millennium J 4 and J 4 Plus had joined the lineup. They had two similar "J-style" pickups instead of the one-"MM-style"-and-one-"J-style" pickup layout of other Millennium basses, and were priced lower than the original versions.

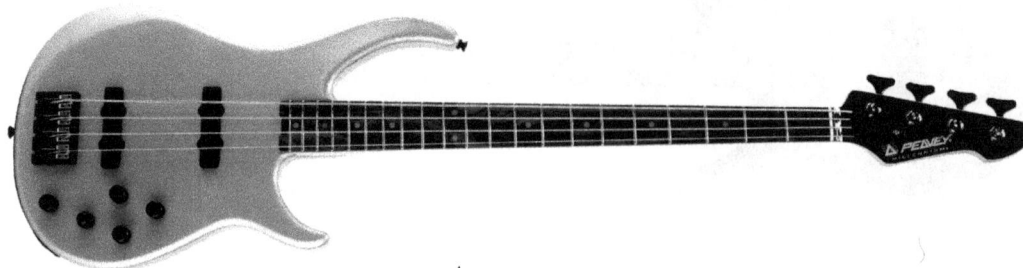

Millenium J 4

Like the Cirrus, the Millennium bass series would eventually end up with imported versions.

CHAPTER 15
Fighting the good fight

At the advent of the new century, Peavey was called upon for delicate "surgery" on an iconic guitar that was located in Meridian.

Jimmie Rodgers's 1928 Martin 000-45 (which was insured for $1 million), had reportedly been Rodgers' favorite instrument. It had been used by Ernest Tubb for four decades following Rodgers' death, and was later donated to the Jimmie Rodgers Museum in Meridian.

The legendary guitar was now in disrepair, and the museum honoring the country music legend asked the local guitar manufacturer to restore it.

"That guitar had degenerated to where it was literally falling apart," Hartley said. "They wanted us to restore it, but I hesitated, but I finally asked Mike Powers to get it back into condition."

Powers had the guitar for three days, and spent over 17 hours of labor on the restoration. His effort was chronicled in a meticulous day-by-day, step-by-step article in a 2001 issue of *Monitor*. Numerous photos accompanied the article, one which showed a note pasted inside the soundhole that read "To Jimmie Rodgers, America's Blue Yodeler, with all good wishes, C. Frederick Martin III, July 27, 1928."

Jimmie Rodgers with his Martin 000-45 *Jimmie Rodgers Museum*

Ernest Tubb with Rodgers' Martin guitar *Google images*

Hartley with the restored instrument

Peavey's moves towards imported instruments had begun, as noted earlier, with parts, including hardware, pickups, and bodies.

"Initially, we'd had our hardware made domestically, particularly at a machine shop in Chicago," DeCola reflected. "We also got parts from companies like Kahler—not just vibratos, but things like bridges for Generation models. But we had to look at how to cut expenses, and some of the hardware started coming in from overseas. Then, it was items like pickguard assemblies or pickups for entry-level guitars like the Predator or Reactor. At that time, we were fighting fire with fire, because other companies were getting into imported parts, and even imported instruments."

"The market speaks to you," Hartley said in a 2000 interview, after Peavey had begun importing complete instruments. "Everybody may say, 'Yeah, I want somethin' made in the U.S.,' and I'd say, 'Here, I've got it,' but then they'd say 'Fine, but this import's cheaper.' I'm as patriotic as they get, and my career has been dedicated to doing it better in the U.S.A. When everybody else over here was using antiquated pin routers and still doing hand-sanding, I'm the one that went to copy lathes and CNC machines. Hell, even Martin is making their stuff that way now!"

The middle of the new century's first decade saw the company actively pursuing a "Custom Shop" designation (with capital letters) for its higher-end American-made guitars and basses. The Custom Shop became "official" in 2002 (when the EVH Wolfgang was still the frontline instrument), and price lists began noting certain upgrades and options that were available from that particular facility.

"The Peavey Custom Shop was the real deal, not a marketing ploy," Jim Beaugez said. "Peavey was digging in as the last great American great company that was still owned one hundred percent—and was *guided* one hundred percent—by its founder. We were staking a claim."

And when Peavey first began to face the inevitability of marketing imported Asian instruments, Mike Powers had traveled to the Far East to examine manufacturing options.

"We tried to remain all-U.S.A. up until the '90s," Powers recounted, "but too many sub-vendors closed up in the U.S. due to labor costs. I was one of the first people in the company to travel to Taiwan, Korea, Japan, and Vietnam. We bought guitars as well as parts from these areas, due to costs, and to be able to compete. I was traveling three, maybe four times a year to those areas."

The company finally committed to production facilities in China, and Powers would move again—this time, halfway around the globe.

"I was asked if I would relocate for a period of time and oversee the production from these factories," he said in a 2011 interview. "Our intention was to make better products from the beginning, and to also speed up delivery times. The only way to accomplish that was to have someone or a team of people dedicated to Asian factories and production, not only for guitar, but for other products as well. While it was not necessarily an easy re-location, I was used to the travel."

An emerging manufacturing nation like China had many facets of industrial production to coordinate, and Powers was constantly busy working with numerous factories, as well as developing new products. He pointed out, however, that many of the styles of Peavey instruments had stayed in the line for a long time in domestic and imported models—the basic body silhouette for Millenium and Cirrus basses were been in existence since the late Nineties, and the venerable Foundation Bass (one of Powers' all-time favorite instruments) had lasted almost 20 years.

Mike Powers tunes up a bass in China

Another new bass series appeared in the Peavey lineup in the latter half of 2001. The Grind series was noteworthy for the differences between the four-string and five-string models—the Grind Bass 4 had a 34" scale and a P/J pickup configuration, while the Grind Bass 5 had a 35" scale and two J-style pickups.

Grind bass four-string

Grind bass five-string

Both models had maple necks with 24 frets, and the tuners were similar to Millennium series tuners. The bridge, however, was technically comprised individual bridges installed on the top (string loaded through the rear of the body). Such an arrangement was dubbed "fingerstyle" on the price list.

Closeup of body showing "fingerstyle" bridge *eBay*

The electronics were hyped as "onboard active or passive 3-band EQ w/ push/push active treble boost, master volume and blend controls." An 18-volt battery system powered the circuitry.

One of the unique (and practical) aspects of Grind basses was their fretboard inlay, which consisted of markers on the bass side that were visible from not only from above the fretboard, but from a player's perspective as well; i.e., the inlay was also on the side of the fretboard.

While the Grind won more than one award in its time, its U.S.-made variant stayed around for less than three years; by mid-2004, the Grind lineup consisted entirely of imported instruments.

Tony Moscal joined Peavey in 2001, initially as a consultant.

"I had my own company that designed an internet program that allowed manufacturers to give their retailers 'website stores'; we literally went from 'zero presence' to over a thousand dealers selling Peavey in one day."

Moscal was later designated as the company's Senior Manager of Marketing and Product Development, followed by another step up to General Manager of Business Development and Marketing.

"When I first came to work here, we were at some weird price points," he remembered, "and I was able to convince Hartley that we needed to get more aggressive on pricing, across the board, and that we needed to have more 'flagship' pieces, to give us even more of a 'credibility aspect', and what the guitar guys did over in Plant 2 really accomplished that."

Peavey had a very unique opportunity when the company hired David Ellefson, bassist for heavy metal band Megadeth, to work in Artist Relations after the band broke up in 2002. The bassist had been familiar with Peavey gear for decades.

"I saw the ad in *Guitar Player* as a teenager, with Hartley Peavey sitting on his amp, holding the T-60 guitar. [That] must have been around 1980," Ellefson recalled. "I grew up in a rural farm community of Minnesota, so all I heard was Country & Western music everywhere. It seemed most every band in the area had some type of Peavey gear on their stages, be it amplifiers or PA equipment. My family would watch the TV show 'Hee Haw' every Saturday night, and Peavey amps were always on the set. Peavey had a definitive look and it was attractive to me, especially once I saw harder-edge, guitar-driven rock bands like Lynryd Skynyrd and Molly Hatchet using their amps."

Ellefson didn't recall the exact date and place he first tried out a Peavey amp (or P.A. system), "…but I *do* remember knowing it was a moment that I felt like I had 'arrived' as a musician, especially because so many working musicians and bands in my local area were actively using Peavey gear. I recall the Tolex on their amps was different and very durable. And, they had speakers with silver dust covers that shone through the black grill clothes. Basically, they just looked very cool."

The aspiring bassist also remembered his first encounter with a Peavey bass:

"I was on a family vacation to Florida around 1980, and I stopped into a music store in Atlanta, and saw the Peavey T-40 bass guitar. I clearly remember it was marked at $240 brand new! To me, it felt great, and the price was incredible, especially compared to other basses I was considering at the time. I never did purchase that bass, but it gave me a lasting impression of quality, great tone, features, and likeability."

"I think Ross Vallory of Journey was the first notable bassist I saw with a T-40 bass. That impressed me, because they were a huge rock band, and they proudly had Peavey amps behind them, and now Ross had the bass, too. While I was just starting to be stung by the more wild and pointy heavy metal guitars coming onto the market, the Peavey T-40 had a look of being innovative, and a serious bassist's axe."

Ellefson had written a book titled *Making Music Your Business* back in 1997, which took a practical/pragmatic attitude towards the business facet of popular music; i.e., it didn't address scales or tunings. At the time, he didn't necessarily envision that he would end up employed by an amplifier and guitar manufacturer.

"Once Megadeth ended in 2002, I really felt like my time as a full-time musician might be over," he recounted. "I knew from first-hand experience how much work, luck, and good timing go into a successful band, so I was pretty certain I wouldn't be able to capture that same lighting twice."

"So I thought about other ventures in which I might be able to parlay my professional musical experiences to benefit other people, or even companies. I thought about doing A&R [artists and repertoire] for record companies, but then suddenly the thought hit me about doing artist relations for a musical instrument company."

The bassist knew Tony Moscal from a stint as an endorsing artist for another amplifier brand a few years earlier. Moscal had just started working with Peavey, and Ellefson was currently a Peavey bass amp endorsee who had a very pleasant relationship with the company.

"Tony told me to sit tight, as he thought this could become a great opportunity for both Peavey and me," Ellefson recalled, "and a few months later it all fell into place for me to work for the company under Tony's direction in the marketing division. That's how I ended up doing Artist Relations for the company from 2002 to 2010."

And even the rock-star-turned-prospective-employee had his eyes opened when he visited Meridian for the first time:

"I had never been to the Peavey facility before I interviewed for the Artist Relations job in 2002," said Ellefson. "Needless to say, I was beyond impressed the first time I went there, especially to learn that it is privately-held and solely-owned by Hartley Peavey himself. There are many companies the size of Peavey which are publicly held, but to see such an empire in the music business of that magnitude was almost beyond belief.

"My interview was with Mary Peavey, the president of the company. She had a very sweet candor, as you might expect from a Southern lady. Yet, she was bold and powerful in her business ideals. I think she liked the idea of having a worldly artist like me in an Artist Relations position for their company. In fact, it was the very first time I had ever prepared a résumé, and I put everything in there that I had ever done in the business. She actually commented on it in my interview. But, I realized that most every thing I had ever done as a professional artist was really just marketing—every interview, photo shoot, TV interview, press campaign, etc was really just marketing and promotion. So, I think it was a really great match for me to take on the job."

Ellefson was hired on October 29, 2002. One important point about his position is that it was not involved with product design; his job was to recruit endorsers for numerous Peavey products.

"Some of my early recruits were A-list artists such as Nickelback, Slipknot and Kid Rock," he remembered, "and we renewed a long-standing affiliation with legendary Peavey artists Lynyrd Skynyrd. Mike Kroeger of Nickelback and Paul Gray of Slipknot were especially appreciative—if not somewhat star struck—that I was their Artist Relations contact. They both grew up on—and were heavily influenced by—Megadeth. So, in many ways I was the 'right thing at the right time' for Peavey's huge impact into the artist community."

While he originally didn't collaborate with R & D on any new products, Ellefson did deal with Litchfield, Pope, and Powers regarding instruments for notable artists.

"Tim Litchfield became a close ally of mine during my AR tenure because the Cirrus bass guitars were a very sought-after instrument by the professional artist community," he said. "Tim and I would have many discussions about new instrument designs and during those discussions he got me hip to the incredible depth of Peavey's instrument offerings over the years."

Another Tony, this one with the surname of Pasko, joined Peavey in 2004 as Product Manager for the guitar and amp division at Peavey. Pasko was another Chicago transplant of Italian heritage, so he and Mike Powers immediately became *amici*.

Pasko noted that Van Halen's popularity—the guitarist *and* the band—was connected to sales of Peavey guitars and amplifiers.

"In 2004, Peavey still had the Wolfgang, but sales had slowed because Van Halen wasn't touring, nor had they put any new music out for a while," Pasko remembered. "When Van Halen toured, you could follow the sales by their tour schedule; if they were going to play New York, all the dealers would order 5150s, Wolfgangs, accessories etc. So having the band out on the road was a great thing for Peavey."

Pasko also clicked with Ellefson:

"Dave and I got along right away, and he also shared the same ideas about artists as I did, so we worked very well together. Having Dave was great because he brought his rock star status with him, so it was a bit easier to get guys to take Peavey."

A mid-2004 price list saw the HP Signature Series and the Jack Daniel's Series being introduced. The new series were listed ahead of the Wolfgangs, which seems to have been a hint that the EVH endorsement was about to expire, or that it had already happened.

The HP Series was first listed with a U.S.-made frontline model and several imported versions. The American versions were finely-crafted instruments that was developed by Tony Pasko, Tim Litchfield and Ed Pope, with input from Powers, and were designed to compete with high-end, handcrafted "boutique" guitars.

"My game plan was to go with what people liked about Peavey," Pasko detailed, "and go with the company's strengths, which is manufacturing in the U.S. We had the infrastructure already in place; all we needed were products."

"I was told 'Make it the best it can be', and 'Put everything into it'," said Pope. "We also made some improvements; there were some players that didn't like the blocked tremolo that the Wolfgang had, and they wanted a floating tremolo. We had coil tapping. We used the same neck shape as the Wolfgang, and a different peghead."

The HP Signature had a one-piece set-in mahogany neck, an ebony fretboard with 24-frets and light maple binding, and a one-piece mahogany body with a carved maple top.

HP Signature

HP Signature—sunburst *Heritage Auctions*

HP Signature—custom variant with no fret markers

Electronics included two humbucking pickups with individual volume controls and a master tone, plus a three-way toggle switch. The pickups were patented with what was named 'dual wind' technology. Two bobbins were wound in a manner that meant if they were switched/tapped to single-coil mode, there would not be any hum.

The HP Signature's gold-plated hardware included a recessed intonatable bridge and a "Dual Compression tailpiece with individual string tubes." This system meant that strings could be loaded through brass ferrules/bushings on the rear of the body or through the tailpiece itself. The tailpiece was also recessed.

The January 2005 price list announced the addition of the HP Special Series. The CT USA and USA versions came in transparent or solid colors (the "CT USA" indicating "carved top," while the "USA" variant had a flat top). Like the EVH Wolfgang Special, it was a lesser-frills instrument with master volume and tone controls, and each model came with a high-tech vibrato or tune-a-matic bridge and stop tailpiece. The Special had a bolt-on maple neck that was installed on a basswood body with five bolts, and a large "scoop" was found on the back around the neck joint, to allow higher access to upper frets.

HP Special—figured maple top *Zinkif*

HP Special carved top

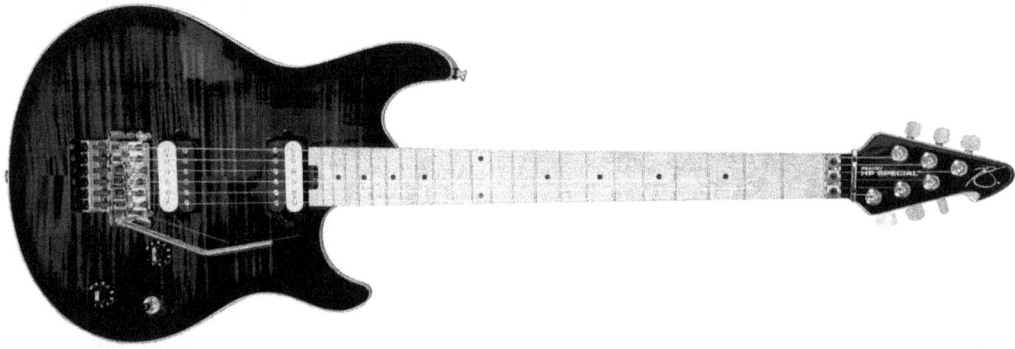

HP Special flat top

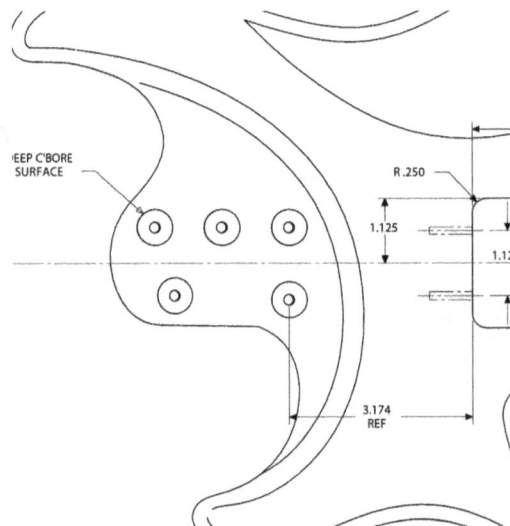

Line drawing of back of HP Special showing five-bolt neck attachment and "scoop"

A year later, the HP Signature Series offered a "Select" all-mahogany variant, at a much-lower price point.

HP Signature Select

Jim Beaugez remembers the switch from Wolfgangs to HP models as "…an exciting time. Hartley seemed energized about shaking things up and making some changes. One was the balance of the guitar. Hartley was in his element; he is a tinkerer at heart, and this was a new toy to tweak. We had a fresh marketing team that was ready to make a big splash with the guitars, too. It was a fun time. We invested a lot of marketing resources into the HP Series launch. We had a lot positive feedback from media, as well. *Guitar World* gave it their Platinum Award, for example."

"There's no question that the HP Series was developed to become our new flagship instrument," said Moscal, "since the Wolfgang wasn't going to be continued. Hartley decided that he was going to make the kind of high-end guitar he'd always wanted to make."

One HP series "guitar" is on permanent view on the Mississippi Gulf Coast—it's a 122-foot tall sign that was installed in front of the Hard Rock Casino and Hotel in 2005.

The sign was acquired through the direction of Gregg Giuffria, the erstwhile musician with whom David Sikes had gigged over two decades earlier. Giuffria was now a successful businessman in the gaming industry.

Peavey and some of the principals who were working with the design of the new facility negotiated a unique arrangement that included the installation of Peavey sound gear throughout the building.

"I told them that since it was a Hard Rock, if the sign was a Peavey guitar, I'd sell them the audio gear at just above our cost," said Hartley. "They hesitated, but we worked out a deal, and an outfit in Louisiana put [the sign] up."

"It was basically 'We'll pay for the sign if you use our gear'," Moscal said. 'We gave them a good deal, and they saved a lot of money."

"Shortly after it was installed, [Hurricane] Katrina came through," Hartley recalled. "The casino had been about a week or so from opening when Katrina hit, and since it's right on the beach, they had wave damage up to the fifth floor. But the sign actually survived, and the only reason it did was because it was edge-on to the wind."

And Hartley noted that he is prone to proclaiming that the gaming business landmark in Biloxi is his greatest erection.

Willie G. Moseley

The Jack Daniel's series of instruments were Tony Moscal's "baby," and would be the harbinger of other licensing deals for guitars and basses.

"We were approached by a licensing firm that represented Jack Daniel's," Moscal recalled. "They were also talking to an Asian company about making Jack Daniel's guitars, but we convinced them to go with an American company."

"Tony had a vision for the Peavey brand that saw it growing outside of traditional channels," Beaugez said. "He brought in brands that were likely to have crossover with our own market audience, and Jack Daniel's was one of them. The branding campaign started as a way to get our brand and products in the hands of more people. The guitar team designed new guitars, and the premium models were built in the USA Custom Shop."

The Jack Daniel's guitars were decorated with logos and filigrees from the distiller, and not surprisingly, Peavey amplifiers were made and marketed as well. The guitar lineup included a domestic guitar at the outset. It was hyped as having an "archtop body style w/unique cutaway & back heel contour at upper registers." Its body and neck construction were similar to the HP Signature model, but the Jack Daniel's model had 22 frets. The guitars were made in the Custom Shop, primarily by Litchfield and Pope. The Jack Daniels guitars were available in "Transparent Whiskey" and "Transparent Charcoal" finishes.

Jack Daniel's guitar—"Transparent Whiskey"

Jack Daniel's guitar—"Transparent Charcoal"

Underlining the collaboration was the fact that the control and selector switch covers, as well as the truss rod cover, were made from pieces of aged Jack Daniels whiskey barrels.

"We actually got the domestic Jack Daniel's products on the market before we got the imported products out there," Moscal recalled.

The next year, a Jack Daniel's bass had entered the lineup, and that instrument may have looked familiar to some observers. The bass had the same silhouette, scale and electronics configuration as the (discontinued) G-Bass, but its neck was maple instead of composite, and the rosewood fretboard had barrel wood dot inlays.

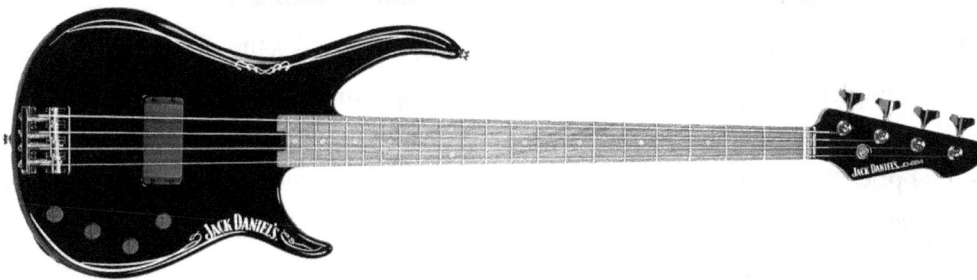

Jack Daniel's bass

The Jack Daniels licensing deal was still in operation as Peavey approached its fiftieth birthday.

And there was actually an American-made "Generation"—the model name having been revived—on the aforementioned mid-2004 price list. The Generation Custom USA w/ ACM (Analog Acoustic Modeling active circuitry) had three large vintage style pickups on an alder body with an all-pearloid top, and a bird's-eye maple fretboard. Its ACM circuitry was designed to emulate an acoustic guitar sound, and was designed in-house by Elon Coats.

Generation Custom USA

"I remember that one being a collaborative effort design wise between Mike, Tim, and me," said Pope. "We made three custom models with pearloid tops with P-90 pickups for the NAMM show—one white, one red, and one blue. They had chambered bodies with separate, glued-on tops."

The mid-2004 price list also included several imported Generation models, and the American-made version would be short-lived.

The Cropper Classic last appeared on a price list in 2005 (in one finish), listed in the "Generation Series" along with several imports. However, another American-made endorsement model was listed (with a "$TBA" price) immediately after the Steve Cropper signature model on the same price list.

The Omniac was the result of a collaboration between guitarist Jerry Donahue and Peavey's Custom Shop. Ed Pope was the luthier who worked closest with Donahue on a traditional-style instrument that was more versatile than it may have looked. Woods included a bound ash body and a one-piece bird's-eye maple neck. It featured pickups made by the Seymour Duncan company, with custom five-way switching. It also had a brass bridge.

Omniac *Heritage Auctions*

"My ace in the hole for the whole project was Ed Pope," said Pasko. "Ed is a great player in his own right, so he had no problem taking the specs we gave him, and he built the prototype Omniac that Jerry fell in love with. My whole goal for this guitar, and working with Jerry, was to get Peavey back into Nashville. The whole 'Eddie (Van Halen) era' put Peavey amps on rock stages, but lots of longtime supporters in country music felt like Peavey abandoned them, so we lost our foothold in Nashville. To address this push to get back into Nashville, Dave Ellefson hired Michael Spriggs, a top Nashville session guy, to be our Artist Relations contact. We set up an office at Sound Check [a Nashville rehearsal/storage facility], and with Michael's contacts we got in front of all the top Nashville players, but for him to be successful he needed the right gear, so I gave him the Omniac."

And the Omniac is indeed the model of which Pope is the most proud, concerning his design work.

"I worked with Jerry several months, sending him copies of body shapes and neck shapes, and the neck didn't have any lacquer," he recalled. "He'd send them back with suggestions and changes. We talked about pickups a lot too; it had a five-way switch, and a circuit design that used capacitors and resistors to get different sounds."

In addition to developing new guitars with artists, Pope and Litchfield continued to build unique instruments in R & D.

"I worked with Tim and Ed personally on the models that we sent to media for review," said Beaugez, "and the artist relations team worked closely with them, as well. We did promotional one-offs to generate publicity and interest in the new USA lines. For example, the HP Signature that had the *Guitar World* logo on the fretboard was featured on the cover and pullout poster of the *Guitar World Buyer's Guide*. Later, we did a one-of-a-kind 40th Anniversary HP Special for *Guitar Player*. All reports I personally heard were positive."

Another new Peavey bass series was announced on a January '05 price list was the Zodiak lineup, consisting of a four-string and five-string model that were to be made in America. Zodiaks were to have a retro-vibe look on an alder body with a maple neck, and a P/J pickup layout with two volume controls and a master tone knob. The price was "$TBA."

The U.S. Zodiak models ultimately didn't get off the ground, but Dave Ellefson then became involved with a signature model Zodiac bass (spelling now changed to a traditional name), and the prototype (built by Litchfield in the Custom Shop) was unique.

"Tim introduced me to the concepts of placing graphite rods under the fingerboard as a way to stabilize the neck," Ellefson said. "It was a genius idea that really worked! He also had an incredible pre-amp that he put in the Zodiac Scorpio DE prototype that he built for me in Meridian's custom shop. He said he only had one, and wouldn't be able to create another one due to time constraints. In the perfect world, all of my Zodiac signature basses would have had that preamp in them, because I really like active circuitry, and that system created a seamless transition into high output tone control, that made it virtually impossible to tell it was active. It had such a tremendous boost without coloring the tone and creating that often-annoying midrange scoop you get with most active circuitry. Tim's pre-amp was more like a power boost than a tone changer."

Ellefson also counted on Litchfield regarding the aesthetics of the instrument:

"Tim taught me a lot about the aesthetic balance of an instrument," he said, "and the importance of a headstock for identity, function, and tone. So, we opted for a large four-in-a-line headstock, which as always been a favorite of mine anyway. Because the instrument needed to be passive for price point concerns, we opted to keep it as a four-string rather than a five-string model."

"Tony Pasko suggested we hot-rod it with the Seymour Duncan line of pickups, even though I must say that Hartley has some of the best bass pickup technology in the business, especially his active pickups and circuitry. But, there was a concern for retail that an artist model should boost outsourced add-ons as a way to create features, benefits, and advantages above the standard product line. These items are most often found in add-ons like pickups, tuners, etc. I always liked the P-bass and J-bass pickup configurations; I think they look cool and offer the retail customer a useable variety of popular tones. So, we used the Seymour Duncan pickups in that configuration.

"From there, the one main aesthetic I wanted to create was the steel mirror pick guard. I'm a huge fan of bass guitars from the 1970s and the mirrored guard was my ode to Phil Lynott on the cover of the Thin Lizzy *Live & Dangerous* album. To me, that is a rock n' roll statement, and I think we created a truly unique bass with the Zodiac DE Scorpio."

The idea of a signature bass with Ellefson's involvement was unique, and was questioned.

"The attitude around Peavey at that time was that Dave was a Peavey employee and not in Megadeth, so why do a signature bass with him?" said Pasko. "But what I saw at every NAMM show we did was hundreds of kids asking Dave for his autograph, and he still was out playing and putting out music with his solo band, so I thought he was a smart first choice."

Ellefson's Zodiac prototype with active circuitry was the only instrument of its kind. It began with a neck that had a maple fretboard, but Ellefson later had a neck with an ebony fretboard installed. The production examples of Zodiac basses would be built in China.

David Ellefson with his prototype Zodiac bass (maple fretboard) *David Ellefson*

Ellfeson in concert with the same bass with a replacement neck (ebony fretboard) *David Ellefson*

One of Peavey's biggest pushes—ever—regarding domestic-made guitars also came in 2005, as the company introduced and promoted numerous models at open-to-the-public guitar shows as well as the first James Burton Guitar Festival, held in August of that year in Shreveport, Louisiana. The legendary guitarist, who backed Elvis Presley, Ricky Nelson, and others, put on a tour-de-force fundraising effort, and Peavey displayed its wares at a trade show as part of the festivities. Hartley, who had known Burton for years, attended the events.

A bronze statue of Burton was unveiled at the Shreveport Municipal Memorial Auditorium, an iconic venue where the likes of Presley, Hank Williams, and other musicians had performed on the "Louisiana Hayride" radio show. A statue of Presley was already on the premises, making the Burton statue even more appropriate.

An all-star concert at the Municipal Auditorium capped the weekend, and featured players like Brad Paisley, Steve Wariner, Eric Johnson, Steve Cropper (playing his signature Peavey guitar), Jeff Cook, Seymour Duncan, Jerry Donahue (playing a prototype Omniac), and others.

To what extent the James Burton International Guitar Festival may have epitomized Peavey's "last big push" regarding domestic guitar production is up for individual interpretation.

"I wouldn't say it was necessarily a 'push'," Moscal said. "It just happened that we had a lot of new products to promote."

Jim Beaugez had a different point of view, but agreed that Peavey was still fighting the good fight.

"In retrospect, I would agree with that sentiment," he said of the '05 effort being described as a 'push'. "It was an opportunity to show the guitar-playing world that Peavey was not only an innovator in musical instruments, but that it was committed to American craftsmanship."

And at the James Burton event, Hartley said that he had probably spent more money on making guitars in the last year than in any other time in company history.

P

In 2006, Peavey created a separate website for their Custom Shop, noting that they could just about anything a customer wanted on a particular model—woods, hardware, finishes, pickups, etc. The web site was the brainchild of Moscal, and orders still had to come through a Peavey authorized dealer.

Custom Shop ad for the Cirrus bass

And while www.peaveycustomshop.com won an industry "best of show" award, sales and production of domestic-made guitars and basses continued to decline.

Ellefson: "I clearly remember samples of various guitars—solid and semi-hollow models—continually showing up at Peavey's headquarters, and someone would put them in my hand, and ask me what I thought the cost of the instrument was. Sometimes they would be as low as $70, and the quality was not too shabby. To me, that told the entire story of the future of the guitar business.

"At the same time, I saw the pained look on Hartley's face as he saw what he called 'the race to the bottom' in China. Here was a man of principle who built his entire company, namesake, and reputation on building what he deemed "a quality product at a fair price" and he did it for 40 years all in the U.S.A. It was his badge of honor. But by 2002, the entire game changed, and everything from mixers to amplifiers, guitars to gadgets were all being made in China. I really felt for Hartley, because he had to make some very unpopular decisions about the fate of his company, and many of those decisions included taking manufacturing overseas."

And Litchfield and Pope continued to develop other prototypes of other artist signature models that, like the Zodiac, would be built overseas. Two latter-day prototype models were created by Pope for Josh Rand of Stone Sour and Mike Stone of Queensryche. Rand's guitar had a camouflage finish, while Stone's instrument had a unique body shape with traditional controls.

"The Josh Rand was basically an HP Special with camo, and a reverse headstock," Pope recalled. "The camo body was sent to a company that applied the camo 'wrap', then it was returned to us, where we sealed and completed the finish. We had to pay some kind of licensing fee to be able to use the digital camo. I remember making at least four Josh Rand models trying to get the camo finish acceptable."

Josh Rand with his signature model Peavey guitar in a camouflage finish

"Mike Stone already had the basic body shape design; I took that and made a 3-D model in Solidworks, a CAD [computer-aided design] program. Then I adjusted stuff like the neck pocket size and angle to make it work with production. The controls were a basic two volume, two tone configuration."

Mike Stone with his signature model guitar

Peavey had begun acquiring smaller, "boutique" companies such as the Budda and Trace Elliot amplifier lines. As the first decade of the new millennium came to a close, the company acquired a small guitar company next door in the Bayou State. Its product was its company name.

Pasko: "Composite Acoustic Guitars was a boutique brand based out of Louisiana, and Hartley loved the idea that the guitars were not wood. Hartley is always on the lookout for new technology, so this company was right up his alley. When we visited the original Composite factory, these guys were building guitars out of an old roller rink they had modified. It was pretty cool."

"I liked the idea that they were doing something new," Hartley recalled. "They're different, and they're high-priced."

After Peavey purchased Composite Acoustic, production of those instruments was switched to Meridian.

In 2008, Peavey discontinued the print version of *Monitor,* switching to an online site exclusively to promote its wares.

The imported guitars conundrum continued to confound Peavey and its founder, and the decision was eventually made to suspend domestic Peavey solidbody electric guitar production. Plant 2 shut its doors in the spring of 2010. The Composite Acoustics venture carried on.

"It seemed like it didn't matter what you did, people didn't really want innovation," Hartley reflected. "The things that we were so proud of—let's say the T-60's tone circuit—people didn't care. And it wasn't a tone control; it was a *mode* control. I couldn't get guitar players and dealers to understand the tone controls on the T-60 and other early models. *Everything* about that guitar was innovative.

"You've got to understand me—I don't want to do it like everybody else. I've always been someone who marches to a different drummer, and I want to do it a better way. But when you're trying to be different in a market that reveres *yesterday*, it's kind of a dichotomy, and you're obviously going to end up frustrated.

"I don't mean this to sound bitter—because I'm not—but putting all of these innovations into a guitar that people don't appreciate is kind of like casting pearls before swine. The Les Paul and the Strat are great guitars, but they're 50 or 60 years old, and they're still the same. The Les Paul's middle pickup position means that turning *either* volume control down means *both* pickups lose volume. That's insane.

"Most people in the guitar business have what I call a 'cow path mentality'. Cows go down the same path time after time, so what you have are hundreds and hundreds of 'Strat-o-copies' or 'Les Paul wannabees'. The frustrating thing is that guitar players keep going down the same kind of path. The guitar business also seems to have 'de-evolved' into a 'limbo dance'—'How low can you go without falling on your ass?' Most American guitar companies have fallen into that."

Beaugez's perspective on the end of domestic guitar production was eloquent and on-the-money: "No one applauded it, but most folks realized that market forces that were out of the company's control dictated how it needed to operate to remain viable so they could keep their own jobs. Hartley is a champion of innovation and change, but one thing he did not support was the music business's move to offshore-sourced products. First it was Japan, then Korea, and then China, and he resisted all of it until he couldn't anymore. He always preached that it could be done, but differently.

"Reference that popular 'Why?' guitar ad from the T-60 days. That's what has always kept him moving. If you tell Hartley that something can't be done, he'll roll up his sleeves and show you exactly how to do it. That has resulted in some failed experiences on the market, even with very good products. It's also resulted in the company's soaring successes.

"Eventually, though, Hartley couldn't compete profitably with the onslaught of offshore guitars anymore. And the quality of those instruments improved, too. He couldn't compete in what was an increasingly commodified market segment. They could import low-end guitars of decent quality for less money; people were choosing price over quality or origin. Ironically, the Peavey brand was founded on the principle of providing quality gear at a fair price. Hartley's commitment to protecting American jobs put him in a precarious spot, and you could argue that companies that weren't so interested in preserving a USA manufacturing base—those that had long since been bought and sold from their founders several times over, or were newcomers with no legacy to support—were beating him at his own strategy. But now they were playing by different rules."

"It was discussed for probably two years before it actually happened," Moscal said of the decision.

So, did Peavey employees in guitar production and the Custom Shop see any "handwriting on the wall" about the future of domestic-made Peaveys?

"Oh, absolutely," said Ed Pope. "I guess we rode it as far as we could, but we all saw it coming."

Key employees were assigned to other tasks and/or other divisions. Ed Pope was assigned to design engineering, and was still there as the 50th anniversary annum in 2015 was pending. Most of what he had been creating in a computer would be manufactured in China.

Tim Litchfield was the supervisor for the production of Composite Acoustic guitars.

"I used to love to go to Plant 2," Tony Moscal said wistfully, almost a half-decade after the facility had closed. "It was my favorite building to visit, because it was a combination of science and art."

CHAPTER 16

Coda

Dr. Hook and the Medicine Show finally made the cover of *Rolling Stone,* and Hartley still keeps in touch with George Cummings.

As of this writing, Cummings plays in the New Jersey area in a blues band called "Mudbelly." He still owns the old Les Paul Special that Hartley painted white, but no longer has the "loaner" Gibson lap steel.

"Like a fool, I gave it to the Hard Rock Café in Berlin in '96," Cummings said. "I have many lap steels now, but wish I still had the Gibson Hartley loaned me…that I forgot to give back to him. I have some old Gretsches and other guitars, but mostly, I'm playing the T-60 [Hartley] sent me in the late Seventies. It's a sturdy instrument."

George Cummings with his T-60 and Les Paul Special *George Cummings*

In recent times, Cummings actually contributed some input to Hartley regarding a modern-day Peavey steel guitar called the Powerslide©, which is played in a standing position. It happens to have the patented T-60-style coil-tap circuitry, albeit in a reverse configuration—fully-clockwise means that both coils are full blast.

Don Belfield is now deceased, as is his brother Bob. However, Don's devil-may-care attitude regarding transportation continued after he left the Peavey rep organization.

"Don left me and moved to Alaska, of all places," Hartley said. "His wife was a nurse, and she'd gotten some kind of job up there. Many years later, he called me and informed me he was in Fairhope, Alabama. He'd bought a sailboat, and had single-handedly sailed it from Alaska, through the Panama Canal, to Fairhope, and this was like in November or December—the middle of winter!"

In the ensuing decades since he left Fender, Chip Todd has been involved in other companies where his engineering skills paid off for him, and he presently builds electric guitars, based on T-60s, on the Texas Gulf Coast. Ever the sonic tinkerer, he has designed an electric bass with a guitar-like scale that he proclaims to have a full and resonant sound.

In 2003, Chip visited Hartley in Meridian, hauling an empty trailer. They visited an attic over one of the Peavey factories that had a lot of prototype/experimental bodies (many of which were inlaid or carved) and necks. Hartley offered to sell Todd most of the contents for $1500, which Chip considered to be too low, so he wrote Hartley a check for $2000, and hauled the items back to Texas.

Hartley and Chip in 2003 *Chip Todd*

"We've still got a bunch of that kind of stuff around, some of which was made by some incredibly talented people," Hartley said. "I just haven't had time to get in there and mess with it. It gets hot as hell up there in the summertime."

On April 29, 2013, Mike Powers, back from China, was at a Choctaw Indian casino in Philadelphia, about 40 miles north of Meridian, and dropped dead while playing a slot machine.

Fred Newell has concentrated on the steel guitar since the late Nineties, and is still in demand in Nashville. As of this writing, his present touring aggregation was Waymore's Outlaws, a band that featured Waylon Jennings' original drummer. He still uses Peavey amplifiers.

"I was a fan of Peavey equipment, and I still am to this day," Newell said. "Hartley has always had equipment that was affordable, and most of all, *reliable.* It's hard to beat that kind of reputation. Thanks to people like him, musicians are able to do what they do."

Mark Farner, now sporting a pacemaker, still performs regularly. He still uses Peavey gear, and still has his custom-made Mystic guitar.

"She's still with me; I call her 'Misty'," Farner said.

Rudy Sarzo is also an active musician, and in 2009, signed back up with Peavey on a Cirrus endorsement version bass, made in China. Acknowledging improvements in overseas manufacturing, he is as enthusiastic about the new version as he was about the original domestic model, pronouncing the Chinese variant to be "an incredible but affordable instrument."

Rudy Sarzo with his new Cirrus endorsement model

After the NASCAR guitar enterprise came to an end, Jeff Carlisi co-founded an all-star band called Big People with Liberty DeVitto (Billy Joel), Pat Travers, Derek St. Holmes (Ted Nugent), and Benjamin Orr (Cars). That aggregation played until Orr died from pancreatic cancer, and the members later became involved with another Jeff Carlisi-Dan Lipson enterprise called Camp Jam, which brought youngsters together for a week-long experience collaborating in a rock band. The camp was capped with a weekend concert. Carlisi was interviewed about the venture on "NBC Nightly News with Tom Brokaw."

Carlisi still stays active in the music business, going at his own pace. His most recent effort has been a partnership with multiple Grammy award-winning recording engineer Phil Tan, in a company called High-tone Talent. One of their recent projects has been the career development of singer Hallie Jackson.

And Jeff still has half a dozen Peavey Mace amplifier heads and his Generation S-1 guitar.

David Sikes departed from the full-time music business and opened a successful insurance company near San Francisco. As sort of a "weekend warrior," he still dabbles in live performances, and has gigged with the Doors' Robby Krieger and Alex Lifeson of Rush.

David Ellefson resigned from Peavey when Megadeth re-grouped in 2010.

"For me, it wasn't so much a learning curve as it was a lifestyle curve," Ellefson said of his Peavey experience.

"It was a tremendous transition for me, from the stages of Megadeth into the offices of Artist Relations, but one that I think I was uniquely cut out for, and it happened at a time when Peavey really needed it to bolster their artist presence. The music business is all about relationships, and being in Artist Relations for Peavey was, in many ways, a very natural fit for me."

"Plus, it helped me understand global marketing and manufacturing, and it also enabled me to finish up my college Bachelor's degree in Business and Marketing while working for the company. I forged relationships with so many great companies and salesmen around the world that I really felt like my horizons as a businessman were largely enhanced. I hope the same is true for Peavey."

Jim Roberts moved from *Bass Player* to the alumni magazine of his alma mater, Cornell University, and retired in 2014.

"It's too bad," he said of Peavey's decision to suspend domestic production of traditional solidbody electric guitars and basses. "They did some great work, both in building solid instruments for working musicians, and in pushing the envelope with instruments like the B-Quad and the Midibase/CyberBass. I'd be glad to see them get back in the game. As Hartley said to me back in 1994, 'It's crazy guys like me who change things and make 'em better.' The music industry needs more of that — there's too much imitation and not enough innovation."

Plant 2 still sat idle as Peavey's fiftieth anniversary year approached.

The company was still developing artwork licensing (imported) guitars in a phenomenally successful effort. Recent licensed series included *Star Wars* and *Spiderman* instruments.

"Hartley doesn't shy away from an opportunity," Tony Moscal said succinctly.

If and when Peavey Electronics Corporation decides to re-enter the American guitar manufacturing business, they have the appropriate facilities in Meridian. However, the company's founder is a realist and a pragmatist, for legitimate business reasons.

"I can always do it," Hartley said, "but the reality is 'Why should I?' If the market wants the same ol' ****, with 1001 variations on a sixty-year-old theme, they can have at it. If you go to a NAMM show, 99% of what you see from guitar makers is the same old stuff. Thank God it isn't that way with amplification, although some of these so-called 'boutique amplifier' guys are charging ridiculous prices to make something that is supposed to replicate an antiquated circuit from the Fifties."

Not surprisingly, however, Hartley still maintains a keen interest in electronics and guitars, even if his company isn't making solidbody/wooden instruments domestically anymore (and he is quite proud of his Composite Acoustic line).

He delights in copying magazine articles (old and new) and other documents to send to friends and business acquaintances.

In recent times, he's distributed a copy of an 1890 patent for an electric guitar filed by an inventor named George Breed, as well as a Photoshopped image of Albert Einstein with a Peavey Razer guitar (T-Model Ford was the actual player onto whose body Einstein's head was "transplanted" in the image).

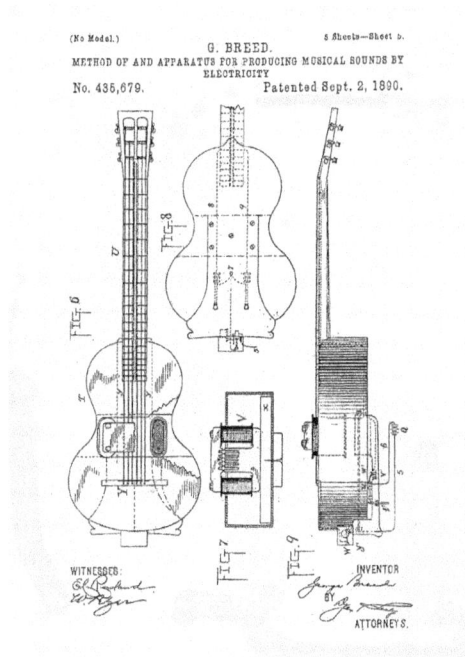

George Breed's 1890 electric guitar patent

Hartley was also philosophical (and plain-spoken) about his company's history as the 50th anniversary approached:

"We've had some 14,000 employees come and go over the decades," he said, "in a town with a population of about 35,000. There's hardly a family—not just in Meridian, but in this part of the world, including surrounding counties, and even in Alabama—that hasn't had someone who's worked here. We've got one guy who drives 85 miles every day, to and from Peavey."

"The one regret I have about my career is that I've always done what most musicians say they want, but most of my competitors have taken advantage of a lot of musicians, because there are people who believe, in their heart of hearts, that the *more* you *pay*, the *more* you *get*. And they assume you can judge something by how

233

much it costs. I like to believe that my customers have a little bit between their ears, and when I've found out that sometimes that's not the case, like with guitars, it's been disappointing. The irony is that when you give them a fair price, they don't believe it, because *everybody else is ripping them off!*"

Hartley also still took immense pride in his manufacturing innovations and accomplishments, regarding his still-vibrant, still-valid drive to maintain his original "quality equipment for working musicians at fair prices" credo.

"My father, having been in retail, was invaluable," he said emphatically. "He always told me, 'Son, if you make a good product at a fair and reasonable price, you'll always have customers.'

"I never assumed that because I made a great guitar and sold it with a case for less than $400, some people would think it was a lesser instrument. And for musicians, to think you can judge the quality, the playability, and reliability by price alone is very, very naïve. To accept that 'you-get-what-you-pay-for' premise 100% of the time, you must assume that *all the other factors* that go into producing a guitar are the *same*, and *all companies are the same!* That's absurd! They're not. But I have something a lot of my friendly competitors don't have, and that's *integrity*.

"We were not trying to make 'our version' of something else," he said Peavey guitars, "and we did it a better way."

Hartley paused.

"We've made a difference," he said quietly, almost as if he was talking to himself.

Among the autographed photos on display in the Peavey museum is one of Mark Farner with his custom-made Mystic guitar, taken when he had received the instrument in the mid-Eighties. Included with his signature is a notation that the Peavey company made "the best gear in the world."

"I didn't say it because I had an endorsement," Farner recalled nearly a third of a century later. "I said it because I believed it."

CHAPTER 17
Rarities and collectibles

Here's the bottom line up front (and to some extent, it should be obvious): Hartley Peavey will declare straight-out that he didn't get into the guitar-building business in the mid-Seventies in order to make future collector's items.

That being said, there are those guitar lovers who genuinely appreciate what Peavey was trying to accomplish at various times in the company's guitar-making history. Hartley has stated that he's heard that some of the earlier T-60s are becoming interesting as "collectible guitars."

But there are also the numerous one-of-a-kind guitars that came out of Peavey's R & D shop over the decades, as well as latter-day Custom Shop instruments.

The two early T-60s with walnut bodies and rear-load controls made for Hartley and Chip Todd are exemplary as primeval Peavey rarities. A similar bass, which had a mineral wood body (naturally-stained ash) and rear-load controls, was made for Peavey's U.K. associate Ken Achard (who later became an author) in 1980.

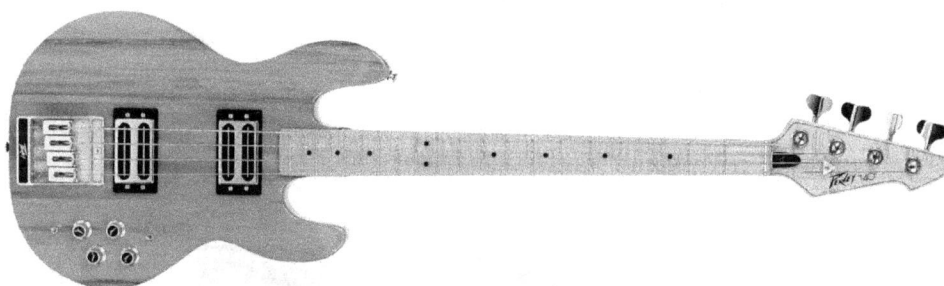

Ken Achard's rear-load T-40 bass

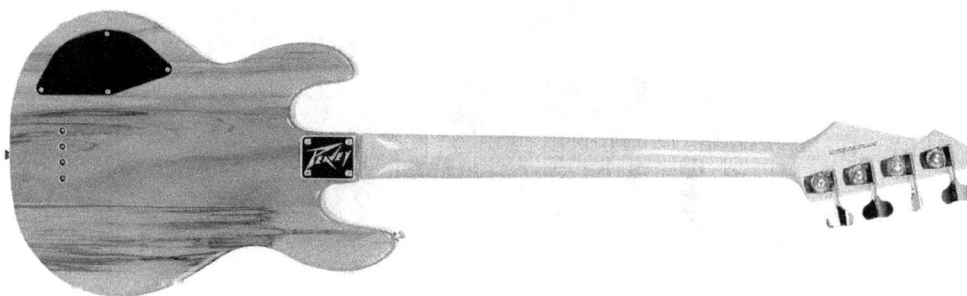

Rear view of Achard's custom T-40

Obviously, many rare Peavey guitars were made for specific artists and/or for specific reasons.

Leon Medica of LeRoux was the recipient of more than one custom-finished Peavey bass, including an all-black T-20 (including hardware), and a bass that was painted in a camouflage color for an overseas USO tour with an all-star band that included members of Cheap Trick, Kansas, and Pablo Cruise.

Medica's custom-made basses included an all-black T-20—*laleroux.com*

...and a bass with a camouflage paint scheme.

"When I got to Okinawa, a friend of mine was a Marine who was stationed there, and I gave it to him and some of his friends," the bassist recalled. "They camouflaged it in Marine colors with Marine paint! So it actually had two different camouflage finishes."

Medica is still a fan of Peavey instruments, and over 30 years after he took the stage with early T-model basses, he still had a large Peavey amplifier in his office in Nashville, as well as a white Dyna-Bass from the mid-Eighties, and his custom-made all-black T-20, which hadn't been modified.

"I would never do that if a company gave me something," Medica insisted. "It was just an honor for me to be asked to work with them. I worked with different staff members at Peavey at different times, but our relationship was always excellent, and that's because of the character of the people there. They really listened to what you said."

One of the earliest fully-custom-made Peavey instruments was one of the most radical. Exploiting an endorsement connection with bassist Ross Vallory of Journey, Peavey crafted an unusual doubleneck solidbody electric guitar for Journey guitarist Neal Schon that had a twelve-string mandolin and a guitar neck. The angular body was a one-off, unique shape, and its silhouette was not interpolated into future production models.

Neal Schon's early Peavey doubleneck *Willie G. Moseley*

Schon onstage

Mark Farner had originally gotten familiar with Peavey amplifiers, and had a stereotypical attitude about the brand's value.

"My friends and I thought that Peavey was good, American-made equipment at a price about any serious musician could afford," he recalled. "It wasn't until later years when I became a Peavey endorsee and got to know Hartley that I had the full inspiration of what this man was all about."

When Farner heard about Peavey's plans to build guitars and basses, he was intrigued, and he would get a special guitar of his own from the company ca. 1983.

"When I found out Peavey was making guitars, I immediately wanted one!" he said. "I had many musician friends who had the early Peavey guitars; they were workhorse guitars for a lot of club musicians who couldn't afford to go out and buy what was most popular. I had an early bass that I wish I would have never parted with. It was very light for a bass, and had a deep bottom end."

When Grand Funk Railroad reunited in the early Eighties (with a different bass player), Mark began using Peavey amps ("We were really impressed that we could get our sound out of them, and that they were tube amps with *balls!*"), and the guitarist also received a specially-built Mystic guitar from the company, which had three single-coil pickups (instead of the standard model's two humbuckers), active electronics, and custom switching.

"It was a spin off of their 'Mystic' guitar design," he recounted, "but with my preference for active electronics, which were designed for me by Jim Fackert from CAE [Custom Audio Electronics], who made and ran Grand Funk's first sound system. The three toggle switches in the bottom horn were three-position to access out of phase and other configurations—your choice—and with the volume attenuator stacked inside the tone control, it was super-fast acquisition."

**Early Eighties: Farner mugs with his custom-made
Mystic in an outtake from a photo session**

And unlike some endorsers of certain guitar brands and models, Farner used his special Mystic extensively.

"That guitar not only saw a ton of Grand Funk Railroad dates, it was used in the infamous [1985] Guitar Army show for Viet Nam vets at Harpo's in Detroit—Dick Wagner, Rob Tyner, Randy California, Brian Pastoria, Scott Morgan, Doug Podell from the [Detroit] Wheels. They were impressed with the look of it, until their ears took over and then they were *really* impressed!"

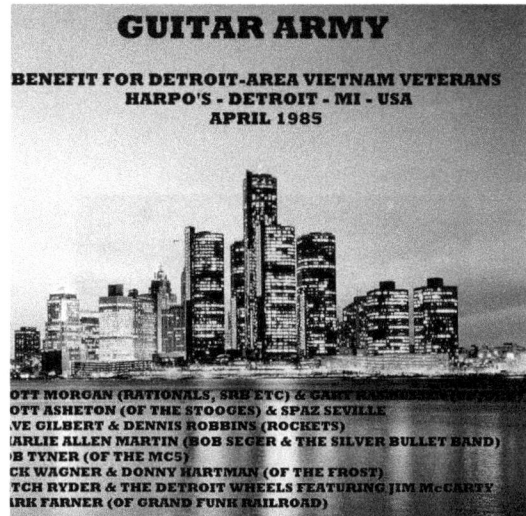

GUITAR ARMY

BENEFIT FOR DETROIT-AREA VIETNAM VETERANS
HARPO'S - DETROIT - MI - USA
APRIL 1985

OTT MORGAN (RATIONALS, SRB ETC) & GARY RASMUSSEN
OTT ASHETON (OF THE STOOGES) & SPAZ SEVILLE
VE GILBERT & DENNIS ROBBINS (ROCKETS)
ARLIE ALLEN MARTIN (BOB SEGER & THE SILVER BULLET BAND)
B TYNER (OF THE MC5)
CK WAGNER & DONNY HARTMAN (OF THE FROST)
TCH RYDER & THE DETROIT WHEELS FEATURING JIM McCARTY
ARK FARNER (OF GRAND FUNK RAILROAD)

Farner recalled that his favorite setting on the guitar was the neck and bridge pickups in phase.

"That configuration is very friendly to my stomp boxes, and I got the most out of her," the veteran guitarist said.

Stone-faced bassist Mario Cippolina of Huey Lewis & the News endorsed Peavey basses, and appeared in an mid-Eighties ad sporting a custom instrument based on the Foundation/Dyna-Bass silhouette. It had a unique cherry sunburst finish, a bound headstock, and four knobs.

Unique doubleneck instruments were also crafted by Peavey luthiers. In the mid-Eighties, Peavey's R & D department built at least two (and perhaps more) special Hydras with two six-string necks (for different tunings) and rosewood fingerboards. One would be seen onstage in the hands of guitarist Barry "Byrd" Burton

(1946-2008), who used the instrument during his tenure with singer/songwriter Dan Fogelberg. Burton had previously been a member of the Amazing Rhythm Aces, a country rock band that charted with hits such as "Third Rate Romance" and "The End Is Not In Sight."

Barry "Byrd" Burton onstage with his double-six Hydra. *Roy Rogers*

The other (documented) double-six—originally a black finish, and now in a twelve/six configuration—has had an interesting history. It belongs to Jeff Carlisi, who had originally ordered it from Peavey as a double-six, with one neck to be tuned standard and the other to be tuned in Open E, for slide. It was intended to be used in concert on "What's It To Ya," a song from .38 Special's 1988 album *Rock and Roll Strategy.*

"We were going to play it live," Carlisi said of the song, "and I told Peavey I needed something where I could just hit a switch and go to another neck for the slide solo. I ordered rosewood fretboards, as well. It was a big guitar, of course, and it had a gigantic flight case."

As it turned out, his double-six Hydra appeared onstage for that tune on one occasion only, after which the decision was made by another band member that the song would be dropped, according to Carlisi.

"The guitar was fine," he detailed. "It played great, and sounded great. But that happened at the beginning of the tour, and it wasn't used any more on the tour. When we got off the road, the guitar went to the warehouse."

The Hydra stayed in storage for several years, and Carlisi ultimately sent it back to Peavey to have a twelve-string neck installed, a la the original design configuration.

The custom flame paint job would also happen later, as a side project to the NASCAR painted Reactor guitars venture.

Carlisi sent his Hydra doubleneck guitar—now in a twelve/six configuration instead of its original special order double-six look—to Wayne Jarrett for a custom paint job of its own.

"Wayne was telling me about a new kind of translucent paint that he had," Jeff remembered. "He said, 'I do flames on motorcycles where you can see through the flame layers'. I was intrigued by that, and I said 'Hey, I've got a big plank of wood!'"

240

The guitarist delivered the instrument to Jarrett, who painted flames on the front, and an image of "Droopy Dog" on the back (Carlisi is known among peers and friends for his impersonation of that cartoon character).

Jeff Carlisi's custom- painted Hydra *J. Kovach*

Back view, showing the Droopy Dog cartoon *J. Kovach*

Peavey's R & D department custom-made a Falcon with a reverse-headstock known as the "Jeff Cook Hummingbird Special" that was played at one of Alabama's "June Jam" concerts, and was later auctioned off for charity. Other similar guitars were reportedly made for Cook for other events and concerts, including other June Jams.

One unique guitar that was based on a G-90/G-Ninety was a natural-finished oddity that the R & D section made for speedster player Jason Becker in 1991. At the time, Becker had been playing behind David Lee Roth, having joined the ex-Van Halen singer's band (replacing Steve Vai) in 1989, at the age of 20.

Becker's Peavey guitar had an ash body with a transparent satin finish in natural. The size of the forearm and belly cut contouring was increased, as was the treble cutaway, to allow access to higher notes. The neck was maple, also in a satin finish, and had a special shape and larger radius for a more traditional feel. Interestingly, the fretboard markers were the most eye-catching items on the instruments—they were large, colorful numbers that were placed on the corresponding fret.

Pickups were laid out in a humbucker/single-coil/humbucker style. The exposed pickup bobbins were also in various colors, and the plastic tips of the tuning keys were bright red.

The text in a sidebar article on Becker's guitar in the Spring 1991 issue of *Monitor* was on the money in its summary:

Result: A totally functional, high performance instrument. Mechanically and electronically straightforward with that natural "woody" appearance; but cosmetically unique (yet functional) and totally unlike any other guitar available anywhere.

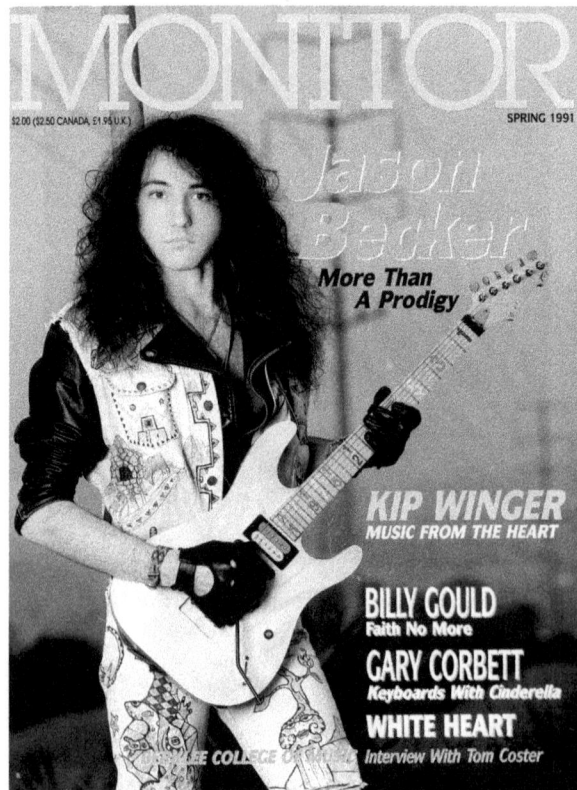

**Jason Becker and his custom guitar were featured as
the cover story in the Spring 1991 issue of *Monitor***

Sadly, Becker was unable to enjoy his instrument for long. Soon after his profile ran in *Monitor*, it was revealed that the talented guitarist had been stricken with amyotrophic lateral sclerosis (a.k.a. A.L.S, a.k.a. "Lou

Gehrig's Disease"). An issue of *Monitor* published later in 1991 would note a benefit concert for Becker that other guitarists had staged.

$\mathcal{F}$

In 1992, Peavey's R & D luthiers created two Generation-based instruments for guitarist Earl Slick, best known for his work with David Bowie. One had a bright red body with binding, a hardtail bridge, and a small pearloid/"mother-of-toilet-seat" pickguard. The guitar also had chrome hardware, and two DiMarzio pickups. The other had a black body with binding and a pearloid pickguard, with three pickups and a vibrato. The maple necks on the instruments had a oiled finish (no lacquer). Slick used the red custom Generation extensively on a 2000 live album called *Bowie at the Beeb*.

Earl Slick with one of his Generation-based custom guitars

$\mathcal{F}$

And in the early Nineties, Peavey also offered to make a custom instrument for Boston's David Sikes, albeit a one-of-a-kind bass instead of a signature/production model (Sikes noted, however, that the company had considered the possibility of turning it into a production bass).

"I jumped at the chance," the bassist remembered, "and was rewarded with a bass that is probably my favorite out of all the instruments I own."

Sikes envisioned his special five-string bass as a "best-of" type of instrument with favorites features he liked on other brands and models.

"I believe it was based on the Tim Landers model," he said. "I was playing one at the time, and liked the feel of it."

The custom bass also had its own unique aesthetics and construction, such as the five-tuners-on-one-side headstock (Most standard Peavey five-string basses had begun with four-plus-one headstock, and later changed to a three-plus-two configuration).

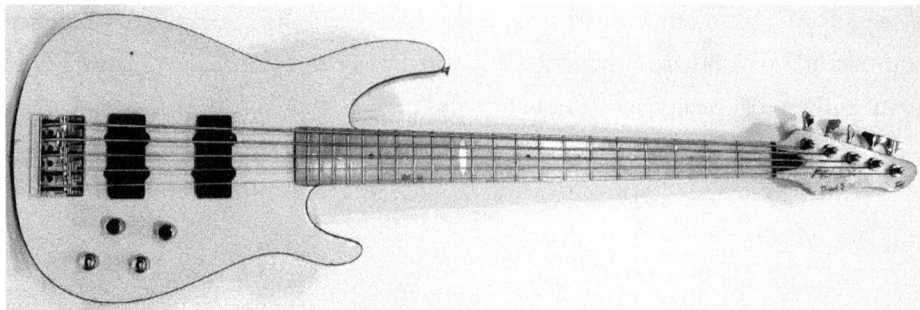

David Sikes custom-made five-string bass *David Sikes*

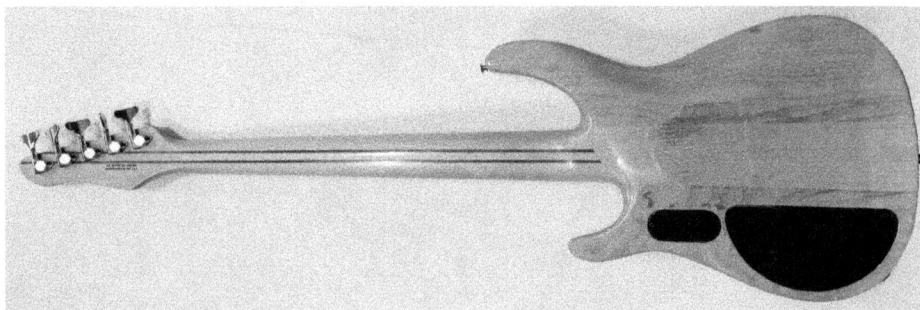

rear view of Sikes bass *David Sikes*

five-in-a-row tuners on headstock *David Sikes*

"I requested the five-in-line tuners, which were made by Gotoh," he said. "I remember it was a bit of a challenge for them, because they had to find tuners that had a small enough 'footprint' to fit."

Jim DeCola recalled that the body shape evolved to balance better with the five-on-a-side headstock. The top horn was extended for balance, and the bottom cutaway was deepened to provice access to the highest frets.

The maple fretboard has pearl inlay, and a silhouette of the Boston logo (a guitar-shaped spaceship) is found on the twelfth fret. That image was a pleasant surprise for Sikes.

Twelfth fret inlay

The body is swamp ash, and is bound in black on the top edge.

As for the electronics, Sikes recounted that he didn't ask for anything special.

"I really liked the sound of the TL bass, so I was happy with their stock pickups," he recalled.

The controls were influenced by a Dyna-Bass layout.

"The large control knobs are volume and blend of the two pickups," Sikes said, "like a pan control on a mixer. The smaller controls are stacked knobs; forward toward the neck is a bass and treble control, and the rear stacked control is a midrange parametric with frequency selection and attenuation plus-or-minus."

Sikes was gratified and delighted with the finished product.

"I loved the bass from the moment I received it," he enthused. "The weight is lighter than many of my instruments, and the playing is excellent, with a flat radius neck that fits my hands. I used it on the *Walk On* album, and on tours in 1995 and 1997. It is my go-to instrument to this day."

Even though his livelihood is no longer music, and he's able to play at his own pace, Sikes is bemused by the reaction of some observers when they discover that his instrument was made by Peavey.

"I have had a lot of compliments about this bass," he detailed. "Guys come up to me all the time and say 'Your bass sounds incredible.' They ask me what it is, and almost always, I seem them with an astonished look when I tell them it is a Peavey bass."

The veteran bassist also sided with Peavey regarding any historical stereotyping about the company's products,

"Peaveys have a reputation with many that they are average or even less-than-average instruments," Sikes opined. "It's really a shame [that] they have not been appreciated for what they are. I think this probably comes from the first instruments they made, which were not held as being worthy instruments by many, myself included. Peavey was a great company to have a relationship with. I found everyone, including Hartley himself, to be very likeable people with a sincere desire to understand what turned us on about our gear."

The EVH Wolfgang series offered numerous examples of one-of-a-kind or minimal quantity instruments.

Of the three-quarter-size EVH Wolfgangs, only about ten were made, and most of those reportedly went to Edward Van Halen himself.

Perhaps the preeminent collector of higher-end Peavey guitars is Geoff Knapp of California, who actually became an online dealer because of his respect for the instruments. Moreover, he eschews the application of the term "collection" to his assemblage of instruments.

"I really don't consider myself a current collector of guitars," he said, "which sounds odd given how many I have. My collection is really the result of 'opportunity' rather than an interest in collecting guitars. It is a very focused collection, and to me, it is really as much of an art collection as a guitar collection."

Knapp's interest first zeroed in on EVH Wolfgangs, and later, HP Specials. He bought his first instrument on behalf of another family member.

"My first Wolfgang was a stop tail, flame archtop that I bought on eBay," he recounted. "I was actually looking for a guitar for my daughter who wanted to learn to play. She was about 16 at the time. That was when I became intrigued with that guitar. Then, I picked up a first-year Quilt Top, and when the Custom Shop opened, I found a dealer who handled my orders and sold them to me at a little over cost. Many of my most interesting Wolfgangs would later be purchased directly from current and former Peavey employees, and referrals from people who learned about me from my website."

Knapp was attracted to Peavey's high-end guitars because of "…the feel, the artistic quality, and a tone that matched the music I liked most. I was very intrigued by what you could get for the money, and the quality of the product. There was also an artistic license there to build whatever you could think up within the parameters of what they were willing to do. And I often got them to stretch that a little, as well."

Knapp became a dealer himself after the EVH Wolfgang was discontinued, and purchased some of the remaining inventory. He later marketed HP Specials, and estimated that 1/3 of his EVH Wolfgangs and almost all of his HP Specials were custom-made to his own specifications.

The Peavey guitar enthusiast also had fond memories of Custom Shop personnel.

"There were only a few guys that made up the Custom Shop at any one time," Knapp recalled, "and they were always great to work with. They had complete passion for the guitars and were willing to do anything if they could fit it within the system at Peavey. They also all seemed to love working at Peavey. They loved trying new things with the guitars. Since my website was essentially a tribute to their great work, they seemed happy to work with me. Even to this day they are able to use the site to show people the cool guitars they created."

Panorama view of part of Knapp's Peavey guitar assemblage *Geoff Knapp*

Another view of instruments in the Knapp collection *Geoff Knapp*

EVH Wolfgang with flame graphics *Geoff Knapp*

Rarities among Knapp's collection include two hollowbody EVH Wolfgangs, made as experimental instruments by the Custom Shop. A sunburst prototype guitar with a bolt-on neck and f-holes shaped like the "F" in "Wolfgang" came first. It had a quilted maple top and back, an ebony fretboard with no inlay, and a matching headstock. Two later examples made by the Custom Shop had flame maple bodies with traditional f-holes, and mahogany set-in necks. The ebony fretboards had pearl dot markers. Knapp owns the original sunburst example and one of the two later prototypes.

EVH Wolfgang hollowbody, bolt-on neck *Geoff Knapp*

EVH Wolfgang hollowbody, set-in neck *Geoff Knapp*

Note the guitar outlines in Knapp's skylight *Geoff Knapp*

Another unique example is the "Luna De Fuego" EVH Wolfgang guitar.

"I am not really into paintings on guitars," Knapp detailed, but I have a lithograph of a painting by Manuel Nunez called "Luna De Fuego" that I really like, and I thought the image would lend itself to a guitar.

"Luna de Fuego" painting by Manuel Nunez *Wikipedia*

"So I ordered it through Peavey, talking directly to the artist, John Douglas, about doing a partial copy of it for me on the guitar. In order to enhance the art and make it a unique guitar, I had it built with only a bridge pickup. This provided more 'real estate' for the art, and eliminated the need for a toggle switch. Since it is a Special, there is also no tone knob, so the only control is a volume knob. It has pearl bar inlays and an ebony fretboard. The body is basswood, and it *does* have a maple top. It is a great guitar, and great art as well."

The "Luna de Fuego" EVH Wolfgang *Geoff Knapp*

In spite of the closure of the Custom Shop and other guitar-making facilities in Meridian, Geoff Knapp plans on leaving his tribute site online, and he still buys and sells instruments.

"I regularly get e-mails to this day, from all over the world from people who have questions about the Peavey Wolfgang and HP Specials, or who have just discovered them," he said. "I leave the site up as a reference for these people. That's been one of the fun things about this adventure—talking to people all over the world about something we have in common. I really enjoyed working with the people at Peavey as well."

"These guitars have never gotten their due because so many people assume that Peavey doesn't or can't make this kind of very-high-quality, custom guitar so they have never tried them," Knapp insisted. "As a point of reference, I would put them up against the top of the line PRS (Paul Reed Smith) guitars any day. And because they are relatively unknown, the HP Specials have never developed much of an aftermarket, and you can thus buy them fairly inexpensively."

Bumblebee inlay on a HP Special fretboard *Geoff Knapp*

"There is a collector value to this instrument now," Peavey rep Roy Rogers said of the EVH Wolfgang, "and they have held up well. I still have three of them."

Quilt-top EVH Wolfgang with wolf's head inlay
(Knapp doesn't own this one) *Heritage Auctions*

Rogers also believes that many Peavey guitar and bass models are still excellent values, even if they're not considered to be so-called collector's items.

"All of the U.S.-made instruments were undervalued," he insisted. "The Cirrus, Wolfies, the Generation, the T-60…even the U.S. Predators were under priced."

In the waning days of domestic guitar production, Peavey's Custom Shop still made prototypes and one-offs. A five-string Zodiac bass, finished in what Dave Ellefson called "battleship gray," was also made in the Custom Shop. It was never intended to be a production instrument, and was made for Ellefson's personal use.

ℙ

Another facet to Peavey's "working musician" approach to guitarmaking was a, er, casual concern about serial numbers and/or dating the production of instruments, since the founder and his company wanted to make utilitarian/"Everyman" instruments.

In fact, the numbers embossed on the back of Peavey guitar headstocks are technically shipping numbers, but it stands to reason that an instrument would most likely have been made a few weeks—max—before it was shipped.

A very generalized list of Peavey guitar shipping numbers from 1978-1995 has been circulating online in recent times, and reads as follows, with the first four digits being cited for early and late examples shipped in each year:

- 8Mxxxxxx 1978
- 0000xxxx t/m 0030xxxx 1978
- 0031xxxx t/m 0047xxxx 1979
- 0048xxxx t/m 0065xxxx 1980
- 0066xxxx t/m 0099xxxx 1981
- 0100xxxx t/m 0129xxxx 1982
- 0130xxxx t/m 0169xxxx 1983
- 0170xxxx t/m 0199xxxx 1984
- 0200xxxx t/m 0239xxxx 1985
- 0240xxxx t/m 0259xxxx 1986
- 0260xxxx t/m 0339xxxx 1987
- 0340xxxx t/m 0359xxxx 1988
- 0360xxxx t/m 0419xxxx 1989
- 0420xxxx t/m 0439xxxx 1990
- 0440xxxx t/m 0519xxxx 1991
- 0520xxxx t/m 0599xxxx 1992
- 0600xxxx t/m 0639xxxx 1993
- 0640xxxx t/m 0769xxxx 1994
- 0770xxxx >>...1995

ℙ

While latter-day Custom Shop EVH Wolfgangs and HP instruments might be among the rarest higher-end Peavey collectibles, Peavey's R & D department was always experimenting, so oddities such as the early Neal Schon doubleneck were always being created. And as the recollections of Hartley and Chip in the previous chapter aver, there are still numerous one-of-a-kind bodies, necks and other parts in storage in Meridian. Whether they'll ever see the light of day as complete instruments remains to be seen.

CHAPTER 18
Outro and acknowledgements

"The john's down the hall, on the right," Hartley Peavey said suddenly, a bemused look on his face.

I must have been fidgeting. Perhaps there have been times where an interview with someone who is as formidable as Hartley has affected my excretory system in that manner.

When interviewing someone who is alleged to have a, uh, strong personality, there can be a fine line between intensity and intimidation, but I don't think I've never crossed it (having survived interviews with Lemmy and Ted Nugent more than once). My style is straight-forward (without coming across as some snotty provocateur, as is often the case in journalism these days), and a lot of preparation also figures into the mix. That being said, any dialogue with Hartley—be it an interview or simple conversation—is also going to be straight-forward; i.e., genuine plain speaking by the redoubtable Mississippi Maverick means you don't get "Hartley Lite."

But I've found that even guys with so-called tough reputations will give you a decent interview if you do your homework in advance, and that's what I've always tried to do when going on-the-record with Hartley.

But that doesn't mean I don't get, er, subliminally worked up about such dialogues.

The incident regarding restroom directions occurred in 1993, during my first interview with Hartley at his Meridian headquarters, on 'A' Street (the new office/tech center hadn't been built yet). I'd already interviewed other legends and captains of industry in the guitar-manufacturing field (some of whom were retired), but Hartley had the largest facilities, and his operation was located in the Deep South, of all places.

Conversing with Hartley has always been an education of sorts. A few of his answers reflect his corporate cosmology (as would be expected from in his position…and from someone who's as busy as he is), but he'll also stick to his guns if he has an opinion about something, because he's always got a strong command of the facts to back up such opinions.

And Peavey Electronics Corporation has always been privately owned, by one owner. Hartley rightfully inquires about how many other major sound reinforcement equipment and/or instrument manufacturers could make the same claim after having been in business for half a century.

And it boggles the mind to take note of the umpteen awards—industry and humanitarian—that the company, Hartley, and others have won. Numerous shelves and display areas in Peavey's headquarters are crammed full of so many cut-glass or gold-plated items with engraved citations on them that perusing the inventory of honors would take hours.

First and foremost, I'd like to thank my wife, Gail, for her perpetual patience and understanding whenever I take on a new book project. Peavey's fiftieth anniversary year also happens to be our thirtieth anniversary year.

I was profoundly grateful that Hartley took the time to sit down with me one-on-one on numerous occasions, to detail the chronology of his company's guitar history.

Conversations with other current or retired or former Peavey employees were also revelatory and very much appreciated, as were the diligent efforts of the folks in Meridian to supply me with a plethora of product information and images.

Ditto the professional musicians who contributed to this effort. Their enthusiasm for Peavey's products validated Hartley's "quality equipment for working musicians at fair prices" credo in spades.

Here's a tip of the headstock to businesses and individuals who contributed photos and/or allowed me to take photos of their instruments. A particular nod goes to Steve at www.vintaxe.com for the plethora of hi-res catalog images.

Thanks also to Neil White and his associates at Nautilus for their willingness to help profile the guitar making efforts of one of their state's industrial icons.

And of course, I'd like to offer, once again, a "read-between-the-lines" salute to the Messrs. Spilman for their ongoing encouragement regarding my writing career. Such recognition will continue until the devil goes ice skating.

One particular notion that validated why I opted to write this book involved citing Peavey guitars and basses as the "Ford trucks of the electric stringed instrument business." No one with whom I broached that analogy—not even numerous employees at Peavey Electronics Corporation—disagreed with such a comparison.

Peavey's half-century mark is the annum in which this book is slated to be released, and as noted in the chronology, Hartley has legitimate business reasons to continue to stay out of domestic guitar production. However, his company is still extraordinarily innovative and viable, and is a definitive example of an American business success story.

Perhaps the best way to sum up the legacy of Hartley Peavey's company is to recall a quote of his from that first interview, now over 22 years old as of this writing:

"Every once in a while someone will still say something like 'You know, Peavey, you build great stuff.' Then they'll add: 'For the money.' Well, bull****. We build good stuff and it holds up. It represents *value*."

It shows.

—W.G.M.

BIBLEOGRAPHY AND PERIODICAL REFERENCES

BOOKS:

Achard, Ken. *The Peavey Revolution—Hartley Peavey, the Gear, the Company, and the All-American Success Story.* San Francisco: Backbeat Books, 2005

Moseley, Willie G. *Guitar People.* Bismarck, North Dakota: Vintage Guitar Books, 1997

Roberts, Jim. *American Basses: An Illustrated History and Player's Guide to the Bass Guitar.* San Francisco: Backbeat Books, 2003

Wheeler, Tom. *American Guitars—An Illustrated History (Revised and Updated Edition).* New York, New York: HarperCollins Publishers, 1992

Wright, Michael. *Guitar Stories, Volume One.* Bismarck, North Dakota: Vintage Guitar Books, 1995

PERIODICALS

Vintage Guitar Magazine issues (chronological order): December 1993, January 1994, January 2001, June 2003, October 2006, October 2007, October 2008, June 2011, December 2011, September 2012

Monitor magazine issues (chronological order): Fall 1982 (Vol. 1, No. 1), Summer 1983 (Vol. 3), Summer 1984 (Vol. 5), 1985—Volume One, Winter 1985-86 (Volume 4), Spring 1987, Winter 1988, Spring 1988, Winter 1989, Summer 1989, Winter 1990, Spring 1990, Summer 1990, Fall 1990, Winter 1991, Spring 1991, Volume 10—Issue 3, Volume 10—Issue 4, Volume 11—Issue 1, Volume 11—Issue 3, Volume 12—Issue 1, Volume 14—Issue 1, Volume 20—Issue 1

(NOTE: Peavey changed its designations for respective issues of *Monitor* more than once in the history of the magazine, and issues that were used in research are noted by the issue date/number that appeared on their respective covers. *Monitor* was discontinued in 2008; like many other companies, Peavey now relies on its web site as the primary source for providing information to consumers)

Peavey price lists, 1978-2011 were also consulted for product information.

9 781936 946518